Extinction and Survival in Human Populations

EXTINCTION and

COLUMBIA UNIVERSITY PRESS

SURVIVAL
in HUMAN
POPULATIONS

EDITED BY
CHARLES D. LAUGHLIN, JR.,
AND
IVAN A. BRADY

NEW YORK 1978

Columbia University Press
New York and Guildford, Surrey

Printed in the United States of America

Library of Congress Cataloging in Publication Data

Main entry under title:

Extinction and survival in human populations.

  Bibliography: p.
  Includes index.
  1. Social change. 2. Man—Influence of environment.
3. Disasters—Social aspects. 4. Starvation—Social
aspects. I. Laughlin, Charles D., 1938–
II. Brady, Ivan A.
GN358.E95   301.24   77–17596
ISBN 0–231–04418–6
ISBN 0–231–04419–4 pbk.

Dedicated to the Memory
of
LAWRENCE SCOTT MAILHES
1940–1965
He
died bravely
in a
needless war

Contents

Editors' Preface

Who knows what form the forward momentum of life will take in the time ahead or what use it will make of our anguished searching? The most that any one of us can seem to do is to fashion something—an object or ourselves—and drop it into the confusion, make an offering of it, so to speak, to the life force.

Ernest Becker, *The Denial of Death*

Death and life, extinction and survival, entropy and negentropy are all dichotomous terms for the polar faces of adaptation—the set of processes by means of which the continuity of human ecosystems is maintained through time in the matrix of an ever-changing environment. Adaptation in human populations depends on the successful operation of a complex set of biological, psychological, and sociocultural processes. The patterns established by the interactions of these processes appear dynamic and systemic as individuals and populations monitor environmental stimuli and attempt to adjust their behaviors accordingly. Both the processes and their products are amenable to scientific discovery and description. Yet the problems involved in doing so accurately and successfully have proved to be enormous.

The study of complex social systems is problematic for several reasons. First, all organic systems are dynamic entities. They encompass space and time dimensions as well as the intricacies of cybernetic processing in the organisms themselves. A problem arises in analysis insofar as the human brain operates to cognitively simplify what it perceives in order to better manage its relationships with the universe of experience. Social scientists thus quite naturally, but often quite unproductively, have been willing to accept simple models of complexity as their forte (see Keesing 1972). The structural relations within and between human societies and their environments form the most complex systems known to science. We have arrived at a point in the development of anthropological theory where the discrepancy between simplistic models and complex reality is no longer tenable (see Geertz 1973). To overcome this difficulty, we may have to foreclose on our simple models of complexity, on our parochial inclinations to explain social and cultural phenomena in terms of themselves, and subsequently broaden our horizons in biocultural, neurophysiological, and evolutionary terms.

Second, the widespread fiscal, political, social, and ethical constraints placed upon researchers in the social sciences make it exceedingly difficult for comprehensive analyses of human social systems to take place. The typical field researcher is sent into the field with little financial support for a relatively short period of time, and is usually alone during the field experience, or at best in the company of a small team of researchers who are generally from the same discipline. He is forbidden for ethical reasons to "experiment" with the system he observes. Nevertheless, he is expected to describe and model the representative interaction patterns of social systems sometimes comprising thousands, or even millions, of persons.

Third, the field researcher generally begins his field experience encumbered by simplistic, synchronic propositions about the nature of social systems that are learned from traditional scholarship and literature. This information has been generated, of course, by previous researchers who have been encumbered by similar constraints. The inevitable result is an enormous body of literature that has much too often described human social systems as relatively static in form, each apparently fixed in time and unresponsive to what we know intuitively to be a dynamic and complexly structured environment. Such models are inaccurate in fact and generally inadequate to the task of explaining systemic change and adaptation.

Finally, the difficulties encountered in observing and modeling complex systems often lead to exceedingly particularistic and trivial research. The common result is to enfranchise a "cult of methodology" ostensibly designed to "control significant variables," but which in fact so limits the bit of reality observed, the conditions of observation, and the problems set as scientifically relevant, that two realities are created: that of empirical reality which resides in the multivariate world of common experience, on the one hand, and that of technical research which resides in an arbitrarily constructed and often severely unidimensional world of social science theory (see Whitehead 1960), on the other. Any theory from the latter set which fails to ground itself in the former set is doomed to failure from the outset. Such a science becomes incapable of asking, much less of addressing, the global, philosophically rich questions that originally gave rise to studies of the human condition. At the other extreme is what might be called "mindless empiricism," where commitments to collecting the "facts" of social life displace the need for a theoretical matrix in which the facts can be placed for systematic interpretations beyond the level of surface structure variations in particular societies.

This book offers no panacea for these deep-seated tribulations of social science method and theory. However, in full view of the difficulties outlined, the contributors to the volume grapple with the complexities of adaptation in several societies as they have existed through time and are presently constituted. The ethnographic ballast of each substantive chapter is set in a framework of contemporary theory. The entire set of substantive chapters is integrated by a still more broadly calculated theory of human adaptation, one which was initially espoused in *Biogenetic Structuralism* (Laughlin and d'Aquili 1974), has since been refined through application in *The Spectrum of Ritual* (d'Aquili et al. 1978), and is further refined with special focus in the introductory and concluding chapters to the present work. The composite result of these efforts is, we believe, a greater comprehension of the dynamics and complexities of human adaptation. It is also clear to us that the macromodel espoused here is incomplete. While it explains many of the features of structure, process, and change in human adaptation, it has also raised more corollary questions than it has answered. This may be the inevitable lot of all productive social theory, that is, to leave the effort forever incomplete. We quite self-consciously, therefore, drop this bit of order into the confusion, and hope that it will be accepted in the spirit in which it is offered—as a gift from all of us to the life force that sustains the best of the human condition.

IVAN A. BRADY
CHARLES D. LAUGHLIN, JR.

Acknowledgments

As is always the case in projects of this sort, our debts to others for their assistance are enormous. In particular we would like to thank Eugene d'Aquili, Robert Dirks, Joseph G. Jorgensen, John McManus, David M. H. Richmond, Robert Rubinstein, and Anthony F. C. Wallace for their many valuable insights, suggestions, and encouragement. One of the editors (CDL) was supported by a National Endowment for the Humanities postdoctoral fellowship for one year during which much of the preliminary work on this volume was completed. The other editor (IAB) was supported by a fellowship and grant from the State University of New York Research Foundation. We gratefully acknowledge the assistance of these agencies. We also thank the many students whose participation in the dialogue of our classrooms encouraged clarification of the content of our project as it developed. In that regard, we owe special thanks to Kathy Pitts and Donald Roberts of SUNY-Oswego. Janie Brady, Dorothy Burke, Kathy Cassella, Pat Kolarik, Jacqueline Lortie, and Kim Skelly helped us immeasurably in preparation of the manuscript.

Contributors

Charles A. Bishop is professor of anthropology at the State University of New York College at Oswego. He has conducted archival and field research among the Northern Ojibwa and Cree Indians since 1965. He received his Ph.D. from the State University of New York at Buffalo in 1969, and has taught at Florida State University and Eastern New Mexico University. He is the author of *The Northern Ojibwa and the Fur Trade*.

Ivan A. Brady is professor and coordinator for anthropology at the State University of New York College at Oswego. Completing his undergraduate work at Northern Arizona University in 1966, he received his Ph.D. from the University of Oregon in 1970. He was formerly assistant professor of anthropology at the University of Cincinnati. His primary work in Tuvalu was done in 1968, 1969, and 1971. He is the editor of *Transactions in Kinship: Adoption and Fosterage in Oceania*.

John Cawte is associate professor of psychiatry at the University of New South Wales. He received his M.D. from the University of Adelaide and his Ph.D. from the University of New South Wales. He is a Distinguished Fellow of the American Psychiatric Association. His fieldwork covers many parts of Aboriginal Australia and New Britain. He is the editor of *The Aboriginal Health Worker*.

John J. Cove is associate professor of anthropology and sociology at Carleton University, Ottawa. He completed his undergraduate work and M.A. degree at Dalhousie University, and his Ph.D. in anthropology at the University of British Columbia in 1971. He is currently engaged in research on the mythic-symbolic systems of the Tsimshian.

Robert Dirks received his Ph.D. in anthropology from Case Western Reserve University in 1972. He is now assistant professor of anthropology at Illinois State University. His field research has been focused on the British Virgin Islands and Belize and has been supported by archival research on slavery and related topics in London and Jamaica. He is presently studying the effects of starvation on human social and biological systems.

Charles D. Laughlin, Jr., is associate professor of anthropology at Carleton University, Ottawa. He completed his undergraduate work at San Francisco State University in 1966 and his Ph.D. at the University of Oregon in 1972. He taught at the State University of New York College at Oswego from 1970 to 1976. His primary fieldwork among the So of Northeastern Uganda was carried out in 1969 and 1970. He is the co-author of *Biogenetic Structuralism*.

Larissa Lomnitz is professor of social anthropology at the National University of Mexico. She completed her undergraduate studies at the University of California at Berkeley and her Ph.D. at the Universidad Iberoamericana in Mexico. Her field research on shantytowns was done in Mexico City from 1969 to 1971.

Colin M. Turnbull is research associate at the American Museum of Natural History, New York, and was recently visiting professor of anthropology at West Virginia University. A graduate of Oxford University, his fieldwork has been mainly in Africa, with special focus on the Mbuti of Zaïre and the Ik of Uganda. He is the author of *The Mountain People*.

Extinction and Survival in Human Populations

Introduction: Diaphasis and Change in Human Populations

Charles D. Laughlin, Jr.
and
Ivan A. Brady

Adaptation in human populations depends on the successful operation of a complex set of biological, psychological, and sociocultural
processes.[1] Generally speaking, adaptive processes are those "by
which organisms, through responsive changes in their own states,
structures, or compositions, maintain [homeorhesis] in and among
themselves in the face of both short-term environment fluctuations
and long-term changes in the composition or structure of their environments" (Rappaport 1971:60).[2] The facility for such responses in
man is embedded in his neurobiological structure, dependent upon
the cognitive and symbolic functioning of his conceptual system, and
expressed overtly in terms of learned and shared behavior in social
groups. From this perspective, the specific culture content and behavior patterns that characterize particular populations are surface-
level expressions of a more complex and primordial structure in
human organisms which can be identified in composite form as a
biogram (Count 1973). The beliefs, recipes, ideas, symbols, and
meanings that define appropriate behavior and that structure the
cognized environment[3] for particular populations, that is, what some
anthropologists are inclined to call "culture" (e.g., Geertz 1957, 1966;

Schneider 1968), are subsumed in this case by the more useful concept of *culture pool* (see Dunn 1970; Goodenough 1971). This diverse pool and all of the behaviors coordinated by it, we shall argue, are produced by the synthetic interaction of the neurophysiological and conceptual structures of individual organisms with environmental events (see also Harvey et al. 1961; Piaget 1971; Laughlin and d'Aquili 1974). Social and biological interdependencies combine individual organisms into groups for purposes of social action. The total adaptive infrastructure of these groups, in turn, mediates responses to environmental stimuli on an ecosystems level. Confronted with this most complex level of human behaviors and adaptations, the ecosystem, the scientific task of the observer "becomes one of investigating the internal dynamics of such systems and the ways in which they develop and change" (Geertz 1963:3).

Why do some sociocultural systems variously persist, transmute, or die out at apparently variable rates in comparable ecosystems and in response to similar stimuli (see Brady and Isaac 1975)? This question is one of the most perplexing in contemporary science, and it is also one that must be answered in terms that transcend functional theories of surface culture variation in particular populations (see Goodenough 1971:122ff.). Without pretending to cover all of the complexities involved, we shall nevertheless provide some answers to the question by: (1) outlining the general characteristics of human adaptive infrastructures and processes; and (2) presenting a biocultural and evolutionary theory of social and cognitive reactions to environmental changes and the stress produced by such changes.

Specifically, we suggest that a society's adaptive infrastructure is both integrated and regulated in large part by the level of cognitive structural complexity operating among the members of that society at particular times. Cognitive structural complexity, in turn, is a product of neurobiological structures and processes that obtain at a deeper level in the organism's biogram, on the one hand, and a product of the range and intensity of environmental stimuli that are perceived as significant by the organism, on the other hand. The model we present is primarily concerned with predictable variations in behavior caused by decrements in the level of conceptual system functioning under conditions of environmental disruption or stress. Some of the social and psychological mechanisms that inhibit decrements in conceptual system functioning are identified, and the importance of expected versus unexpected changes in the environment is emphasized in relation to these mechanisms. We conclude: (1) that successful adaptation depends largely upon the range and efficiency of perceptual, cognitive, and cybernetic synchronization among the members of a given population (see also Chapple 1970; d'Aquili et al. 1978); and (2) that these synchronization patterns are manifested, challenged, and altered most overtly in terms of sociability, exchange, food production, political behavior and ritual action under conditions of environmental stress.

ADAPTIVE INFRASTRUCTURE

A society's adaptive infrastructure may be defined as the total set of constraints imposed by members of the society, either individually or collectively, upon the processing of energy and information necessary for biological survival of the population. By definition, any deep or surface structural elements (including customs, beliefs, attitudes, behaviors, organizational principles, etc.) that have no effect upon the survival of a population are not viable or intrusive elements of that population's adaptive infrastructure. For most human societies, some of the culture pool—and thereby some of the cognized environment held by individual actors—is outside the range of adaptive infrastructure. The enormous elaboration of human conceptual systems beyond the strict demands of adaptation has been shown elsewhere to be a direct function of the evolution of the hominid brain (Laughlin and d'Aquili 1974: article 4).

Primary Subsystems: The three main subsystems of an organism's adaptive infrastructure can be identified analytically as neurobiological, cognitive, and societal (figure 1.1). These subsystems are organized on a common set of principles for synchronized responses to inputs from other levels within the organism or from outside the organism as environmental stimuli. Structural synchronization of this sort is necessary for the successful operation of the organism as a unit or corporate entity. Even the simplest technological skill, for example, requires entrainment of somatosensory, vestibular, cerebellar,

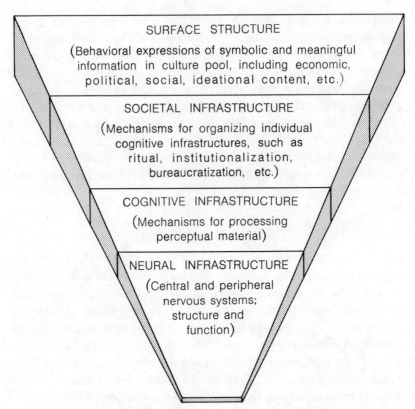

FIGURE 1.1   DEEP AND SURFACE STRUCTURE: LEVELS OF STRUCTURE OPERATING IN THE HUMAN ORGANISM AS ACTOR IN A SOCIAL SYSTEM

and motor functions within the central nervous system. Similarly, effective responses by the organism to external stimuli require synchronization of perceptual, cognitive, and affective capacities. Furthermore, if the stimulus is such that it requires a collective response from individuals as members of a social group, then the group must be capable of entraining perceptual, cognitive, and affective components in the conceptual systems of all or most of the actors. Finally, at the level of societal organization of the adaptive infrastructure, the group must assure that its pool of ideas, beliefs, attitudes, behaviors, recipes, and institutions contains sufficient alternatives and information for synchronized responses to the complex stimuli of environmental shifts. At best, failure to synchronize on this level precipitates fragmentation of the social group, or it may stimulate innovation and reintegration on new premises. At worst, failure to synchronize eliminates the group as a corporate body, and may lead to extinction of the group as a biological population.

The principles that link each subsystem or infrastructural level to the others are cybernetic and organized in a complex feedback system throughout the organism (Powers 1973). Information from the environment may enter the adaptive infrastructure at any level, and each subsystem must be cybernetically structured in a manner that allows for synchronized input from other subsystems as an indirect link to environmental stimuli or for direct input from the external environment (Miller 1964). However, input of the latter type may or may not require active or significant responses from more than the subsystem at the primary point of input in the organism. Information about the environment may enter at the level of subcortical systems of the central nervous system and an appropriate response may be directed, for example, without the organism being conscious of either the information in its original form or the response made. In other circumstances, environmental stimuli may elicit a low-level perceptual response from the organism that requires mediation and synchronization by both the neurophysiological and cognitive-affective subsystems, but without conscious articulation or visible rearrangements of elements on the level of overt behavior and cultural management. These are subtle responses from the standpoint of the external observer, but that does not make them necessarily unimportant from the standpoint of maintaining the adaptive profile of the individual organism.

The third general possibility for cybernetic processing and infrastructural integration in the organism occurs when environmental stimuli are sufficiently massive to require active and significant synchronized responses from all three subsystem levels. Individuals make conscious and deliberate choices from the range of information that is socially and culturally programmed for them in attempts to take "appropriate" action under these circumstances; or they innovate new responses for effective action through a recombination of existing elements in their cognized environments, which may or may not constitute "appropriate" action from the perspective of the group as a whole. Either way, all responses to input on the higher levels of subsystem structure necessarily entail operations by the lower levels. Effective or appropriate social responses require synchronization of individual cognitive operations. These operations, in turn, require synchronization of the neurobiological subsystem of the adaptive infrastructure. Infrastructural subsystems are thereby ordered hierarchically in terms of overlapping cybernetic response principles, and the activity range of these principles depends largely on the initial point of infrastructural input as well as on the particular type and intensity of information conveyed to the organisms by environmental stimuli (see d'Aquili et al. 1978: chapter 1).[4]

Having mapped the systemic organization of adaptive infrastructures in this manner, we should reassert the point made earlier that our concern in this chapter lies primarily with the interrelationships of the two higher levels of adaptive infrastructures, that is, with the levels of cognitive and societal organization of energy, information, and action pertinent to adaptation. A satisfactory understanding of these interrelationships requires that some additional analytic distinctions be introduced at this point. One such distinction concerns cognized versus operational environments.

Cognized and Operational Environments: The distinction between a population's cognized environment and its operational environment is important for understanding the nature and functions of adaptive infrastructures. Rappaport's discussion of these concepts is particularly instructive:

> The operational model [of the environment] is that which the anthropologist constructs through observation and measurement of empirical entities, events, and material relationships. He takes this model to represent, for analytical purposes, the physical world of the group he is studying. . . . The cognized model is the model of the environment conceived by the people who act in it. The two models are overlapping, but not identical. While many components of the physical world will be represented in both, the operational model is likely to include material elements, such as diseases, germs and nitrogen-fixing bacteria, that affect the actors but of which they are not aware.

Conversely, the cognized model may include elements that cannot be shown by empirical means to exist, such as spirits and
other supernatural beings. (Rappaport 1968:237–38)

It is important to underscore the fact that no organism's cognized environment is coextensive with its operational environment. In a very
real sense, adaptation for any organism is the degree of success obtained in coordinating its cognized and operational environments for
continued survival. With restricted reference to adaptation, we call
the process of coordinating the two environments the cycle of *tandem
exploitation*.[5] The process of tandem exploitation involves both genetically based neurocognitive functions (see Laughlin and d'Aquili
1974) and developmental interaction between the organism and the
operational environment in ontogenesis (see Piaget 1971). Theoretically, this process results in behavior that is adaptive within the context of the operational environment and is systematized and coordinated (however indirectly) through the cognized environment and
culture pool of the population.[6]

Under normal conditions, the actors in a society will be unaware of
most of the adaptive infrastructure and its constituent mechanisms.
What is known, conceptualized, structured, and consciously manipulated in the cognized environment can only be effective in the long
run to the extent that cognized elements and relations are systematically linked through tandem exploitation with the key elements
and relations in the operational environment of that society. Surface-
level adjustments in behavior or institutional arrangements that lack
positive cybernetic synchronization with the complexities of the operational environment are therefore either maladaptive or irrelevant to
survival of the population in the long run. *Coordination through tandem exploitation of cognized and operational environments can be
posited, in fact, as the primary function of adaptive infrastructures
in human ecosystems.*

Infrastructure and Sociocultural Content: All human societies
must have some systematic means for getting people to resources
and resources to people, for allocating power and managing constitu-
encies in tasks requiring concerted action, for integrating and ex-
ploiting interpersonal relationships in a manner that facilitates socia-

bility and perpetuates alliance, and for renewing and conceptually stabilizing the place actors perceive themselves to occupy in the universe of natural and supernatural forces. The actual patterns of expectation and action generated in meeting these ends may be distinguished analytically as deriving from the economic, political, social, and ideological domains of the society's adaptive infrastructure. As subsystemic or behavioral domains, each one represents a conduit of cybernetic flow between the society's cognized and operational environments. But it is also important to recognize that none of these domains occurs in precisely the same form on any systematic level other than that of cultural content, which is a surface rather than a deep structure component of the sociey's collective adaptive infrastructure (figure 1.1). The four-part division posed here does not refer to partitions of equal content or scope in the cognitive or neurobiological subsystems of the adaptive infrastructure. As such, the actual content of these four surface domains may be treated as a dependent variable or product of adaptive interactions between organisms and their operational environments, or as an intervening variable between environmental input and behavioral outcomes. Furthermore, we recognize that all four domains are closely integrated in actuality. We separate them here *for analytic purposes only*.

We are now in a position to examine each of these surface domains in more particular terms, and, subsequently, to evaluate their relationships to the cognitive subsystem level of the adaptive infrastructure under conditions of environmental stress.

The Economic Domain: The economic domain of the adaptive infrastructure consists of the means a population has for provisioning itself through the production, distribution, and consumption of basic resources. *Basic resources* are those raw materials present in the environment that are exploited through the prevailing level of information and technology in a given society, and upon which survival of a viable reproductive population depends (see also Fried 1957:24). The term *production* is taken to mean the technological exploitation of basic resources by indigenous members of the society, or by individuals outside the society in a way that alters the subsistence profile of the host population. In the latter case, basic resources generally find their way into the host society through some type of exchange (see

Brady, article 9 below). *Cognized resources* are those resources which are ordered into meaningful categories by the indigenous population. *Operational resources* include all material and non-material resources ". . . that enter a reaction system of the organism or otherwise directly impinge upon it to affect its mode of life at any time throughout its life cycle as ordered by the demands of the ontogeny of the organism or as ordered by any other condition of the organism that alters its environmental demands" (Rappaport 1965:159; quoted from Bates 1960:554), such as living in social groups.

Several points need clarification if these concepts are to be useful to us. First, not all resources exploited in the environment are necessarily basic resources. In fact, some resources that enter into the economic infrastructure may have little or no direct value for population survival. We shall refer to these as *secondary resources*. Second, the environment may provide elements which could be utilized as basic resources if they were exploitable by the local population. Such resources might not be utilized because of technological inadequacy, ideological proscription, or ignorance of their potential utility. Third, not all of the operational resources that enter into the economic infrastructure of a given society are necessarily cognized resources. Some resources or resource cycles that impinge on the survival of a population may not be conceptualized as fundamental or ordered into meaningful categories by the members of that population. Such resources lie outside the cognized environment in the operational environment but still function as components of the ecosystem in which the population participates. Some resources that lie outside the population's cognized environment thus may be basic and strategic for survival but tapped only indirectly or unconsciously through the exploitation of resources that are cognized. This would, of course, provide an instance of tandem exploitation in the economic domain. Fourth, a life-serving element in the population's ecosystem may be a basic resource at one time and a secondary resource at another time. Such changes may be progressive or cyclical, depending on the particular history of the society's sociocultural development in specific environments, and on the vicissitudes of environmental fluctuations over time. Finally, we should emphasize that the economic domain outlined here is *not* a synonym for the economy of a given population, but is rather a more specific network of concepts referring to that portion of the economy which mediates the process of survival between a society and its operational environment. The economic domain of a society's adaptive infrastructure is also closely integrated with its social domain in particular ways.

The Social Domain: The social domain of the adaptive infrastructure consists of the network of interpersonal relations, formal and informal, that operate through the mediation of a population's cognized environment. The *primary* social domain is the network of such relations that actors consider to be intrinsically "own" rather than "other" in their origins and structural characteristics. The *secondary* social domain includes any non-indigenous network of relations that enters into the cognized action system (or culture pool) of the population, regardless of the mode of introduction and of the acceptance or rejection patterns displayed by the host population in its primary domain (see Brady, article 9).

The basic adaptive functions of the primary social domain are to provide: (1) the channels through which basic resources and derivative products are distributed for consumption or reallocation by the population; and (2) the potential structure for amity, altruism, sociability, corporate action, "mass effect" (see Wilson 1971), alliance, and cooperation in such strategic enterprises as shared labor and defense. The latter function is fairly generalized in non-human societies (see Count 1973; Wilson 1975) and forms an important basis for social rather than individuated adaptation. The former function is also found in some non-human societies under certain conditions (see Wilson 1971 for insect societies and Teleki 1973 for chimpanzees). Relative to both functions, there may be infant and adult members of the group who have no direct access to basic resources and thereby must depend for subsistence on their relationships to active participants in the production system. But the range of tolerance for such dependence is greater in human as opposed to non-human societies, especially under normal conditions of resource availability. It is also apparent that human production systems are linked to much more elaborate and complex exchange networks than any found in non-human societies. However, we agree with Count (1973) in asserting that the difference in social domain functions between human and certain non-human adaptive infrastructures is more one of complexity than of kind.

Rights of access to basic resources in human societies are generally predicated on some combination of shared physical, cognitive, and social space that yields specific (though multifaceted) positions for actors in the social infrastructure of the society as a whole. These individual positions may be structured and expressed most overtly in terms of kinship, alliance, and territorial or land tenure patterns (see Silverman 1971; Count 1973; Lieber 1974; Sade 1974; Brady 1974, 1975a, 1976a). The functional integration of these positions is promoted at minimum by the sexual division of labor (Durkheim 1963), by the demands of incest taboos and exogamy (Lévi-Strauss 1949), and by the obligations to give, to receive, and to reciprocate in exchange relations (Mauss 1954). Such positions are also durationally structured insofar as they may change substantially as individual information pools and contributions to the functioning of the social unit change over time. Similarly, individual positions in the social system and concomitant rights of access to basic resources may vary in scope and intensity as the demographic and subsistence profiles of the group fluctuate in response to climatic variations, competition with other groups, or cross-cultural interference, among other possibilities. Within this context, however, actual access to basic resources is largely a function of power allocations and performance in dominance hierarchies, that is, of the network of interpersonal relations that obtains in the political domain of a society's adaptive infrastructure.

The Political Domain: The political domain of an adaptive infrastructure encompasses all of its power relations that influence resource distribution and adaptive action. A *power relation* is defined as the influence one actor or set of actors has over another actor or set of actors by virtue of the control the former has over some set of valuables desired or required by the latter (Burns 1973; Burns and Meeker 1975; Baumgartner et al. 1975a, 1975b). The valuables that are manipulable and desired in this manner are *power resources,* and may be material (such as cattle, gold, money, food) or non-material (such as intercession beween god and man, social solidarity, access to prestige, ritual control). It is also important to distinguish between two types of power resources, those that are also basic resources and those that are not. The set of power resources controlled in any transaction overlaps the set of basic resources available to members of the society, but the two sets are not necessarily coincident in type and distribution (figure 1.2). Obviously, non-cognized basic resources

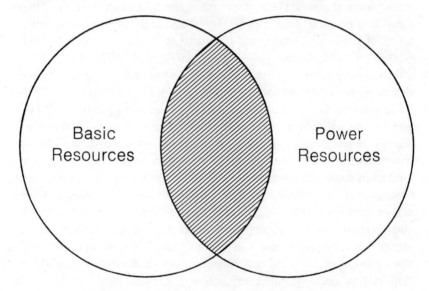

FIGURE 1.2 BASIC RESOURCES AND POWER RESOURCES

may be entailed and transacted as power resources through tandem exploitation with cognized resources. These factors of overlap and entailment are critical features of political responses to resource deprivation, as we shall demonstrate later in this chapter.

Power relations thus are based in part on an actual or potential structure of differential access to basic resources. Where these differences are institutionalized and allocated on characteristics other than age, sex, generation, or personality, the political aspects of the adaptive infrastructure may be said to be *ranked* and *stratified;* they are *egalitarian* in all other instances (see Fried 1957; Service 1975). Basic resource power is generally achieved, shared widely among actors in the society, and situation-specific in egalitarian systems; it is generally ascribed, enhanced by achievement, monopolized or maximized by only a few actors in the society, and generalized to many complex situations in ranked and stratified systems. Either way, the political domain is closely integrated with the regulatory and adaptive functions of the economic, social, and ideological domains of the society's collective adaptive infrastructure.

The Ideological Domain: The ideological domain of an adaptive infrastructure consists of all rational formulae, affective states, symbols, meanings, and behaviors that define, reify, or otherwise reinforce the place actors perceive themselves to occupy in their universe of natural and supernatural forces. A major adaptive function of ritual in particular, as a form of social action and a subset of the ideological domain, is to regulate, reduce, or eliminate altogether psychobiological stress that may develop in individual organisms as a result of real or imagined changes in the environment (see Rappaport 1968; d'Aquili et al. 1978). As an activity domain, ritual intersects with what is normally termed religious behavior and beliefs; it is likely to be concentrated on mediating and manipulating the parameter of indeterminacy that separates the cognized from the operational environment of the population. The most immediate and strategic contribution of ritual to the adaptive infrastructure, however, is stress alleviation.

Psychobiological stress can be defined operationally as any reduction in the functional capacity of the organism to cognitively mediate an adaptive response to its operational environment. *Ecological stress* is any change in the operational environment that represents a potential or actual threat to the continued survival of the organism. Such stress may be caused by a decrement in the quantity or type of basic resources normally available to the population. The decrement itself may derive from changes in the incidence or type of predation, from intensification or alleviation of competition with other human or nonhuman populations in the ecosystem, or from climatic variations such as hurricanes, floods, droughts, and earthquakes. Together with ritual, the ideological domain operates within the adaptive infrastructure to create a buffer mechanism between ecological and psychobiological stress (see McManus 1978). However, the relative effectiveness of the ideological domain as a buffer mechanism for stress depends to a large extent on the psychological impact and general receptivity of ritual formulae and behaviors in the indigenous population, as well as on the source and degree of novelty of the ecological stress input. Through cybernetic linkages, these variables also have a major and determinate effect upon the operative levels of the cognitive infrastructure, which is the most immediate deep structure level and the one that mediates all of the surface material from the culture pool, as well as corporate responses from the various social domains of the adaptive infrastructure.

Cognitive Infrastructure: The cognitive infrastructure of a society is a collectivity of individual and biocultural elements linked through a network of synchronized conceptual systems (see figure 1.1). Any variable affecting the functions of a society's cognitive infrastructure does so by influencing individual conceptual systems or the patterns of their synchronization. All adaptive actions and decision-making are mediated through the cognitive infrastructures of individual organisms but constrained by the position of those organisms in the wider cognitive network of the group. Cognitive infrastructures thus have a complex ontogeny that results from the synthetic interaction of individual organisms with their cognized and operational environments.

We know from the work of various psychologists (Piaget 1952, 1971; Harvey et al. 1961; Kohlberg 1969) that the development of complexity in conceptual systems occurs in a series of stages. The development of cognitive complexity in individuals—which refers to the number of differentiated elements in perception and conception, as well as to the number of alternative patterns of integration of those elements through conceptual transformations (Schroder et al. 1967)—is marked by a series of ontogenetically "sensitive" periods that are presumably matched to optimal environmental input. A developing individual progresses in his ontogeny from one stage to the next higher stage of cognitive complexity *only* when structuring at the previous stage is completed. If the actor experiences some deficit at the previous stage, progress to the next higher stage will not occur. Furthermore, individuals do not skip stages. The development of cognitive complexity is an orderly, lawful progression through stages of increasing complexity until some maximal stage or peak is reached. The actual maximum stage reached, relative to those theoretically possible, depends on several critical variables, however, including the individual's neurogenetic endowment, the presence or absence of optimal environmental complexity for input at each developmental stage, and a complex set of sociocultural factors in the socialization process (see Dasen 1972).

The complexity of each progressive stage in individual cognitive development is defined by the degree of differentiation and integration exhibited in the cybernetic and behavioral functioning of the organism. That is, in estimating the complexity of cognitive functioning of the organism, we want to know the number of different kinds of information being processed and the number of different ways in which that information may be linked for optimal performance, as suggested above. However, it is important in this regard to distinguish between perceptual and conceptual complexity. Differentiation and integration in perceptual structure refer to the variety of things and relations perceived by the actor in his operational environment, as well as to the number of ways these elements may be linked for alternative recognition. On the other hand, differentiation and integration in conceptual structure refer to the quantity of information considered and the number of alternative ways of combining or associating that information relative to decisions about the operational environment (Schroder et al. 1967). It is also important to note that no conceptual system operates constantly at maximal complexity (Schroder et al. 1967). There are conditions under which it might prove maladaptive for actors to be operating at maximal conceptual complexity (see McManus 1978). Optimal operative complexity is selected for at a level lower than maximal complexity in these instances.

What do levels of cognitive complexity mean in terms of actual information processing in the adaptive infrastructure? If we treat the various levels of cognitive functioning as a series that ranges from simple to very complex, we may characterize structures at the simple pole by perceptual "compartmentalization and by a hierarchial integration of parts (rules). Regardless of the number of dimensions or the number of rules and procedures involved, the integrating structure is absolute. It lacks alternate interacting parts. When the structure is hierarchical, the dimensional 'readings' of a range of stimuli are organized in a fixed way" (Schroder et al. 1967:15). Persons operating at the simple structural level tend toward perception and conceptualization that is very concrete. Objects or events in the world are rigidly categorized into systems of identification with little conflict or ambiguity. Simple structuring results in "either-or" dichotomies and minimal conflict in reasoning. Most importantly for our purposes, simple structuring tends to result in stimulus-boundness. The individual is or becomes a more passive recipient of external stimuli as cause. His behavior is often determined by what is happening in his environment as concrete input at the moment, rather than by a more complex and algebraic range of reasoning that might provide for a different response level (see Schroder et al. 1967:16–17; McManus 1978).

Although it is not essential that we describe each ascending level of cognitive complexity possible in the organism, it will be useful to contrast simple, concrete structures with higher-level structures in general. Schroder et al. suggest that:

> Increasing levels of information processing involve the emergence of more complex and interrelated schemata. In turn, more dimensions are generated, and discrimination between stimuli becomes more linear. If the adaptive significance of moderately low structure is the delineation of alternate rules, the significance of moderately high structure may be described as the initial emergence of rules for identifying more complex relations than alternation. (1967:20)

Persons operating at higher structural levels thus respond out of less concrete perceptual and cognitive categories. They are able to integrate material stored in their cognized environments and derived through perception from their operational environments in a variety of ways, with a number of possible interpretations of stimuli that enter their reaction system. Such persons generally perceive themselves as active agents in their cognized environment. They may also consider events, conditions, and goals that are not a part of their immediate operational environment and integrate these elements in decision-making.

The relationship between environmental and conceptual complexity is illustrated in figure 1.3. The complexity of events in the cog-

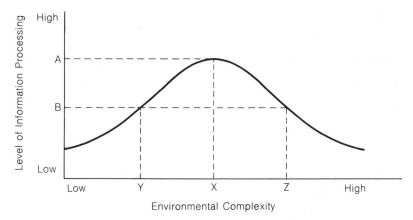

FIGURE 1.3 GENERAL RELATIONSHIP BETWEEN ENVIRONMENTAL AND COGNITIVE COMPLEXITY (FROM SCHRODER ET AL. 1967:37, REPRINTED WITH PERMISSION OF THE PUBLISHER)

nized portion of the operational environment has a determinate effect on the level of cognitive structuring that obtains in the actor's adaptive infrastructure at that time, and the actor's behavioral responses are modified accordingly. If the environment is perceived as too simple (point Y), the actor's response (B) will reflect concrete structuring to that degree. If the environment is too complex (point Z), on the other hand, the response will be the same. There appears to be an optimal degree of environmental complexity (point X) that will stimulate optimal cognitive complexity (A) in the actor. The actual level of optimality is, of course, relative to the actor's overall cognitive profile; that is, optimal complexity will be lower and occur more rapidly in actors with low cognitive structuring potential than among actors with higher cognitive structuring potential. The potentially complex conceptual system will just be reaching optimal functioning at the point where the simple conceptual system has "bottomed out" on the superoptimal side of the curve.

ADAPTIVE DIAPHASIS: A FUNDAMENTAL PROPOSITION

We have now outlined the four major societal domains of adaptive infrastructures in human societies, and we have discussed the inherent structure and operation of cognitive subsystems underlying these domains from the perspective of conceptual systems theory. Before proceeding to delineate the major mechanisms and modes of change in these components in changing environments, we need to distinguish between two types of ecological stress, namely disaster and deprivation.

Disaster may be defined as a significant decremental shift in resource availability which is considered unique or novel by all or most actors in the system. Disaster represents an event, in other words, for which the adaptive infrastructure is *conceptually* unprepared. *Deprivation,* on the other hand, is a decremental shift in resource availability which is perceived by most or all of the actors as being cyclical or repetitive and therefore at least partially predictable in occurrence. The event that causes the decrement may have key elements that are not cognized and thereby exist only as elements in the broader operational environment of the population's ecosystem (such as trophic level disruption in symbiotic species, depletion of soil nutrients, etc.). But a culturally specific interpretation of both the form and the causes of the event is inevitable as the members of the population attempt to make sense of the disruption. The difference between disaster and deprivation is thus primarily one of information content and structuring in the cognized environment of the population. It follows that the same event (such as an earthquake, epidemic, drought, flood, or warfare) may constitute a disaster for one society and only a deprivative phase for another, depending on the novelty of the event in the perception of the populations involved (see Lang and Lang 1964). If a certain type of decremental event is a regular occurrence in an area in which a particular society has been located for several generations (such as a Pacific Island society in the tropical cyclone belt, an East African society confronting drought, a town on the San Andreas fault confronting earthquake), then the event is likely to be perceived as a deprivative phase in a larger cycle of known events rather than as a unique disaster. Magnitude or intensity, of course, can also produce novelty in the upper or unexpected extremes. But we are concerned here primarily with the level of preparedness of a society's adaptive infrastructure for particular *forms* of decrement in basic resources.

Both disaster and deprivation pose threats to the survival of the individuals and groups who experience them. A failure to respond selects for extinction in both cases, but the risk of responding inappropriately would seem to be less under conditions of deprivation than under conditions of disaster. The problem for the observer becomes one of isolating and analyzing the empirical response levels of a society's adaptive infrastructure under these conditions, and of specifying the processes and patterns of change involved.

Adaptive Change in Complex Systems: The biocultural capability of human social systems to respond to ecological stress has enormous ramifications for the study of social structure, some of which have been posited here and will be explored at length in subsequent chapters of this volume. We have already outlined some of the structural complexities of this capability in terms of adaptive infrastructures. However, given that adaptive infrastructures are also dynamic and durationally structured as complex systems, what remains to be specified here is the nature of changes in such systems in the context of particular environmental relationships over time. It may be expected that such changes are patterned, biocultural in scope and content, linked to varying degrees with tandem exploitation cycles, and generally represent positive contributions to the problems of maintaining population survival and sociocultural continuity.

Short-term changes in complex social systems are generally not radical in the sense of altering the fundamental structure of the system itself. They usually amount to changes in the degree of internal cognitive differentiation and integration of information, or, in a broader sense, to changes in the specific alignment or orientation of the system to its cognized and operational environments. The cumulative effects of such changes in the long run, however, represent an effort to maintain adaptive isomorphism with the operational environment. By *adaptive isomorphism* we mean that the elements and relations of the adaptive infrastructure are arranged in a way that permits a high degree of synchronization with the variable demands of the operational environment (see also d'Aquili et al. 1978: chapter 1). Obviously, with a change in the operational environment, a reciprocal and coordinated change may be required in the adaptive infrastructure of that population in order to maintain the adaptive quality of its actions. The process of maintaining adaptive isomorphism between a population's infrastructure and its operational environment can be labeled as *equilibration* (after Waddington 1957). The state produced by equilibration is *homeorhesis* rather than homeostasis, as we suggested at the beginning of this chapter. Homeostasis implies return of the adaptive infrastructure to a static point after undergoing change, while homeorhesis connotes a return to a more dynamic course (Piaget 1971). The notion of dynamism as a state of affairs in adaptive infrastructures is more consistent with the realities of human social systems.

Generally speaking, equilibratory mechanisms within the adaptive infrastructure of a given society must respond to two types of environmental change. The first type may be termed *progressive change:* it is ongoing, more or less constant, and non-repetitive change such as one might observe in the alteration of a river's path, in the development of a progressively drier climate, or in the increase of a population's density. Progressive change may also be introduced through cross-cultural interference by other populations, and such changes may lead to a greater abundance, to a greater decrement, or to a different inventory of basic resources. The adaptive infrastructure operates within its own constraints as well as those of the physical environment in adjusting the patterns of social action in the population in response to such stimuli. At minimum, there is selective pressure to make adjustments that accord with local demands for maintaining population survival and sociocultural continuity. As Piaget has said, "The adaptation process intervenes inevitably as soon as the environment undergoes any modification, and where the life of the organism is concerned it is perpetually undergoing modification, at varying speeds according to its place on the evolutionary ladder" (1971:171). The tendency for an adaptive infrastructure to maintain isomorphism with a progressively changing environment may be called *simple* equilibration.

The second type of environmental change is *recursive:* it occurs in a repetitive sequence and has a more or less predictable range of frequency, character, phase, and amplitude from the standpoint of the actors who perceive it. Recursive changes may derive from purely natural processes, such as those underlying annual agricultural cycles or those that produce the regular but infrequent tropical cyclones of Micronesia; they may also derive from sociocultural circumstances, such as those precipitated by cross-cultural interference and ritualized warfare, among other possibilities. It should be noted, however, that the cross-cultural interference characteristic of contact between industrial and non-industrial societies in the developing Third World tends to be of the progressive sort.

Recursive change is adaptively critical to an adaptive infrastructure when the change produces a sinesoidal fluctuation in the availability of basic resources, that is, a significant oscillation in range or quantity of subsistence items and other strategic goods or services. If a society has been located in an environment marked by adaptively significant recursive change for a long period of time, we would expect the population's anticipation of such change to be manifest in the flexibility of constraints placed on behavior and sociocultural alignments in the adaptive infrastructure of that social system. Furthermore, we would expect that any constraints placed on social action under these circumstances will never be so stringent that effective responses to anticipated change in the environment are precluded. Patterns that fall short of these expectations run the risk of being maladaptive and thereby selecting for extinction rather than survival in the long run, all other things being equal.

The tendency for an adaptive infrastructure to integrate constraints on social action and coordinate them with recursive environmental change may be called *diaphatic* equilibration, or simply *diaphasis*. Examples of social diaphasis in response to recursion in the environment include the ritual warfare complexes that obtain among the Tsembaga and other related tribes of New Guinea (Rappaport 1967, 1968), the seasonal coalescence of numerous small hunting bands among the traditional Ojibwa (Bishop, article 7), the decrement and reestablishment of widespread sharing in response to drought among the So of Northeastern Uganda (Laughlin, article 3), adaptation to differential frost intensity by the Fringe Enga of Highland New Guinea (Waddell 1975), and seasonal patterns of resource exploitation among the Bushmen (Lee 1966). Several points need to be clarified, however, to make diaphasis a useful (and we think powerful) analytic construct against which disaster, deprivation, and other substantive ecological data may be weighed.

We should emphasize, for example, that both diaphatic and simple equilibration may operate simultaneously to maintain or stimulate adaptive isomorphism between infrastructures and their environments. In fact, where diaphasis is distinguishable as a quality of equilibration in the system, it will most likely appear as an epicycle in the process of simple equilibration. Furthermore, recursive change will usually result in diaphasis under one of two conditions.

First, diaphasis will occur in cases in which the periodicity of cycles is sufficiently clustered in time so that actors in the system perceive the recursivity to some degree and integrate it consciously as an attribute of their cognized environment. Such patterns are part of the more general phenomenon in which all organisms with brains conceptualize their environments in a way that maximizes redundancy and minimizes novelty, leading to the recognition of patterns in time as well as in space (Whitehead 1960; Laughlin and d'Aquili 1974: chapter 4). Nevertheless, certain cyclical environmental events occur with such infrequency (such as glacial oscillations) that they are perceived as progressive changes or they are not perceived as environmental change features at all, which brings us to the second condition under which diaphasis may occur. The initial set in a recursive environmental series might cause morphogenesis in an adaptive infrastructure in such a way that the actors never become conscious of the forthcoming set in the recursivity series.[7] Diaphasis is not integrated in the cognized environment of the actors under these circumstances, and even simple equilibration may go unrecognized as a low-level response to whatever progressive change stimuli the long-term recursive cycle produces. Yet the recursive cycle remains as part of the operational environment of the population, and it may be mediated indirectly through tandem exploitation cycles in the long run.

Adaptively significant recursivity is generally of the first type, however, insofar as it is anticipated, cognized, and managed through consciously shifted responses in such things as cultural content, personnel alignments, and social behavior as parts of the total adaptive infrastructure in that society. Disaster emerges from this paradigm as an abrupt and noxious form of progressive change in the environment, and deprivation can be identified as a noxious form of recursivity. Deprivation is clearly a diaphatic stimulus in the short run; disaster may be diaphatic in the long run. Both engage cognitive engineering through the adaptive infrastructures of the societies that experience them. We concentrate in the following section on the effects of deprivation on adaptive infrastructures. Our intention is to exemplify some of the complexities and processes that can be triggered in adaptive responses to environmental stimuli generally, including those presented by disaster.

THE EFFECTS OF DEPRIVATION ON ADAPTIVE INFRASTRUCTURES

As we have said, infrastructural response to environmental change frequently requires manipulations and adjustments in surface structural features. We may now examine some of the specific kinds of variations likely to occur under conditions of deprivation in the different domains of a society's adaptive response, and then analyze the relationship of these variations to the functioning of cognitive subsystems as the latter mediate between environmental stimuli and adaptive responses generally.

Deprivation and the Economic Domain: The diaphatic effects of economic deprivation (deprivative fluctuations in basic resources) in human societies vary enormously. More than any other animal species, man has developed a vast array of means to exploit his environment for survival. He has done so in niches ranging from the arctic tundra to tropical rain forests, from low-lying Pacific atolls to the high mountain valleys of the Andes. Much of the adaptive success that has been achieved in these disparate regions derives from remarkable plasticity in technological development and tool use, from the algebraic and symbolic capacity to cognitively "map" an environment, and from the physical and social abilities to equilibrate production strategies in response to environmental fluctuations. Man is able to shift his goals from the ultimate to the immediate for purposes of adaptive social action, and he is able to maintain extremely flexible and alternative channels of interpersonal relations without necessarily sacrificing the cooperation and cohesion needed for survival in social groups.

Nevertheless, the range of survival strategies extant in a given society at particular times forms a finite set. An unforeseen proliferation of adaptive innovations may take place under special environmental and psychobiological circumstances, but the processes of adaptive change always begin in a context of constraints on actions in the societies affected (see Barnett 1953; Carneiro 1970; Service 1971; Brady and Isaac 1975). The upper limits of technological capabilities, territorial expansion, cooperation in burgeoning social groups, among other considerations, impose constraints on the plasticity of adaptive infrastructures as they attempt to meet the problems of changing physical or social environments. Concomitantly, the inherent capabilities of adaptive infrastructures to respond to environmental stress are also limited in this highly relative and immediate sense, and these structures are therefore quite susceptible as a general rule to disruptions from innumerable external sources. Such disruptions may also function as important stimuli for adaptive change, of course; but the actual outcome in terms of survival or extinction of the groups affected depends largely on the cybernetic wherewithal and kinds of responses generated by the adaptive infrastructures operating in those groups.

To illustrate some of the variety of economic responses we might expect to find in societies confronting ecological stress as a result of fluctuations in basic resource availabilities, we may imagine two different sets of environmental conditions. First, a cyclical decrement may occur in the number or variety of basic resources available to a group without a corresponding reduction in the quantity or quality of nutritional material consumed. Seasonal fluctuations in the flora and fauna strategic to hunting and gathering societies, or crop failure in a society that also has access to cattle or produce from hunting and gathering activities as alternative sources of nutrition are exemplary of this first condition. Second, as a more extreme possibility, a cyclical decrement may occur in the variety and the overall quantity and quality of resources that particular groups depend on for nutrition and survival. Such changes cover alternatives known and utilized under partial change circumstances in these groups, and the result is generally widespread deprivation. An example here might include an agrarian society faced with crop failure because of blight or drought where access to produce from domestic animals or hunting and gathering is limited or not included in the traditional repertoire of subsistence modes and may in fact be impossible in that particular environment (see Laughlin, article 3). A similar circumstance obtains in societies with diversified production and subsistence modes where the cyclical decrement in resource availability is unusually intense and covers the entire exploitative repertoire. Intense tropical cyclones frequently create such conditions on the coral atolls of the Pacific by spoiling fresh water supplies, decimating land-based resources, and interfering with the availability of marine resources (see Brady, article 9).

Some of the adaptive responses we might expect to find in economic domains under the less severe circumstances of the first condition outlined above are compared to some we might expect to find under the second condition in table 1.1. Generally speaking, societies confronted with cyclical deprivation under the more severe circumstances of the second condition may be expected to develop a varied set of techniques that are geared to exploit the widest possible number of potentially available basic resources in their environment. This may include an increased or new exploitation of resources which are not directly consumable, but which may be used for obtaining consumables through external exchange and conversion into subsistence items (see Brady 1972a; Laughlin 1974b). Societies faced with cyclical fluctuations under the first condition are not subjected to precisely the same selective pressures, although such societies may develop similar response patterns through parallel innovations conceived in response to other stimuli in their environment, such as cross-cultural competition or interference.

Similarly, we might expect actors under the second environmental condition to be especially open to new economic alternatives if experimentation with these alternatives is not perceived as interfering with "tried and true" practices to the point of eliminating the latter entirely. The ideal circumstance here is often to develop internally or to incorporate from outside sources a battery of alternatives for eco-

TABLE 1.1 SOME ECONOMIC AND RELATED RESPONSES TO TWO VARIED CONDITIONS OF CYCLICAL DEPRIVATION

Response Category	Condition I (shift in no. of basic resources w/o shift in quantity)	Condition II (shift in type and quantity of basic resources)
Technology	Limited technological means	Large variety of technological means
Production strategies	Intensified exploitation of existing alternative native resources	Intensification, search for new alternatives
Knowledge of basic resources	Knowledge of limited set	Widest knowledge of available resources
Conceptualization of basic resources	Fundamental, stress on integration of spheres of conversion and exchange; involuted versus outside orientation	Elaborate, stress on compartmentalization of spheres of exploitation and exchange, including external resources
Production of surplus	Limited pressure for stockpiling	Maximal pressure for stockpiling
Territory	Little pressure for expansion	Expansion if possible through alliance, warfare
Long-range versus short-range maximization of payoffs	Mixed with little or minimal alternation	Extreme alternation
Mythology	Stress on inherent order of cosmos and long term survival	Stress on fragility of cosmos and codes for alternative survival strategies
Social organization	Emphasis on internal solidarity at expense of external or wider alliance	Emphasis on flexibility, widest possible alliance, and integration at expense of inherent structural continuity inside

nomic action that will represent the widest possible range of exploitative opportunities, and perhaps to do so by compartmentalizing the new from the old (Barnett 1971) in order to increase the overall diversity of survival strategies available to the population.

Compartmentalization of cultural elements in the economic or social domains generally represents a transformation of expansion of the range of adaptive strategies, whereas substitution represents a transformation of replacement in the same context (see Brady, article 9). Both modes of conceptual and social integration may represent successful responses under conditions of environmental flux. But, specifically with reference to the second type of environmental condition outlined above, the homogeneity perceived in substitution as a possible response may give way to greater selection for compartmentalization as a point of ecological conservatism, and as a more obvious way of expanding heterogeneity in the population's repertoire of economic action. Direct substitution of new patterns for old ones may in fact be selected for at the expense of compartmentalization only under special circumstances of progressive environmental changes where the older patterns are no longer perceived as viable, or under cyclical conditions where the new alternatives conflict in principle with the old ones and are clearly perceived as more powerful and successful adaptations. It should be noted that we are talking about a difference in degree of emphasis and institutionalization of these integrative modes, however, since some measure of both is likely to be entailed in all adaptive responses that include new alternatives (see Brady and Isaac 1975).

We might also expect actors faced with deprivation under the second environmental circumstance outlined above to retain and cultivate knowledge of the fullest expanse of resource alternatives within their territory of normal exploitation, and, where possible, to expand the range of this territory through alliance, sociability, exchange, or warfare with neighboring groups. Similarly, although the concept of "surplus" is fraught with conflicting interpretations which we shall ignore for the moment (see Sahlins 1958; Harris 1959; Orans 1966; Cancian 1976), we might expect societies confronted with inevitable and cyclical deprivation to produce and stockpile the largest surplus of basic resources possible within the limits of their existing technological capacities and environmental opportunities.[8] Finally, the payoffs maximized by individuals and groups in production and allocation strategies under conditions of cyclical deprivation may be calculated explicitly for short-term benefits, such as satisfying daily hunger or clothing needs, at the expense of longer-range goals that might be maximized by the same individuals and groups during periods of relative abundance, such as saving basic resources for bridewealth, building a house, accumulating cattle, and so on (see Laughlin, article 3).

We have emphasized adaptive responses to the two previous conditions primarily because they are common in occurrence and frequently cited in the ethnographic literature. There is a third and less common condition confronted by adaptive infrastructures, however, which can be identified as *unremitting deprivation*. This form of deprivation results from a dramatic and progressive decrement in the resource base of a given population. It is marked by periods of deprivation that predominate over periods of abundance to the extent that abundance rather than scarcity is perceived by the actors as an environmental aberrancy (see especially Turnbull, article 2; Cawte, article 4). Under these circumstances, the range of possibilities for transformations of replacement *and* expansion are generally perceived as exhausted, and experimentation by individuals in attempts to achieve new options are minimized for fear of high personal or social costs, including extinction. Individuals usually maximize the most immediate payoffs possible in production and allocation strategies on a day-to-day survival basis. Societies caught in this seemingly intractable web have adapted to minimal conditions for maintenance of a viable reproductive population, and usually at considerable cost to sociability and integration with other individuals and groups. As we shall see below in the discussion of hoarding and sociability, societies on the brink of extinction may manifest some rather remarkable attributes in infrastructural responses to such environments. For now, it is pertinent to reassert that these and other possible responses to cyclical and progressive changes in basic resource profiles are closely integrated with the elements, processes, and responses of the social domain.

Deprivation and the Social Domain: As suggested previously, the social domain of a society's adaptive infrastructure consists of a network of interpersonal relationships, formal and informal, the basic adaptive functions of which are to provide: (1) the channels through which basic resources and derivative products are distributed for consumption or reallocation by the population; and (2) the potential structure for amity, altruism, sociability, corporate action, and so on. One of the key variables for understanding the impact of deprivation on this domain is *social cooperation,* which may be defined operationally in terms of the degree to which strategic goods and services—that is, goods and services required for survival—flow through the network of interpersonal relationships in the primary social domain of a given population.

The reciprocal sharing of food and other resources fundamental to survival has long been recognized by social scientists as a primary strategy of adaptation in human populations (see, for example, Malinowski 1922; Mauss 1954; Lévi-Strauss 1963, 1969; Sahlins 1972). The collective endurance of households as viable units everywhere depends on an internal pooling and sharing of the fruits of domestic production. Larger social action units similarly may depend for their survival on a generous and predictable flow of strategic resources from the "haves" to the "have-nots," that is, on a regular diversion of some household produce, personnel, or services for wider socioeconomic ends in each community (see Service 1966; Lee and DeVore 1968; Sahlins 1968; Brady 1972a, 1976e; Laughlin 1974b). At an even deeper and more primordial level in the adaptive infrastructure, it is in the interest of any population to assist the survival of its members, if for no other reason than to ensure the perpetuation of its gene pool (see Trivers 1971; Giesel 1974). Thus, in the broadest sense of the term, social cooperation is the essence of society itself; as Rousseau would say, it requires a subordination of individual desires from time to time for the benefit of the commonweal.

The major adaptive principle underlying sharing, sociability, and social cooperation in general can be identified as *reciprocal altruism* (cf. Trivers 1971). However, by "altruism" we do not mean to imply that it is behavior motivated by compulsive or socially contrived generosity with absolutely no expectation or realization of the return— Malinowski's (1922) "pure gift" category. Pure gifts of this sort probably do not exist in the reality of "give and take" economics that governs exchange in human societies. *Some* obligation to reciprocate, no matter how indefinite or generalized in kind, is always implied in the transaction (Mauss 1954). Nevertheless, a failure to reciprocate for gifts given or services rendered does not necessarily stop the donor from giving more in the future. Wherever there is a structural and moral mandate for generous giving, goods and services may move in one direction, in favor of the "have-nots," for long periods of time (Sahlins 1965a:147). Furthermore, it is important to recognize that the principle of generosity in reciprocal altruism "can create conflict as well as contribute to solidarity, and can also be manipulated to secure an advantage over one's fellows" (Cook 1968:214).

In a problematic examination of similar problems, Trivers (1971) argues that genetic and behavioral selection can operate against the non-reciprocator or "cheater" in social action systems involving reciprocal altruism (cf. Sahlins 1976). But he also adds to his argument the following:

> The human altruistic system is a sensitive, unstable one. Often it will pay to cheat: namely, when the partner will not find out, or when he is unlikely to survive long enough to reciprocate adequately. . . . Given this unstable character of the system, where a degree of cheating is adaptive, natural selection will rapidly favor a complex psychological system in each individual regulating his own altruistic and cheating tendencies and his responses to these tendencies in others. As selection favors subtler forms of cheating, it will favor more acute abilities to detect cheating. The system that results should simultaneously allow the individual to reap the benefits of altruistic changes, to protect himself from gross and subtle forms of cheating, and to practice those forms of cheating that local conditions make adaptive. *Individuals will differ not in being altruistic or cheaters, but in the degree of altruism they show and in the conditions under which they will cheat.* (Trivers 1971:48, emphasis added)

Cheating in this case denotes a failure to reciprocate, and, whether or not it stops the donor from giving, it is an important form of hoarding that is likely to appear under conditions of resource scarcity and deprivation.

As Brady has argued elsewhere (1976d), if sharing and reciprocal altruism are the essence of social contract and collective endurance in society, then hoarding represents the antithesis of this process. Hoarding maximizes self-interest against the interests of the wider group. It is antithetical to widespread interdependence in human groups (see Lomnitz, article 6). Where solidarity and subsistence are governed by the sharing of strategic resources, hoarding represents anarchy and fission. Hoarding may be institutionalized and expressed formally in a dominance hierarchy where rank and stratification (if not brute force) protect differential access to strategic resources (see Washburn 1961; DeVore 1965; Reynolds 1966; Van Lawick-Goodall 1968; Sahlins 1972). Even under these circumstances, however, there are usually tolerance limits beyond which individuals and groups are not allowed to pursue their self-interests in a peaceful and socially sanctioned manner. Hoarding beyond the normal tolerance limits may be mitigated ultimately by the communal demands of the social system itself, perhaps by the need to preserve a balance of cooperation over competition for functional purposes such as defense, among other possibilities (see Mead 1966; Trivers 1971; cf. Sahlins 1976).

It may also be that there is greater tolerance for hoarding everywhere in times of plenty than is permitted or even practical in times of scarcity. But there remains in all societies as well the distinct possibility "that structural compulsions of generosity are unequal to the test of hardship" (Sahlins 1965a:158). Prolonged resource deprivation resulting from either cyclical or progressive alterations of basic resources may trigger a deescalation of the normal patterns of sharing resources. Individual or small group hoarding units may surface where structural obligations to share once prevailed, and widespread cooperation may give way to active competition between these units for differential access to the strategic resources that remain. This degeneration of solidarity can be expected under the conditions we identified above as unremitting deprivation. This is admittedly an extreme condition for human adaptation, yet it is one pregnant with implications for scientific study of the human adaptive infrastructure, as we shall see in the articles by Turnbull (article 2) and Cawte (article 4), as well as in the concluding article of this volume.

The most common pattern to be found in the ethnographic literature, however, is one of solidary response to adversity. Initially, at least, the range of generalized sharing is *extended* to include persons and groups who are socially and perhaps genetically distant (see Danielsson 1955; Demerath 1957; Schneider 1957; Baker and Chapman 1962; Lessa 1968; Kates et al. 1973; Waddell 1975; Sahlins 1976). It appears to be only as the resource deprivation level becomes more protracted that the extended parameters of sharing may collapse into hoarding units that are *narrower* than those within the normal range of sharing (see Brady 1974; Laughlin 1974b). Furthermore, the sphere of generalized exchange for food may be even wider than the sphere of generalized exchange for other kinds of things, both as an ordinary circumstance and in times of scarcity (Sahlins 1965a:172; Brady 1972a:310ff.). This adds the dimension of the *kind* of items shared or hoarded as a critical consideration for understanding social cooperation patterns and infrastructural responses to environmental stress generally.

The combination of expansion and retraction phases in the range of generalized sharing of basic resources of all kinds produces a cybernetic flow pattern and structural effect over time that Laughlin (1974b) has called the *accordion effect*. The social segments traversed by a full cycle of this effect are sociability sectors (see Sahlins 1965a:144, 151–52; Brady 1972a:293–94), each of which is more or less expendable in times of basic resource scarcity. Determining exactly which segments are expendable and when varies according to the society's particular structural plan and the intensity and type of deprivation that it encounters. However, since hoarding appears to be inversely related in frequency and scope to sharing behavior, that is, hoarding does not vary independently relative to sharing in the same sociocultural system, it may be expected that the retraction phase of the accordion effect is calculated on the same structural grid or scale of relative social distance that is used to calculate the expansion phase. If so, we should be able to predict the patterns of structural deescalation in the retraction phase from knowledge of the structure of sharing in the expansion phase, all other things being equal (Brady 1976d).

Following this reasoning, the individuals and groups who represent the periphery of the maximal expansion phase should be the first to be excluded as the motivations for sharing give way to the demands for hoarding in the retraction phase; persons and groups who represent the next least solidary level relative to the hoarding unit would be sloughed off second, and so on down the sliding scale of relative social space until the level of hoarding produces a satisfactory subsistence profile for the participants. The hoarding unit should stabilize at this point until the level of resource deprivation changes for better or for worse. This is a fundamental pattern of social and economic equilibration through environmental change, although it is presented here in a highly idealized form. Laughlin's (1974b; see also article 3) study of diaphasis and deprivation among the So of Northeastern Uganda provides a concrete example of this pattern that departs only in minimal ways from the version proposed here.

Theoretically, the upper limits of the expansion phase are set only by the common interest obligations and desires of the population, by the inventory of strategic resources that the population controls at the time, and by the particular type of ecological stress, if any, the population is subjected to through change in the operational environment. Conversely, the range of shrinking sociability and cooperation that is associated with hoarding in the retraction phase can be reduced ultimately to the last survivor of an afflicted population. However, an absolute and long-term retraction of the reciprocal flow of strategic resources would in most cases prove maladaptive. Lost would be the flexibility of social response characteristic of diaphasis in systems confronting recursive environmental change, a resiliency that some human societies retain under even the most marked deprivation (see Gould 1970 for an example of Australian Aboriginal response to extreme deprivation). For one thing, not all members of a society are equally equipped to provision themselves, especially the old, the indigent, and the very young; and the survival of such persons will, under most conditions of ecological stress, increase the maintenance of cultural and infrastructural continuity. For another thing, the functional requirements of keeping incest taboos and managing sexual reproduction at the same time set certain vital demographic and infrastructural limits on sociability reductions below the level of small groups (see Bishop, article 7). If for no other reasons than these, a total retraction of sharing behavior is unlikely in populations facing even the most extreme periods of deprivation—unlikely, that is, in all cases save those of unremitting deprivation in which some strong measure of "every man for himself" may become the only apparently viable strategy available to the organism (see Turnbull, article 2). Yet even in such rare cases as these, one may find pockets of cooperation in such fundamental activities as construction of shelter and defense. We may view such societies as having become transfixed at the lowest point of their retraction phase, just as societies may become transfixed at the high point of their expansion phase with either the cessation of environmental recursivity, or the inception of an innovation that buffers the intensity of such recursive effects.

In terms of social cooperation generally, of which sharing, hoarding, and the accordion effect are important but not the only indices, the relationship between cyclical decrements of basic resources (one indicator of ecological stress) and the degree of social cooperation elicited at the level of adaptive infrastructure may approximate the relationship shown in figure 1.4.[9] We hypothesize that there is some point of average resource availability under normal conditions in all

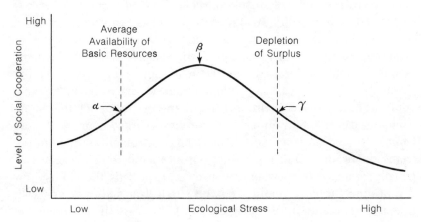

FIGURE 1.4 RELATION OF SOCIAL COOPERATION TO ECOLOGICAL STRESS IN A SOCIAL ACTION SYSTEM

societies that corresponds to an average level of *suboptimal* cooperation (point α). The beginning of a deprivative phase caused by a perceived decrement in the availability of basic resources should produce an increment in social cooperation that parallels the expansion
phase of the accordion effect (point β). If the deprivative phase lasts
long enough or is severe enough to cause the level of surplus to approach zero, the degree or incidence of social cooperation theoretically should show a comparable and progressive decrement toward
zero at approximately the same time (point γ).

Points α, β, and γ are necessarily imprecise. The factors determining the exact value of each point vary according to the situation at
hand in specific social and ecological contexts. For example, the
slope may depend directly on the nature, quantity, perishability, and
distribution of surpluses in the afflicted society; it may also be
influenced by the existing range of alternative resources available to
the population, the type of political control exercised over resources,
the constraints placed on social action by physically debilitating factors such as disease and dislocation of the population, the values regulating hoarding behaviors under normal conditions in that society,
and so on. However, one of the most important variables affecting
point γ, if not *the* most important one, is the perception of depleted
resources in the absence of a perceivable end to the deprivative
phase. Furthermore, we expect that societies confronted with deprivation are generally able to maintain a higher level of social cooperation at the outset, if not in the long run, than are societies confronted
with disaster. Point γ should be reached in the latter case more
quickly than in the former.

Social cooperation at the level of economic exchange is not the
whole story, of course, as we shall see in later sections. But it is a critical chapter in this thesis and worth documenting as far as we can.
Aside from the evidence and hypotheses presented in this volume on
social cooperation, some interesting data are supplied by social psychologists, particularly by the work of Muzafer Sherif.

Sherif and his group (Sherif 1967; Sherif and Sherif 1953, 1969)
have been concerned in large part with the factors leading to increased intergroup cooperation and decreased tension and conflict
under variable conditions. In a series of experiments with small

group interaction, often called the "Robber's Cave" experiments (Sherif and Sherif 1969), Sherif demonstrated that the major variable underlying intergroup cohesion is the presence of what he calls *superordinate goals*. These are defined as "goals which are compelling and highly appealing to members of two or more groups in conflict but which cannot be attained by the resources and energies of the groups separately" (Sherif 1967:445). Groups tend to unite around such goals and the cooperation engendered thereby has a cumulative effect on reducing conflict, minimizing competition, and enhancing intergroup identification. On the other hand, rewards or incentives for individual achievement may be interjected into group interaction with the ultimate effect of disrupting cooperation, reducing orientation toward superordinate goals, and creating individual goal maximization even at the *intragroup* level.

Applying Sherif's conclusions to the present thesis, that is, to environmental effects on social infrastructures as networks of interpersonal relations that provide for exchange and corporate action, the social fabric of a society can be viewed as a systematic integration of groups within groups in a scheme of ever widening co-membership spheres. As Sahlins puts it: "the household, the local lineage, perhaps the village, the subtribe, the tribe, other tribes—the particular plan of the course varies. The structure is a hierarchy of levels of integration, but from the inside and on the ground, it is a series of concentric circles" (1965a:151; see also Evans-Pritchard 1940:144). Social cooperation at any of these overlapping points is action in pursuit of superordinate goals, and the pursuit of such goals is subject to the same constraints and processes outlined by Sherif in terms of small group interaction processes.

In broader terms, another way to interpret this model is that at point γ in figure 1.4 both deprivation and disaster create conditions conducive to intergroup or even interindividual competition, and they select for a suspension of superordinate goals, especially those involving long-term payoff maximizations. We argue below that primary and determinate transformations for these operations exist at the level of cognitive infrastructure in the organism. The effects are quite clear, however, at the level of social infrastructure: a decrement in social cooperation occurs down the gradient of social cohesion toward the individual and his primary social unit. Sharing or hoarding behaviors are employed accordingly. Disaster, of course, usually disrupts the matrix of superordinate goals and social cooperation more rapidly than deprivation does, insofar as the society is at least minimally prepared for the latter. An entire infrastructure may be disrupted by disaster, perhaps irretrievably so. The changes induced may be drastically equilibrative, leading to morphogenesis or extinction. In the case of deprivation, the social infrastructure is prepared and selects for successful diaphasis. The matrix of superordinate goals is temporarily suspended for the duration of the deprivative phase, and is generally reestablished with the return to relative abundance of basic resources. We can add, then, the dimension of superordinate goal maximization or suspension as a critical part of the accordion effect outlined previously.

Lest we perpetuate a serious misinterpretation of this model, let us stress that we are not suggesting that societies confronted by disaster or deprivation necessarily "atomize" or fall apart (see also Bishop, article 7). We do argue that societies confronted with intense or prolonged ecological stress tend to reduce both the incidence and range of social cooperation that normally prevails in their social systems, and that the maximization or suspension of various hoarding, sharing, superordinate goal and corporate behavior patterns are important indicators of such responses. What remains to be specified is the role of political action, ideology, and cognitive infrastructures in the development of such responses.

Deprivation and the Political Domain: As outlined earlier in this article, the political domain of a society's adaptive infrastructure encompasses all of the power relations that influence resource distribution and adaptive action by the members of that society, including the production, distribution, and consumption of basic resources and the defense of the members as a corporate action unit. The importance of this domain to adaptation is especially poignant under conditions of deprivation in societies where the set of power resources upon which the structure of power relations is grounded overlaps to a significant degree with the set of basic resources upon which the biological survival of the group depends. We hypothesize in this regard that *a complete overlap between power and basic resources will never occur in such societies, primarily because the maintenance of social cohesion under changing environmental circumstances requires flexibility in the differential allocation of such resources* (see Burns and Laughlin 1978). At the perceived onset of a deprivative phase (point α), for example, especially if the period of deprivation is expected to be severe and prolonged, the members of the afflicted group may increasingly look to their leaders for definition and initiation of a coping response. These leaders are expected to take whatever action is socially defined as appropriate or adequate in order to alleviate the disruptions of the moment. Leaders may be expected to take action that will reduce suffering, redistribute surpluses, protect or expand the existing range of basic resources, and otherwise end the phase of deprivation. These attitudes and expectations tend to increase in intensity until a return to abundance is apparent, or point γ is reached and surpassed. The return to abundance generally reduces reliance on leaders in the group; reaching or surpassing point γ leads to an optimal reliance on the actions of such persons.

It is virtually axiomatic that groups under stress tend toward greater political centralization and reliance on basic norms and traditions, at least initially. This means that the variety of alternatives for effective and appropriate action by leaders under ordinary circumstances may be diminished under conditions of ecological stress. Some social psychological data on the effects of stress on centralization tendencies are pertinent here. After three laboratory studies and one study of natural groups, Fiedler (1962) suggests that highly directive leadership is more effective under artificial stress conditions while non-directive leadership is more effective under more pleasant circumstances. Hamblin (1958:334), drawing data from research on twenty-four laboratory groups, suggests that leaders tend to have more influence during periods of crisis than they do under other circumstances. Tuckman's (1964) study of the relationship between levels of cognitive complexity of group members and tendencies toward hierarchization provides additional support for this proposition; and Schroder et al. conclude at one point in their research that, "like individual systems, group systems become hierarchial under stress . . ." (1967:101).

In a very real sense, deprivation represents the crucial test for adaptive diaphasis in the political domain, as in the others we have outlined for adaptive infrastructures. In stimulating the tendency to move toward greater political centralization in the short run, or perhaps to group fragmentation in the long run, deprivation also forces people to define within rather precise limits the problems confronting themselves and their leaders. Leaders who do not have obvious solutions to problems, who fail to mediate stress properly in terms of directing concerted action, or who are otherwise found to be inadequate under such conditions, are replaced quickly as a general rule (see Hamblin 1958: 334; Sherif and Sherif 1969:534; also Sahlins 1963; d'Aquili et al. 1978).

We have again directed our emphasis toward societies faced with the two more common conditions of environmental recursivity noted in table 1.1. Societies that become successfully adapted to unremitting deprivation, such as the Ik, the Kaiadilt, and seventeenth-century slaves in the West Indies (see articles 2, 4, and 5), may manifest a partial or total diminution of power relations and political action. Some societies may exhibit few power relations beyond the most fundamental level of "the most goes to the strongest." It is critical to understand that the stress engendered by resource scarcity may at the same time cause a tendency toward enhanced centralization of authority and an exacerbation of interpersonal conflicts due to differential access to strategic resources (Robert Dirks, personal communication). A reasonable inference from the data on West Indies slaves, the Ik, and the Kaiadilt, is that if leaders are perceived as incapable of an adequate coping response to deprivation, then the opposite, conflicting inclination will disrupt the structure of power relations in that society. More particularly, the structure of power relations will tend to disintegrate under unremitting deprivation when: (1) the payoffs underlying non-basic power resources become partially or totally devaluated under the pressure of a continuous, day-to-day struggle for survival; and (2) basic resources are so scarce and dispersed that little or no differential access to them on an orderly basis is possible. In the absence of alternative power resources, the channels of differential influence underlying the political domain of the adaptive infrastructure may become attenuated or may cease to function altogether.

Putting all of this in perspective, we predict that where there is a large overlap between power and basic resources in a society, the initial period of enhanced social cooperation between point α and point γ (figure 1.4) will mandate some redistribution of surplus basic resources from leaders to group members. So long as the redistribution is perceived to be adequate by the group, the structure of power relations vis-à-vis the existing leadership will be reinforced. If the deprivative phase outlasts the supply of redistributable basic resources under the control of leaders, any one of several things may happen. The leaders may abdicate their positions, they may be replaced, or they may shift the emphasis of their actions to control over power resources the availability of which is not affected in any direct way by deprivation. We would expect the last alternative to occur most often in societies that are diaphatically structured for deprivation as opposed to those societies experiencing disaster. In fact, the value of the power resources to which the leaders turn may be enhanced in some cases by the decrement in basic resources, that is, they may become more readily available, more desirable to the actors, and so on. Leaders of a more complex, pluralistic society may be in control of military and police forces, a power resource that may acquire an enhanced value to many actors during a deprivative phase. Through the use of coercive forces, leaders may take significant action to protect the remaining surplus of basic resources from "plunder" by individuals within the group or by alien groups. Coercive power may also be used by leaders to increase the input of basic resources to their groups through raids for resources controlled by other groups, or by territorial aggrandizement through warfare with other groups.

Societies facing disaster are placed under an even greater adaptive test as they are, by definition, forced to respond to conditions for which they are relatively ill prepared.[10] These more intense and disruptive conditions may increase or exaggerate the movements toward greater centralization and rapid replacement of ineffective leaders, and may place an even heavier reliance on internal coercion by leaders in efforts to maintain their own positions.

Disasters also tend to provide fertile ground for the development of "revitalization" movements (see Wallace 1956; Demerath and Wallace 1957; d'Aquili et al. 1978). Such movements may have political and economic repercussions, but they are primarily attempts to equilibrate stress through the ideological domain of the adaptive infrastructure.

Deprivation and the Ideological Domain: We would expect much of the ideological domain in a society confronted by deprivation to focus on defining the precise nature of the deprivative condition, solutions to attendant problems, and proper action coordination. Often mythology will depict dire consequences of improper action under such conditions, thereby reinforcing or directing appropriate action. Such is the case for Tsimshian and Kaguru survival myths (Cove, article 8), as well as for the Buffalo Calf Pipe mythology and associated ritual among the Sioux (Brown 1953). In general, myths may contain statements of appropriate action for allocating goods and services, guidelines for appropriate, ceremonial response, justifications for ritual action, specifications of the correct relationships between actors and leaders under deprivative conditions, and perhaps also important information concerning the cosmic forces that are believed to affect resource availability in times of plenty or scarcity.

A fundamental means by which the ideational domain of adaptive infrastructures may counteract the potentially divisive effects of deprivation is by presenting a cognized environment in which the deprivative phase itself is interpreted as punishment for or a reaction to social individuation. This point is emphasized by Schneider (1957) in his discussion of the social effects of hurricanes on Yap and the social effects of disaster in a number of Western societies. Similarly, Firth notes that on Tikopia, "natural order and prosperity were related to social harmony. Disorder in nature, untoward events [such as hurricanes, drought, tidal waves, epidemics—all infrequent but regular occurrences on this island], lack of prosperity, were to be related to social defects such as the religious division of the society or the feebleness of its premier chief" (1959:80). Hurricanes, drought, and resulting disorders such as famine are defined on Samoa as the punishment of angry spirits and gods to which the Samoans respond with communal ritual (Mead 1930:16; see also Stair 1897:238; d'Aquili et al. 1978). These are brief examples of the means by which the ideological domain may encode and anticipate recursivity in the environment, and also embed such events in a symbolic structure that results ultimately in corporate rather than individuated action, ritual or otherwise.

Under certain circumstances, access to ritual may be restricted by maximal leaders. Where this happens and the performance of ritual is also necessitated within the context of the cognized environment, we may speak of ritual as a power resource (see Burns and Laughlin 1978). This will very likely be the case in societies where the leaders are religious specialists. In any event, we would expect the control of ritual to form a subset of power resources for leaders in societies confronting deprivation. It is precisely through ritual that leaders may demonstrate their capacity for appropriate action—action that is perceived by all concerned as necessary and sufficient for the return to abundance.[11]

Cognitive Infrastructures and Deprivation: The effects of deprivation on perceptual and conceptual structures are of special interest here because an understanding of change at this infrastructural level provides, at least in part, some important information concerning the causal mechanisms that produce changes such as those discussed above in the four principal domains of societal infrastructure. We have defined cognitive infrastructure as synchronized conceptual mechanisms that mediate perceptions and decisions pertaining to the availability and use of basic resources. We have also mentioned that such structures are most accurately modeled as a sequence of stages in the ability of individual organisms to differentiate, integrate, and act upon perceptual information.

Levels of cognitive complexity appear to function in a curvilinear manner relative to perceptual input. That is, from an experimental standpoint, there appears to be a level of optimal complexity of environmental input which will arouse sufficient interest or attention in the individual to deal with input at peak cognitive capacity (Schroder et al. 1967:90; see also Miller 1964). However, if the complexity of the input is increased beyond this optimal point, a rapid decrement may occur in the level of cognitive complexity, as evidenced by the response displayed in behavior. If the input is sufficiently complex in a superoptimal sense, the complexity of the response may be quite concrete (figure 1.5). Concrete structuring of the perceptual field is somewhat analogous to looking at the field through the wrong end of

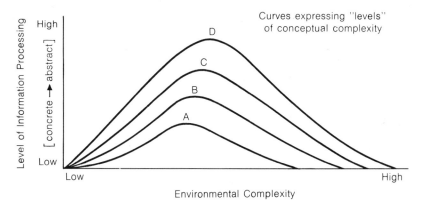

FIGURE 1.5 INCREASING INTEGRATION INDEX OF STRUCTURAL PROPERTIES (FROM SCHRODER ET AL. 1967:52, REPRINTED WITH PERMISSION OF THE PUBLISHER)

a telescope. The amount of information, as well as the number of distinctions and levels of integration involved, is reduced relative to optimal structuring. Concrete structuring in decision-making is generally indicated by simple yes-no, right-wrong, black-white distinctions, that is to say, it is almost exclusively dyadic and binary in nature.

It will also be remembered from our previous discussion of ecological stress that environmental input may be noxious or unpleasant to the organism. Such is the case with a perceived decrement in basic resources and all of the problems that accrue from deprivation. Yet, even here, the evidence would suggest that a similar curvilinear relationship obtains between the level of cognitive complexity and the level of complexity or degree of noxity in the environment. Noxity stimulates optimal complexity in cognitive responses, up to a certain point. If the noxity is increased beyond the optimal, a decrement in cognitive complexity generally follows (figure 1.6; see also Keys et al. 1950, Manocha 1972).

These findings from cognitive psychology relate to our present thesis on deprivation in the following ways. We may argue that deprivation creates enormous noxity or stress in the perceptual environment of the organism. The increment of stress is not sudden, as in the case with disaster, but is more or less gradual and predictable.

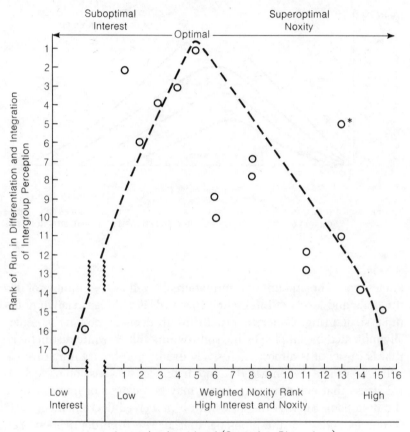

FIGURE 1.6 RELATION BETWEEN LEVEL OF SECONDARY DIMENSION INPUT (NOXITY AND REWARD) AND AVERAGE PERCEPTUAL COMPLEXITY IN ALL RUNS OF THE INTER-NATION SIMULATION (FROM SCHRODER ET AL. 1967:80, REPRINTED WITH PERMISSION OF THE PUBLISHER)

For an initial period of time, the increment in stress enhances attention and interest in individuals, especially for persons in leadership positions, and it may also increase the maximization of long-term superordinate goals. At point γ (see figure 1.4) the stress produced becomes overwhelming (superoptimal) and results in a decrement in structural complexity of both perception and cognition. As Schroder et al. (1967:77) suggest, "Too much noxity may induce a decrement in *all* aspects of structure, particularly of internally generated dimensions (thus leading to more stimulus-boundedness)." It is also important to note from their research that perceptual structuring tends to diminish in complexity before cognitive or decision-making structuring (figure 1.7).

Problem solving under severe deprivation is affected by a decrement in cognitive structuring, that is, responses are characterized by a reduction in the number of alternative actions perceived. Both the perception of the problem and the generation of solutions to the problem become increasingly simplified, progressively reducing the number and type of creative or novel solutions that might otherwise

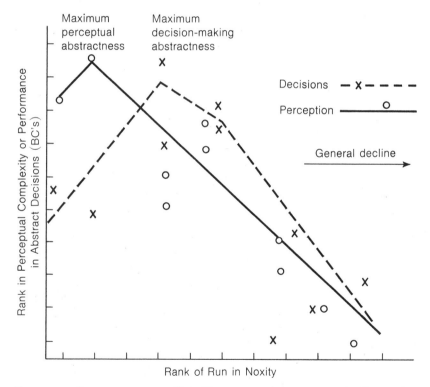

FIGURE 1.7   RELATION BETWEEN TWO MEASURES OF ABSTRACTNESS (IN PERCEPTION AND IN DECISIONS) AND NOXITY IN TEN BALANCED HIGH-INTEREST RUNS OF INTER-NATION SIMULATION 8 (FROM SCHRODER ET AL. 1967:98 (REPRINTED WITH PERMISSION OF THE PUBLISHER)

be applied (see Fiedler 1962; Tuckman 1964). Concomitantly, individuals look increasingly to persons in authority for solutions to their problems, thus giving rise to greater centralization. Furthermore, the reduction of cognitive complexity to concrete levels diminishes the likelihood that long-range strategizing and superordinate goals will be realized or even pursued.

Finally, not only is the role of leaders as decision-makers made more adaptively crucial by a shift in structural complexity, the role of tradition is enhanced as a provenience for proper decision content. Individuals who are influenced by structural decrements, including leaders, tend to focus attention on the "tried and true" solutions to previous problems of a similar nature that have been included in the society's culture pool. The point is more critical than it may appear to be at first glance. We have argued that both deprivation and disaster tend to produce a decrement in social cooperation in the long run. This process, taken alone, selects for atomization and social disintegration. However, societies that have adapted to deprivation as recursive change in their environment are likely to incorporate a set of norms in their ideological infrastructure that defines appropriate behavior under deprivative conditions. These norms, whether embodied in "survival" myths, the structure of appropriate ritual, codified law, or general cosmology, are increasingly attended by persons under prolonged or intense deprivation, especially if the application of the norms is accompanied by social coercion from leaders. The most important effect of concrete attention to tradition is to enhance social cooperation and thereby mitigate tendencies toward social disintegration under stressful conditions. Furthermore, structural decline and enhanced attention to tradition are major and fundamental causes of diaphasis in adaptive infrastructures. That is, these are mechanisms of transition from one phase to another in the diaphatic equilibratory cycles that adaptive infrastructures display through time.[12]

SUMMARY AND CONCLUSIONS

The relationship of diaphasis and deprivation to infrastructural organization and change may be summarized in a general proposition: *If a decremental shift in basic resources is due to recursivity in the en-*

vironment of an individual organism or society, then the adaptive infrastructure of that organism or society will at all times be organized to respond and adapt to that eventuality. This proposition may be referred to as the *Principle of Adaptive Diaphasis.* A first corollary proposition explored in this article is that: *The particular form and content of the adaptive response generated under such conditions will be determined in part by the prevailing level of information flow and balance of cognitive structural complexity brought to bear on the problem at particular points in time.* A second corollary proposition is that: *If an organism or society is confronted by unremitting deprivation such that the periods of minimal resource availability significantly predominate over periods of maximal resource availability, then the adaptive infrastructure of that organism or society will tend to lose its diaphatic characteristics and become stabilized in the homeorhetic state appropriate to the minimal phase.*

Infrastructural response to environmental change frequently requires manipulations and adjustments in surface structural features. We have argued that, where new alternatives for action are perceived and implemented in a given society's culture pool, then compartmentalization of the old and the new, as opposed to direct substitution, may contribute more to enhancing adaptive diversity in that population and thus may carry a heavier ecological load than direct substitution in many circumstances. We have also argued that the structural decrements associated with prolonged or intense deprivation put special pressures on leaders and special focus on tradition as a source of decision-making content. In terms of socioeconomic responses to deprivation, we have identified sharing, hoarding, and superordinate goal behaviors as key elements of social cooperation patterns, and we have traced variations in these elements and their distribution through adaptive infrastructures under conditions of ecological stress.

These principles, processes, and propositions are evaluated in various ways in the ethnographic articles that follow. To coordinate the relevance of each article with the present model, we have introduced each selection with a brief headnote. An overview of the work encapsulated in this volume and some implications for future studies of human adaptation and evolution are presented in the final article.

NOTES

1. We wish to express our gratitude to Robert Dirks, John McManus, Robert Rubinstein, and Tom Burns for their stimulating commentary and criticism of an earlier draft of this article.

2. We have substituted our term *homeorhesis* for Rappaport's term *homeostasis* in this passage, for reasons that are made explicit in a later section of this article.

3. *Cognized environment* is defined below and contrasted with *operational environment* as a fundamental point of analysis in our model.

4. The philosophical problems related to bridging levels of systemic organization in scientific explanation have been discussed in detail in Rubinstein and Laughlin (1977).

5. Tandem exploitation is a special application of the more general neurophysiological process that Laughlin and d'Aquili (1974:84ff.) have called the *empirical modification cycle.*

6. Members of the same social group generally reside in the same operational environment and adapt to it in part by using information grounded in a common culture pool. We may thus speak of a society's (or population's) cognized environment as a convenient label for the collective and synchronous aspects of the cognized environment developed within each individual's brain.

7. Buckley (1967:58ff.) distinguishes two general types of mechanisms that can be applied to systemic changes in adaptive infrastructures: (1) *morphostatic mechanisms,* which function within and between systems to preserve their primary structures; and, (2) *morphogenetic mechanisms,* which function within and between systems to alter their primary structures. The resulting conditions are termed *morphostasis* and *morphogenesis,* respectively.

8. Maximizing alliance and social cooperation between groups and societies may be especially important under such conditions in societies lacking technology for long-term storage, as on many of the Pacific Islands.

9. The two-dimensional graph in figure 1.4 is insufficient in sensitivity to depict many of the subtle interactions involved in our model. The graph is intended solely as an illustration of several major relations discussed in the text. A more satisfactory mathematical representation of our model might be found in catastrophe theory, a simplified offshoot of topology that facilitates the modeling of rapid change in systems (see Thom 1975; Zeeman 1976).

10. As Cohen (1971:9) suggests, "There is no such thing as an adapted organism; there are only organisms that have adapted to particular habitats." Such habitats do not include disaster as a general condition, although they may include deprivation as a form of cyclical fluctuation in basic resources.

11. Our treatment of ritual here has been necessarily summary. Readers wanting a fuller treatment should see Wallace (1966), Shaughnessy (1973), and d'Aquili et al. (1978).

12. It has been argued elsewhere (McManus 1977) that many institutions provided within the culture pool function as buffers inhibiting the complete collapse of individual conceptual systems under stress. An example of one such set of institutions is ceremonial ritual (d'Aquili et al. 1978). In formation encoded and stored in the society's culture pool may also operate as a buffer when it pre-structures the interpretation of potentially stressful events in such a way as to reduce the noxity perceived in the event. Lazarus (1964) has shown in a series of experiments that the same stimulus may cause more or less stress in subjects, depending upon the nature of information accompanying the stimulus.

2

Rethinking the Ik:
A Functional
Non-Social System

Colin M. Turnbull

The following account of the Ik by Colin Turnbull offers a synopsis of one of the most extreme cases of unremitting deprivation yet documented in the ethnographic literature (see also Cawte, article 4). The deprivation suffered by the Ik has been unremitting to the extent that resource abundance is conceptualized by them as an "abnormal" condition of temporary duration. Their life styles and survival strategies are geared closely to the problems of resource scarcity, and much of the traditional sociability and resource sharing employed under more abundant circumstances has been sacrificed as a result. The Ik plainly do not represent what anthropologists are accustomed to calling a "well-adapted and progressive society." But their marginality can be illusory in important respects. The Ik are in fact adapted and adjusted to prolonged environmental disruption and stress. They do not thrive under their present living conditions, but they have managed to survive. In fact, the Ik exemplify much of the profound resiliency of human adaptive infrastructures in selecting successfully for some measure of population survival and sociocultural continuity under extremely adverse environmental conditions.

The Ik (also known as Teuso) of northern Uganda represent an extreme end of the spectrum of change, deprivation, and disaster, so it is important that the factors leading to their present condition be considered as fully as possible. Information is regrettably minimal and eyewitness accounts of the process are virtually nil. The only facts that amount to a concentrated study are those that I collected during an eighteen-month stay from mid-1964 to the end of 1965, and during the summer months of 1966; and those collected by Joseph Towles during three visits during this same period and another brief survey in 1971. However, the following description, and the account given in *The Mountain People* (Turnbull 1972), make it plain that conditions for gathering data during this period were just about the worst imaginable. The Ik were already highly fragmented, and most activities, especially those related to subsistence, were pursued individually and in isolation. The only relatively localized segment of the population was that of the older men and women, who, together with the sick, were unable to go far from the villages. Even they engaged in little communal activity, so again we were reduced to following, as best we could, individuals living in relative isolation. While this fact is in itself significant as a measure of extreme social fragmentation, it means that even our joint observations over the two-year period are much more meager than would normally be the case from the point of view of the social anthropologist and are further weakened by the necessity of dividing our attention among individuals instead of villages or other social units in studying the Ik population.

Further, it was impossible to follow the younger men and women on their long and solitary treks toward and into the Sudan in search of food and water. The same conditions that demanded that each Ik spend days (sometimes weeks) wandering on his own made it impossible for us to follow them for more than a day or so. Except when visiting other villages, we were never away from our base village for more than a week at a time; the longest we ever pursued any individual Ik into the Sudan was usually for a day or two, five days being the maximum (three out, two back).

Despite these and other drawbacks, the information gathered is of vital importance in telling us about the process of desocialization that can accompany prolonged and severe deprivation. While our interpretations of the facts may be questioned, the facts themselves raise a number of critical issues concerning our understanding of human behavior and sociality.

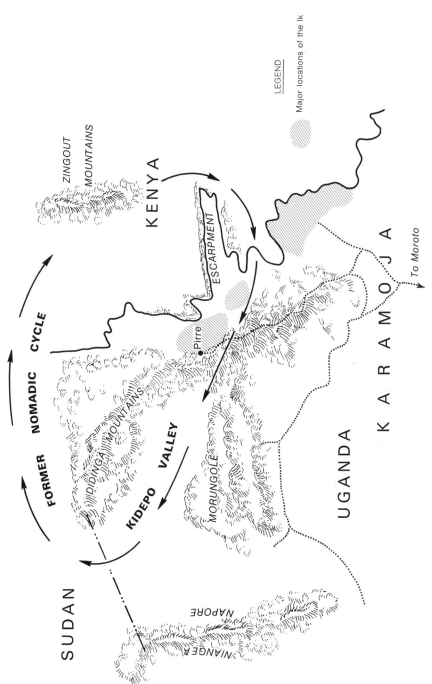

MAP 2.1 PRESENT LOCATION AND TRADITIONAL NOMADIC CYCLE OF THE IK

HISTORICAL BACKGROUND

It is, of course, impossible to say when the changes leading to the present situation began, since change is an ongoing process. But from the descriptions provided by the oldest Ik I met, which refer back to some time in the 1920s, it seems safe to assume that at that time they were still following their traditional nomadic hunting cycle successfully and doing so without any definite administrative or environmental stimulus to change. Nevertheless, using a number of chronological markers, it is plain that deprivation had consciously impinged on the population before the outbreak of World War II.

The people between forty and fifty years of age when I was there (placing their birth between 1914 and 1924) agreed that they had looked after their children in the traditional fashion but that it had been "difficult."[1] They all made the point that they parted ways with their children earlier than *their* parents had parted with them (at puberty). But they were unclear as to just how young their children had been when they began to find their own food. The youngest person I could find who had been cared for by her parents beyond the age of three was eleven or twelve years old in 1964 and she was exceptional. People born in the 1930s recalled the problem of having to find their own food, without help from parents, "long before puberty." When the old people died, and all except two died during my two years with them, nobody was left to remember the days when children were an integral part of the family unit. Most of those surviving said that in putting their own children out to forage for themselves at the age of three they were merely doing what had been done to them; it had worked for them, so why should it not work for their children?

The old people were also unsure about the cause of such changes in parental responsibilities, but drought and the increasingly effective national boundaries were cited. Both were certainly contributory causes then, and they continue to be major factors in the lives of the Ik today.

Their former nomadic cycle led the Ik to hunt for the bulk of the year in Kidepo Valley. However, when rains came and the valley floor became treacherous for heavy game, the Ik followed game up into the Didinga Mountains to the north and into the Sudan; they then descended into what is now Kenya where they gathered honey and bartered it with the Turkana before climbing up over the escarpment, crossing over to the Morungole range and down into Kidepo again. This cycle was apparently being discouraged for administrative reasons during this whole period, but probably did not become totally disrupted until the 1940s.

It is reasonable to assert, then, that the changes leading to the present disintegration of Ik society have been at work at least since the 1930's, and very likely were already at work, though with little noticeable effect, before that. If, as I suspect, the two years (1964–65) covering my field experience marked a critical moment in the process of social change—a moment at which a new, nonsocial system was recognized by the Ik to have evolved and was consciously accepted by them as effective—then the time span we are dealing with in considering the overall process is probably a minimum of forty years, including a minimum of thirty years of the process actively "cognized" by the Ik. My claim is that during this time span the change was continuous, predictable, and gradual enough to permit systematic adaptation. The most recent account of the Ik (Joseph Towles, personal communication) indicates that the system established by 1966 was continuing four years later, and despite a slight improvement in environmental conditions, was found to be satisfactory by the Ik: they saw no reason to change that system because of what they considered to be only a temporary amelioration of their circumstances. The present system enables them to survive with predictability, although with a greatly reduced population size and individual life span. This is preferable for them to the hazards of adapting to better conditions, for if better conditions should prove temporary, then the change back to sociality would have been from their survival point of view, maladaptive.

Borrowing the model of Laughlin and Brady (article 1), the Ik situation represents a deprivation extreme insofar as it includes a "significant decremental shift in resource availability" for which the people seem conceptually prepared. Both Towles and I feel that they seem satisfied, if not content, with their situation, at least insofar as they have faced a problem and apparently found a workable solution. What makes the Ik situation so extreme is that positive fluctuations in basic resources (that is, the periods of greater abundance of resources) are the exceptions rather than the rule. The Ik expect deprivation to continue, with no return to former sufficiency. They are prepared for the minimum, and they maintain their preparedness by systematically refusing to allow maladaptive regression to their former sociality. In essence, the Ik have encountered a series of deprivations, the cumulative effect of which has been to convince the Ik that deprivation itself is the only predictable feature of their environment in the long run.

The overall pattern has been a progressive, non-repetitive series of short-term changes in the environment, heading predictably over at least thirty years in the direction of the present situation of permanent hunger and frequent starvation. But, again, it must be emphasized that the Ik have come to accept this as the norm, so that to some extent their system is still flexible enough to restore the norm whenever it is breached, as by an exceptional year of sufficiency or even abundance. They may confidently expect a reversion in subsequent years to insufficiency. When Towles visited them again in 1971, they were demonstrating the effectiveness of their system by allowing self-seeded crops to rot in the fields, each Ik taking what he needed for the moment only so that there was no danger of having enough to share. Sharing represents an abnormal situation for which the present system is not adapted. It was the same in 1965 and 1966 when I saw them consciously disposing of government famine relief as rapidly as possible, as if recognizing that it posed a structural threat to the existing system. They treated famine relief, probably correctly, as they treat a year of sufficiency or abundance. They treated both as an abnormality, unpredictable, and therefore not to be relied on or formally integrated into the system.

BIOLOGICAL CONSIDERATIONS

Unfortunately there have been no biological studies of the Ik, so far as I know. Two attempts of my own to get qualified specialists into the field failed. Similarly, there have been no psychological studies. Despite frequent suggestions, usually by those who refuse to accept that the Ik *can* be considered in any way normal, that their nonsocial behavior must be due to some kind of mental or physical aberration, I have been unable to justify any such explanation. Qualified doctors have suggested a variety of possible causes, from insomnia, through malnutrition to madness. I saw no signs of insomnia; malnutrition was confined to the youngest children (generally in the three- to eight-year-old bracket, with a smaller proportion among the eight- to twelve-year-old category), the old (since life expectancy was not much more than thirty years, anyone over twenty-five was effectively "old"), and the sick of any age. Since systematic sharing structures (to beg the question for a moment) had been broken, and subsistence activities were individual enterprises, to be malnourished was an indication of weakness, ineffectiveness, and failure. More frequently than not, malnutrition led quickly to death. Only the healthy of any age survived, and, as stated previously, the weeding out process was for the most part completed in early childhood. Since food and water were not systematically shared, those that survived were disproportionately healthy, a few were even plump, though such an abnormal condition never lasted during my stay for more than a few months, and was to be found only among the older teenagers, the most active, the strongest, and therefore the healthiest age group. This seems to make biological sense; the breeding group was not only alive, but healthy and far from malnourished. The expenditure of energy to maintain this condition, however, was excessive and was probably a major factor in leading to an early decline and old age. All that is required to accept the situation is to accept that for the Ik sharing was no longer a positive value, empirically or conceptually. For them there was no anomaly and certainly no sense of moral impropriety at finding two brothers or sisters, or kin of any kind, side by side, with one in an advanced stage of starvation (as distinct from mere malnutrition), the other healthy and well-fed, and the latter eating without giving even the smallest morsel to the former. In fact, under their present value system, moral outrage would be felt if the healthy individual *did* share with his starving kin.

Yet I saw no sign of mental aberration or psychological stress. The difficulty in accepting this lies simply in the fact that there have been few examples known to us of adaptation to such extreme conditions over a period of time long enough to allow for the conceptual system to adapt along with the changing conditions. The only sign of mental disturbance among the entire Ik population (some two thousand when I arrived) pertained to an eleven- or twelve-year-old girl named Adupa. Adupa was already in an advanced state of malnutrition, however, so it was not surprising to find her apparently retarded. Her reactions to any situation were excessively slow. When she found food she frequently was unable to consume it in time to prevent it being taken from her by other children. She was also unsuspecting, it seemed, and therefore easy prey, allowing herself to be attacked with little resistance. The only really unusual thing about Adupa was that she had survived long enough for the malnutrition to affect her mind, if this was indeed the cause of her retardation. Other Ik who were unable to get sufficient food generally died long before any mental deterioration set in. But Adupa was the victim of parents who had not accepted the adaptive changes that all other parents of their age accepted and who continued to try to share what they could with their daughter, prolonging her life and thus allowing for the effects of constant malnutrition to become manifest. (I shall have more to say about this and some related sexual factors in a later section.)

The very fact that the Ik were able to accept with apparently total equanimity the juxtaposition of starving and well-fed kin, sick and healthy, living and dying, without making any effort on the part of the "haves" to share with the "have-nots" is strong indication of a highly functional conceptual adaptation. The fact that there was already, while I was there, a whole generation of adult Ik for whom such behavior and thinking were perfectly normal is an equally strong indication of the functionality of the system through time. The continued success of the system over an even longer period of time can only be determined, of course, by further investigation. Political considerations have thwarted two attempts I have made to get such further research done by others. The facts that follow, however, should further testify to at least the short-term effectiveness of the non-social adaptation of the Ik.

ENVIRONMENTAL CONSIDERATIONS

Progresssive dessication of the environment has been a constant factor in the decline of Ik society over the period considered here. Overgrazing by surrounding pastoral peoples has contributed to this condition, and the recent attempts of the Ik to take to farming have only aggravated the situation. When burning their fields they allow the fires to spread unchecked, destroying precisely those areas of greatest foliage density (the ravines and gulleys) that were relatively wooded and up which the fires spread with ease, frequently continuing down the other side of a hill or mountain after reaching the crest.

From their experience the Ik have come to expect little from their environment. Those that survive see the environment as being "adequate." The attitude that is held by the sick and dying is difficult to ascertain. Those I questioned did not blame the natural world as being inadequate; rather, they blamed their own inadequacies. Even when on the point of death they were able to point to the efficacy of the system, a system which in fact reduced the population to a size the environment *could* support, and which maintained that level. They saw their own death, through sickness, or premature old age, as being part of the system. This was evidenced by criticisms leveled at me when I gave food and water to sick and old or dying people, and also by the frequent requests of the sick and dying themselves for me not to "waste" food on them that could be better allocated by giving it to healthy persons. The population diminished by almost half during my two years with the Ik, and while this led me to think that they faced almost certain extinction, it seems from the report brought back by Towles in 1971 that the population level of about one thousand reached in 1966 was in fact ecologically compatible with their environmental context, and at least until 1971 it continued at that level with no further diminution. Just as important, the fragmented and highly individuated system of interpersonal relations has also continued.

One environmental factor of crucial importance lies in the realm of ideology. While those surviving are able to regard their world as adequate, it is extremely difficult to assess the role played by their former religious beliefs concerning that world. It could be argued that those beliefs were at least in part responsible for their refusal to accept government offers to relocate them elsewhere, where survival might not have been at the expense of sociality. However, it could also be argued that their continued sense of religious dependence upon their particular mountain homeland has had adaptive value under the

present circumstances, since they *do* continue to survive, and the
fact of survival seems to outweigh, in their estimation, any consideration of the degree or quality of survival. This is another problem that
I shall return to in a moment. For now, it is important to note that, in
addition to resolving certain economic problems posed by their environment, the Ik have also conceptually reconciled their place in the
wider environment and do *not* regard it with hostility. They can
hardly be expected to consider the environment as responsible for
their plight, since they do not cognize their condition as a "plight."
This, then, is another aspect of the adaptive normality of the Ik.

THE FAMILY

While economic factors are obviously of paramount consideration in
this thesis, it is probably best to deal with the adaptivity of the Ik
familial system at this point. We must simply accept for the moment
that the economic context is one of reduction to the barest minimum
adequate for physical survival, and that this has not been the result of
a single disaster, but of a series of deprivations of increasing intensity
over a period of at least thirty years. In response to this situation the
family itself has, *as a socioeconomic unit,* become dysfunctional. It
simply does not exist in any form recognizable to us as such. Even
the conjugal pair, whether formally married or not, does not form a
cooperative unit except for a few specific purposes. The Ik themselves say, in explanation of why they get married, that one person
alone cannot build a house. This may be a reflection on the fact they
now (since their compression into the Morungole escarpment region)
build more elaborate houses of Karamojong style rather than their
former dome-shaped grass huts. Their present houses are made of
a circular frame of poles, embedded in the ground, lashed together,
mudded, and surmounted by a conical roof thatched with grass. The
whole construction is greatly facilitated if there are two people working together and certain phases would be impossible without such
cooperation, especially the mudding and the roof raising. The conjugal pair further cooperated, up to 1964, in work associated with the
fields then maintained by most Ik. However, such labor was exces-

sive in proportion to the returns, was abandoned during the course of my stay, and had not been revived at the time of Towles's visit in 1971, other than in the form of a small amount of clearing and haphazard replanting done by individuals on their own.

Fields were cited as a reason for having children, but not in the sense that involved any concept of children as being a part of a family. The fields of a conjugal pair were worked and guarded by that pair, if at all. However, if any field came to fruit, the children, organized into age gangs, scavenged there and in so doing *incidentally* helped keep away birds and baboons, which would have done much more damage than the children did by their pilfering. Children were in no way expected at any time to assist their parents, either in house-building or in the fields. Their collective existence as a category of scavengers, however, was recognized to have some utility and this, as I have said, was a reason cited by most Ik for having children. I do not imply that this was the extent of their feeling in the matter. All I can say is that I saw nothing to indicate otherwise, other than in the case of the girl Adupa and in the weaning process which displayed conscious recognition of affective bonds that had to be broken.

Village construction also indicates the fragmented nature of Ik life, that is, with each conjugal compound being stockaded against the others, each having its own private entrance, so that there is no central meeting place within the village (see figure 2.1). All compounds face outwards, there is no access from one compound to another except for tiny holes in the stockades through which children can pass, and even these were extremely rare. The Ik compound may be contrasted with the more open compound typical of other Sudanese tribes (see figure 2.2).

Children were allowed to sleep within the compound of their parents, but not inside the house once they reached the age of three. They had to provide what shelter they wanted for themselves. Meals were not consumed within the compound or house unless the consumer found himself or herself alone. An adult might bring food back to the compound, but only if reasonably sure that his or her partner would not be there. If both were there, each ate separately, neither provided food or water for the other, and neither provided anything for the children.

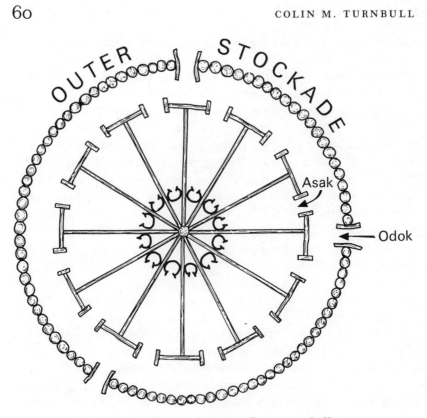

FIGURE 2.1   THE PRESENT IDEALIZED FORM OF AN IK VILLAGE

SEXUALITY

Before describing the life cycle of the Ik it is pertinent to consider the sexual life of the adults, since the very manner in which each child is conceived affects the life cycle, at least in terms of attitude toward family. I have said elsewhere (1972) that the first reaction of a woman on finding that she is pregnant is one of anger, quickly followed by a boredom that is relieved only by anxiety. In a precarious position herself, however healthy she might be, childbirth is an additional hazard and the subsequent necessity of feeding the child for the minimal three-year period constitutes an additional burden and threat to her own survival. The only Ik of any age or either sex to

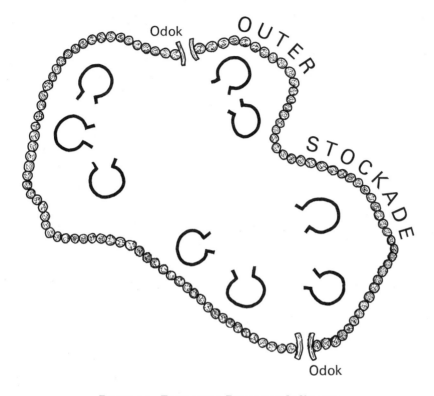

Odok

OUTER

STOCKADE

Odok

FIGURE 2.2 TRADITIONAL FORM OF AN IK VILLAGE

discuss their sexual exploits among themselves were the younger women and girls (married or single) who used their bodies as a means of obtaining food, usually by prostitution to cattle herders when drought forced the male herders on long drives into Ik territory. These exploits were not discussed by others and were discussed only rarely among the girls and women, and even then not for sexual interest but in terms of success as a subsistence activity. If any pleasure was expressed, it was in light of the amount of food obtained. Neither adults nor youths of either sex expressed pleasure in the sexual act. Most said, simply, that it was too tiring and they needed their energy for getting food and water. It is, of course, likely that physical strain and nutritional deficiencies reduced the sex drive. When asked

"If they did not find pleasure in sex, then where did they find it?" the Ik were prone to reply that defecation was a comparable sensation, another form of excretion, and much less tiring. These attitudes were born out in observable interpersonal relationships between husbands and wives, and between boys and girls, that seldom if ever were marked by any action that could be interpreted as affectionate, let alone loving. But when we consider that in the Ik language as in other African languages the word for "love" is the same as for "want" or "need," the attitude is comprehensible. Love can have no meaning if there is nothing to share and so no possibility for sharing. A sense of social or sexual dependence, or interdependence, is dysfunctional under such circumstances.

I have absolutely no way of determining how many children were deliberately conceived and how many were the result of a "mere excretory act" the Ik consider comparable to defecation. Nor can I give significant figures on childbirth or abortion; there was simply no way of obtaining such information. When a child was born, however, it was an unremarked event. The child was breast fed for three years and accompanied the mother everywhere. The infant was given plenty of opportunity to either adjust to the environment or die during this period. Moreover, if it reached the age of two, it was subjected to deliberate abuse as part of the weaning process. This seemed excessive and brutal at times, as did the apparently malicious pleasure derived from the child's pain or anxiety by the mother and other adults present. In fact, though, both were integral and essential parts of the child's education. In this way a responsible Ik mother taught her child, as best she could, the value of independence. She knew that after three years, if she and the child both survived, there would be no possibility of her continuing to nourish the child. She also knew that in adult life the child would spend much of his or her time away from all others on the solitary quest for food and in difficulty or danger, or in cases of accident, there would simply be nobody nearby to help. The apparently malicious pleasure was also functional, for it taught the child that even if anyone were nearby he or she would not care. It helped the mother at the same time begin to wean herself from the child, breaking the affective bonds that were inevitably, however minimally, established by having shared so much of each other. Until a child reached the age of two, mothers could very rarely be seen to fondle their children with affection, but after that, never. The process of separation thus began most conspicuously when children were about two years old, and it was completed when children were put out to fend for themselves at about three years of age.

The child then entered an age gang of other children whose age ranged upwards to seven or eight years old. The same educational process was continued systematically. The gangs did not exist as an age group or age set might, for cooperative purposes, except for the solitary purpose of protection against predators—including adult Ik. A new meaning of *marangik* "goodness" emerged in this predatory context: any adult who found a child with food and could take the food and eat it was a "good" adult. That was the system. But since adults normally pursued their food quest alone, only a solitary child was in danger. Hence, the formation of gangs of children can be viewed as an adaptive response to wider threats in the population. I never saw a gang actually exercise this one cooperative activity, however, and never heard of any adult rash enough to take food from a child with a gang nearby. The gangs roamed the ravines and when food was seen; the first child to reach it consumed it instantly. The others did not expect it to be shared and only fought over it if there was more than could be consumed at once by the finder. The fastest and strongest survived; the others died. When a child reached the age of seven or eight and was strong enough to climb the large fig trees that could be found in certain ravines, that child was thrown out of his junior age gang and joined a senior gang, becoming once again the weakest member, the least likely to get food before the others, and the least likely to survive. If the child survived until about twelve, he (or she) was considered to be an adult and was once again thrown out. The child theoretically had learned all he needed to know at this point: to survive one had to depend on himself, expecting no help from others, except on rare and unpredictable occasions where there might be some mutual profit. He had to want to survive and to be prepared to survive alone, in relative isolation. There was nothing in his experience in either age gang to encourage him to look further for the relationship of dependency he had found at his mother's breast.

He learned that cooperation was rarely beneficial—a temporary expediency at best—and that the unpredictability of circumstances that could make it worthwhile meant that there was no value in establishing permanent bonds with others on grounds of age, sex, or kinship. He learned that systematic sociality itself had no value.

Puberty was not marked, either formally or informally, except by some girls who chose to change their style of aprons at their first menstruation. I saw only one marriage during my entire stay. This bond lasted one week and followed the traditional pattern only in part. A couple wanting to set up a household simply did so by cooperating in building a house together without any intergroup discussion or exchange of goods, symbolic or otherwise. Death was similarly no longer marked by formal mourning or burial rites. Since there was nothing to inherit, such as goods or social status, and no affective bonds to reinforce, there was no point to any group gathering on these occasions. Further, as the Ik pointed out, the old tradition required a feast which, of course, was impossible under the present circumstances. More important than that, however, was the clear recognition that there was nothing conceptual to share. Death was as solitary as the rest of life. In a few cases among the older people, I saw evidence of personal grief; but in the one instance when there was an attempt at a formal burial, it was because the dead man had acquired some possessions. On that occasion, no sign of grief whatsoever was shown by those who attended.

In sum, since there were no enduring social action networks and groups on the premise that they would plainly be dysfunctional, societal and sexual interdependencies were reduced to an equally temporary and expedient nature. There was no adaptive function to any network of interpersonal or intergroup relationships, so it should not be surprising that such a network did not exist. The justification for this can be found in subsistence patterns.

ECONOMIC CONSIDERATIONS

Some of the most startling (yet logical and consistent) elements of the economic system are embodied in the almost total absence of sharing of food or other vital resources. Food was consumed privately and was not exchanged. Moreover, abundance was systematically destroyed when, by accident, it occurred. Yet with all this the system is not profitably viewed as maladaptive, nor does it represent "a system failure of the gravest sort." Such judgments apply more to the maladaptiveness and failure of the former system, when sociality was sometimes disrupted but nonetheless greater than in the period under discussion here. The system that has emerged with its almost total retraction of the reciprocal flow of strategic resources is, in fact, highly adaptive under the circumstances. People who are ill-equipped to provision themselves are, it seems, very expendable; indeed, their expenditure is a necessary part of the system. There is, in times of plenty, no "resurgence of the expansion phase" of sharing and sociability, yet the population does *not* die. Some cultural, if not social, continuity is achieved in addition to at least marginal physical survival.

These patterns derive primarily from two factors: the extreme nature of resource deprivation, even for the minimal size to which the Ik population has been reduced, and the predictability of the continuity of that condition. Deprivation has simply become the new normality. The Ik are nothing if not pragmatic. The So, among whom Laughlin worked and saw something of the same process in operation (Laughlin, 1974b; also this volume), were able to maintain the essential phase of "systematic fluctuation" back to reciprocity, probably not only because of greater resource availability and the presence of reserves such as cattle and goats, but also because of their much greater proximity and access to the regional administrative center of Karamoja at Moroto, a center that did its best to provide material security and thereby provided an additional source of conceptual security. The only conceptual security for the Ik was their traditional place of origin, Morungole, the mountain on which they believe God (*Didigwari*) first set man (the Ik) down on earth, which has provided for them ever since, and which they still could claim in 1971 (Towles, personal communication) as a source of subsistence provisions. The Ik had revised their concept of "being provided for" to the barest minimum necessary for biological survival; they no longer thought in terms of social survival.

I have already tried to indicate that unless we see, as anthropol-

ogists, that our own Morungole is that mystic mountain called Statistics, there is no point in playing the numbers game with the information available on the Ik. It is perhaps unfortunate that we do not have
adequate data on Ik for reliable statistical analysis. This lack is certainly not for want of effort, for in the field there was frequently
nothing to do but count, and at one time for want of anything better
to do I even counted raindrops. The most reliable data I can supply
are the direct observations of what took place and the connection between what took place in the case of one individual had little or no
social relationship to what took place in the case of any other individual. Such data were not used by the Ik in planning their own lives,
which they regarded as individual and isolated enterprises.

Data that I consider significant and adequate in this respect are,
for instance, that in the two years of living among the Ik and covering several thousand miles on foot (five miles a day minimum, sometimes thirty), I seldom saw vegetable food supplies in any one place
that could support more than one individual for one day. Such supplies (clusters of berries, nuts, roots, leafy vegetables, edible bark,
wild grass seed) were almost always some miles distant from the
nearest source of water, which again was infrequently available in
sufficient quantities to supply the needs of a group. In fact, the only
places where water was available in such quantities were at a half
dozen water holes (three on the Pirre side and three on the escarpment side), all of which save two were polluted and used only by the
sick and old, thus hastening their death. There was no food close to
these holes, so the food quest necessitated setting out alone, in the
knowledge that this maximized the chances of finding enough for everyone; having found food, the individual then wandered on in
search of water. Water was generally found by digging a shallow hole
in the ground where it was sandy (butterflies settling on the sand indicated the presence of sub-surface moisture) and allowing the water
to accumulate. A cupful of water twice a day was about as much as
could be expected from such a hole. To reach more reliable water
resources the Ik had to trespass in Kidepo, or illegally enter the
Sudan.

Thus the family compound was more than frequently deserted or inhabited by only one member of the family. Each member went his or her own way and was likely to be away from the village for anything from a few days to a few weeks. If they were both present at the same time it was by chance rather than design. I have been out on such food quests when we have seen other Ik similarly scouring the countryside. Rather than make contact, however, each would veer away from the other. Success in food quests was more important than social communication, which amounted to a frivolity; it did not even have the value of being a luxury.

Reciprocity is not totally absent, however. People do talk to each other and communicate in other ways, services are rendered (frequently despite the vigorous objections of the recipient), and it is possible that affection of a limited sort exists for brief periods of time. Conscious pleasure is taken (as stated by the Ik themselves and as seen in countless daily examples) in the misfortunes of others, which is a form of negative reciprocity. However, the significance of this does not lie in the gloomy picture of a loveless people so much as in the fact that organized reciprocity, formal and enduring bonds that relate people or groups in predictable ways and for predictable goals, is structurally unsound and is dispensed with. This was, to me, nowhere more evident than in the solitary consumption of food. Even when several people were eating in each other's presence, the usual tendency was to turn away so that there would be no visual communication, and there was certainly no verbal communication. The often stated preference was for eating alone, and the reason given was that in this way lay the greatest safety, since it was a "good" act for anyone to take the food even from your mouth, if they could.

Some qualification needs to be made here, though it has to be made in light of the fact that my own observations were made at the time in which the emerging system was likely being consolidated and during which certain former values and attitudes still persisted in attenuated form. For instance the bond of *nyot,* a form of exchange relationship, was still recognized but was seldom implemented. It mainly existed between Ik and Karamojong from whom they could expect to profit. Among the Ik the only times I saw it implemented was in the frequent demand for tobacco. However, tobacco was lo-

cally grown and was more plentiful than food. Even so, we have to
ask ourselves what was the significance of establishing or maintaining an exchange relationship of any kind? It did not serve as a model
replicated in other contexts. Did its significance lie in the nature of
the commodity, its availability (hence the likelihood of later return),
its effect as a pain or hunger suppressant, or in the pleasure its consumption gave by smoking or chewing? What in fact was being
shared? Pleasure, of course, is as practical and effective as the sup-
pression of pain or hunger, but of a very different nature. A hint lies
in the fact that if such tobacco was given on demand (and it was
refused as often as it was given when available), it was not com-
munally consumed, but consumed apart. The emphasis seemed to be
on the acquisition of a desired commodity, not on the sharing of anything useful or pleasurable, and the gift did not, in any of my observations, lead to future exchange or reciprocation of any kind; it certainly did not lead to or correspond to any other acts of reciprocation
between the individuals concerned.

Yet there was recognition that a prestation implied reciprocation of
some kind at some time. I believe this to be because reciprocation
and reciprocal patterns and bonds were still remembered as having
once been functional, for otherwise surely some model for reciprocal
relationships would have been established earlier in the life cycle,
especially in the age gangs. It is significant that demand and acquies-
cence were to be found primarily among the older Ik, whose memory
stretched back to rather more plentiful times of mere scarcity when
reciprocation was still both possible and functional. The only two
demands frequently made were for tobacco and food, and the overt
demand for tobacco was far more frequent than that for food. The
demand for food was recognized to have validity only between adults
of the same sex. It was never made between children, or between
children and adults or between young adults and the old. Between
adults it was only made when there was a surplus, such as when one
person found more food than he could consume at the time. The Ik
did not resort to violence to protect such a surplus, nor did they wel-
come other consumers, nor did such "sharing" establish any reciprocal bonds, effective or affective. It is doubtful, then, that we should

even consider such instances as "sharing"; perhaps they should better be considered simply as acts of hunting and gathering with the focus clearly on immediate profit on the part of the taker and with little or no thought of future return on the part of the "giver," and no importance being placed by either on the act itself.

Similarly it is difficult to accurately assess the exchange of services. Among the older Ik particularly, a clearly recognized obligation was incurred if services were accepted. For this reason most Ik consciously avoided accepting such services, and even sought to perform activities on their own that could much more simply and effectively have been performed with help. I have seen men endanger their lives in this way, as in the attempt to haul a heavy wooden beehive single-handed to the top of a tree. Again, however, the recognition of reciprocity seems to have been a recollection of the past rather than an institution of the present, and was never observed among the younger Ik, for whom the non-social system was plainly adaptive, and who were not hampered by memories of anything different. For them, their experience in the age gangs taught them that the only benefit that lay in sharing lay in such strategic enterprises as mutual protection against predators. They learned that cooperation *can* be effective for all individuals concerned in rare and specific situations, but since such situations could not be predicted, neither could the nature of the cooperation nor the identity of the cooperators, so the age gang experience did not result in any formal exchange relationships. The most significant act of sharing or communication that I could discern was conceptual. It had nothing to do with kinship, or even with amity or sociality. It had to do in part with a sense of common history and identity, certainly with common language (which sharply differentiated the Ik from their Karamojong neighbors), with their self-concept as a mountain people,[2] and above all it had to do with the fact that they shared a common relationship with their sacred mountain, Morungole. Even the Ik now established on the escarpment side of their territory spoke with feeling about Morungole. If we can speak of the Ik as a social or political group at all, it is in light of this sense of identity and unity, not in terms of any "truly social" organization.

POLITICAL CONSIDERATIONS

We are accustomed to thinking of societies as consisting of various levels of political grouping, from minimal to maximal; family generally representing the minimal political unit and tribe or nation the maximal. It seems that only at the maximal extension of tribe do the Ik see themselves as in any sense a political unit, and it is significant that there the distinction between "political" and "religious" is more than usually blurred. The family at the minimal end of the scale has no structural significance. At one moment in its existence it consists of a man and his wife without children. At another moment, with the birth of a child, it consists pragmatically of a mother and that child, since the father plays no role in the support of the child beyond having helped the mother build the house that will shelter them all until the child is three. At three, the child is effectively excluded from the family, which reverts to its former existence comprising only the husband and wife, until the birth of the next child.

Above the family, one traditionally finds the lineage and then the clan as having vital structural functions as political units, though this is generally less so with hunter-gatherers than with others. But whereas the Ik have clan names, they have lost whatever structural significance they had and have fissioned to allow for the greater degree of inbreeding now necessary, to the point where some formerly exogamous clans now consist of three or even four intermarrying segments, differentiated by different totemic affiliations. With hunter-gatherers it is normal to proceed from family at the minimal level to band, which effectively is the maximal level, the tribal level having conceptual rather than political reality. For the Ik, villages have replaced bands as units of cohabitation and, to some extent, of territorial exploitation, but an Ik village can hardly be said to have political significance. A village never acts as such. It has no exclusive claims to land, food, water, or other resources. It does not even have a conceptual center and, as already shown, has no geopolitical center since every village radiates outwards from a hub at which all compounds converge, or, in the case of larger villages, several such hubs. Can the *di* "sitting place" that is always found outside the village be said to represent its political unity? I think not, though at one time it may have done so. At no "sitting place" are you likely to find a group of men or women all of whom come from the same village. A "sitting place" is more a place where itinerant people congregate for no easily discernible purpose, certainly not to discuss village business, but merely to be in the company of others, regardless of who they are or where they come from. The "sitting place" seems to satisfy a gregarious rather than a political urge. Gregariousness is not a term for which we are accustomed to finding much use in social anthropology, but in looking for significant forms of grouping among the Ik it assumes vital significance. The kinship, social, and political groups that are normally so powerfully if flexibly structured in most small-scale societies are not to be found, but we do continually find spontaneous though not frequent formations of gregarious groups among the Ik.

We cannot dismiss political considerations with that, however. We must look further to see how political factors have been adapted to the conditions of stress that the Ik have faced during their process of change. The general model proposed by Laughlin and Brady would suggest that at some point the chronic inability of the previous Ik socioreligious structure to cope with the progressive decrement in strategic resources resulted in the demise of the traditional system of authority. If this indeed did occur, we unfortunatly have no record with which to document the event. We do know that the colonial government introduced the institution of *niampara* "village headman," and even of *mkungu* "tribal ruler." At one time these leaders might have played an internal role within Ik society as well as an external role, mediating between Ik and administration, though no information could be found to show that this was so. All the information gathered tends to show rather a progressive *weakening* of the traditional role of family, lineage, and clan elders until today, where they are no longer leaders in any sense at all since those units no longer exist even conceptually, except in the most minimal way in which clan names are recognized and passed on. Alternatives to traditional responses to situations, far from being reduced, have been increased to the point at which from the position of the Ik it could be argued in a poetic sense that greater centralization *has* taken place, for each Ik has become the ultimate and sole ruler of his own actions and each individual Ik is a virtually autonomous political unit. Ik society could also be said to be ranked or stratified, since power over basic resources is ascribed to the fittest, enhanced by achievement, and monopolized by only a few.

We plainly have to stop thinking of the Ik as a society in the traditional sense, for only then does their system become comprehensible. It is here that the blurring of the distinction between political and religious aspects of their system assumes major importance. The distinction is of course never or seldom more than a conceptual one, useful primarily for analytical purposes; but with the Ik it fades away almost completely. Since the Ik have revised their concept of normality to fit their present context they do not see themselves as being under stress (see Cawte, article 4, for a similar situation). Even young people dying of starvation seem remarkably well adjusted to their situation and see nothing abnormal about it. With the imposed shrinkage of their territorial space, so has their concept of time shrunk, and both are still in proportion to each other. While we do not know what occurred during the process, there is again no evidence that ritual played a significant role in stress alleviation. The process was probably too steady and predictable and relatively gradual. Perceptual, cognitive, and affective capacities are as perfectly synchronized as in any well-functioning society. But since no collective response is mandated by external stimuli, no group entrainment is required. Leaders, charismatic or otherwise, political or religious, are no longer necessary. Synchronized responses are seen only in light of the one dominant value of individual survival by which all actions are judged. But it was not a failure to synchronize that precipitated the fragmentation that characterizes the Ik today; the two went hand in hand in the ongoing process of functional adaptation.

IDEOLOGICAL AND COGNITIVE CONSIDERATIONS

Ik cognition coincides with the operational reality of their situation. The reality is stark but cold and clear; the cognitive model is similarly devoid of imaginative frills and is essentially pragmatic. There is no room for ideals, no need to explain the inexplicable by reference to gods or spirits. There is no need for ritual to mediate between the cognized and operational environments. The Ik seem to have traditionally had a higher level of ritual specialization than other hunter-gatherers, though we have no way of knowing for how long this was so. But during my stay there the last such ritual specialist died unmourned, for he was no longer needed. This does not mean that their ideological world is empty, however, nor that the Ik have no belief; rather, it means that they have almost no place for ritual. Since the operational environment for each Ik is his own personal environment, so is his cognized environment a highly individuated phenomenon. He does not need to relate himself to other Ik in his cognitive world any more than he does in his operational world. All that is required is that there is a common sense of identity so that the dominant value of "goodness" is recognized equally by all. That this is achieved is amply demonstrated by the lack of physical violence or hostility among the Ik. It is here that I believe Morungole plays an essential role, providing a common focus of attention for all Ik, serving as a symbol of order.

In the absence of ritual there are no common or communal observances, no shared acts, but there is a common and powerful respect for the sacred mountain. The respect is manifest in the accepted prohibition against hunting there, but even more, if I interpreted it correctly, in the way that eyes are directed toward the mountain whenever there is nothing else to look at or look for. A group of men at the "sitting place" might sit for a day without saying a word while looking intently at Morungole. Even the young seem respectful of the mountain, but this even more than other factors is one that desperately needs to be checked again now that those young have themselves become old, that is, to see what respect the young of today have for the place where Didigwari set man down on earth, if that story is still remembered at all. At the time of my own stay among the Ik, the sentiment evoked by the mountain was certainly as ideologically coercive as the physical environment was structurally coercive. The peculiar power of a commonly held belief lies in the fact that, while it is learned through shared experiences, it is cherished by each individual as his own private belief; it is the very core of his conceptual world. Even though he may recognize that others share the same belief, that is not the essence for most individuals. The more intensely it is held, the more private and personal it is felt to be. While common actions and responses arise because of the commonality of the belief, this is in a sense incidental. Each actor acts in that common way because he has a personal and private urge to do so. He does what he wants to first and foremost, and it turns out to be a shared response only secondarily, if at all.

In this manner Morungole mediates between the two political units found among the Ik—the individual and the tribe—and gives each its identity and meaning, assuring relatively conflict-free operation of the survival system. It should no longer seem strange to us that the Ik do not regard their environment as noxious and are reluctant to leave it. Theirs is a cold but systematic adaptation, conceptual and structural, affective and effective, that has steadily accompanied environmental change, both natural and imposed. Morungole is the one constant factor in their world.

CONCLUSIONS

To some extent at least the Ik may be said to conform to the model of adaptation proposed in article 1—that is, if one assumes that they represent the results of a long period of unremitting ecological stress. Table 1.1 of Laughlin and Brady can be applied only if we accept that the Ik have undergone such a severe shift in both the type and quantity of basic resources that no potential for producing a surplus exists, and if we give a rather broad interpretation to the phrase "widest possible alliance and integration" in the social organizational response category.

The Ik have been observed only over a two-year period and, again, in a brief survey, after a five-year lapse of time. While the latter visit provided invaluable confirmation that the system was continuing despite certain fluctuations in basic resource supply, it does not mean that there will be no further change. The change has been unidirectional thus far; the difficulty, of course, is that one can never say when a "cycle" is complete. What if it is only part of another cycle? Even if we see certain processes begin to repeat, that is no excuse not to continue to follow them and to see if they repeat yet again or proceed further or in a different direction. We must observe all we can, and for as long as we can, and still be aware that however full and prolonged our observations, they can only be partial at best. Nonetheless, despite the manifold imperfections of the Ik study, the facts illustrate the extremes to which adaptation to deprivation can lead a human society, extremes at which sociality becomes extinct for all intents and purposes, but the people survive.

NOTES

1. I doubt very much that my oldest informants were above fifty years old. Two of my eldest informants said they were born during the First World War. This was further corroborated by the age of their eldest sons. The sons were just beginning to copulate (by their own and their fathers' statements) when Kidepo was made into a national park in 1946. Other indicators of chronology were World War II, Ugandan independence, and Mau Mau.

2. The Ik saw their language as linking them to other mountain people such as the Niangea and Napore—linguistically and culturally related peoples on the far side of Kidepo Valley. They were curiously reluctant to link themselves to the So in this way; see Laughlin (1975) on this issue.

Adaptation and Exchange in So: A Diachronic Study of Deprivation

Charles D. Laughlin, Jr.

As Turnbull notes so insightfully, it is difficult to know when one short-run cycle of environmental change leaves off and another begins. The following article by Laughlin reaffirms the importance of viewing adaptation through the diaphasis and equilibration of adaptive infrastructures in relation to environmental change cycles in the long run. The article deals specifically with the manner in which a small society in a marginal environment adapts simultaneously to progressive and recursive environmental change. Viewed only in the short run, one might infer considerable discontinuity in the social behavior observed in a time of severe environmental stress relative to the previous period of resource abundance. The overview taken by Laughlin shows plainly that behaviors in both kinds of environmental cycles are expectable and predictable variations on a common set of institutionalized techniques for adaptation, many of which are reflected directly in social exchange patterns. The changes manifested in behavior by the So through such fluctuating resource cycles are monitored and regulated by the same culture pool. Different aspects of the pool are emphasized as "appropriate" behavior according to the changing profile of environmental constraints. There is continuity in such changes. Moreover, aside from the structural and cognitive integration displayed by the So in moving from one resource cycle to the next, the actual results of behaviors manifested in each cycle may include some nuances against which behaviors engineered in succeeding cycles may be weighed. Progressive changes in sociocultural content may be instituted in this manner as a means for equilibrating the demands of a progressively changing environment, thereby facilitating survival of the group in the long run.

Many of the world's societies may be found in a state of equilibration to both progressive and recursive environmental change.[1] Quite commonly, this will be the case for societies adapted to both the cyclical recurrence of seasons and the progressive interference of Western technology. Less commonly, there are societies that must, in order to survive, adapt to more serious extremes of recurrent change and a progressively deteriorating basic resource base. The present article is a study of one such society in its struggle for existence.

PROGRESSIVE AND RECURSIVE CHANGE IN SO

The So are a small tribe related to the Ik (see article 2) who inhabit three mountains (Mounts Moroto, Kadam, and Napak) in Karamoja District, Uganda.[2] The tribe is comprised of the remnants of a population that once inhabited much of Karamoja. Today they are surrounded by the Pakot and several Paranilotic groups (Karamojong, Turkana, and Teso) and occupy only the small area provided by their mountains.

Prior to 1880, the So subsisted upon abundant wild flora and fauna, honey production, and slash-and-burn cropping. Non-agricultural subsistence resources were of greatest importance during time of drought, which occurs once in every three to four years and results in at least partial crop failure.[3] The So kept no cattle in the early days and few goats. The tribe was endogamous and spoke a language unrelated to any other language in the area (see Laughlin 1975 for two exceptions) and had little communication with any of the surrounding peoples.

Around 1880, game on the plains and in the forests of Karamoja was abundant, so much so that one early observer could write, "I have seen herds on the plains below Mount Elgon in which the total number of elephants would well reach 2,000."[4] This date marked the approximate inception of the ivory trade in Karamoja, and as the hunting became more intense, hunters, in blatant disregard of protective legislation, shot whole herds at a time (Laughlin 1972:25). By the end of the ivory trade (around 1910) there were virtually no elephants surviving in the district. The elephant was not the only species thus decimated. Few of the larger game animals were left in any appreciable numbers, and many became extinct.

As mentioned, the So in traditional times relied heavily upon non-agricultural resources (especially wild game) during periods of drought and crop failure. Game animals on the plains, also affected by drought, would move to the mountains where some water and grazing could be found even during the worst droughts. Here they fell easy prey to So hunters and provided much-needed sustenance. There seems to have been a relative balance in So ecology, a balance which clearly combined diaphatic structuring of So production activities with environmental recursivity. However, this balance was rapidly altered by the ivory trade and "big game" hunting mania that predominated during the final decades of the nineteenth century. The result was the removal of a major subsistence resource from the limited set of resource alternatives available to the So.

Ironically, the So themselves became immediately and directly involved in the ivory trade, a factor that both exacerbated the ultimate scarcity of game and gradually provided them with a basic resource alternative to game. Because they were skilled hunters, they had little trouble killing large numbers of elephants and trading ivory for livestock with neighboring groups and itinerant traders. They quickly accumulated large herds of cattle and goats, thereby providing a subsistence resource that replaced dependence on wild fauna for survival during drought.

So herds prospered during the first half of this century largely because they were protected from raiding by the Pax Britannica. However, protection faltered in the early 1950s owing to both an increase in human and stock population in the district and a fundamental change in colonial administrative policy (Barber 1968:217). The Karamojong, Turkana, and Pakot initiated a gradually accelerated program of cattle raiding which had reached a rate of at least one incident per day by the end of the decade (Dyson-Hudson 1966:246). The So, of course, have been a more than tempting target for raiding activity because they are confined to the lower slopes of their mountains by administrative decree and are, therefore, vulnerable to attack. So herds were subsequently depleted—whole herds having been lost in a single attack. In 1970, a lineage owning fifty head of cattle was considered wealthy. Yet such a small herd could hardly be long relied upon for total subsistence by a lineage of the size found in So (see Allan 1967).[5]

Raiding has become so fierce, as a matter of fact, that most So have moved their compounds close to administrative centers. The competition for available planting, grazing, watering, and foraging resources in such areas has, therefore, increased. Women must often travel far afield if they choose to exploit edible wild flora. The progressive decimation of available subsistence alternatives—the reduction and extinction of wild game herds, the reduction of livestock herds, the greater scarcity of wild flora, and continued vulnerability to crop failure—has caused conditions of extreme ecological stress for the So during periods of drought.

A few other changes require our attention before we move on to other matters. As the So came to accumulate and value cattle, they also began to exchange women with surrounding tribes (principally with the Pakot and Karamojong) for livestock. For some time this was a one-way exchange, as So women were highly valued as wives (see Laughlin 1974a; Gray 1960, describes a similar situation among the Sonjo). The exchange, however, had wider implications. It opened a channel for wholesale cultural and material borrowing from the Karamojong by the So, particularly in language, social institutions, and technology.

Finally, a series of water pumping stations was completed in 1966 in the Lia Valley of Mount Moroto, an area where a significant proportion of the So population dwells and the area most widely studied during fieldwork. The function of the pumps is to supply water to the district headquarters, a town of approximately 10,000 (1970 figure) that lies at the mouth of the Lia Valley. The pumps have apparently lowered the water table in the valley sufficiently so that during the dry season, water no longer flows above ground on the valley floor. Whereas water was once an abundant resource there, it has become a seasonally scarce resource.

Table 3.1 summarizes the various changes that have occurred in the environment of So. It also distinguishes changes that are progressive from those that are recursive. The recursive changes listed are all drought-related variables. Some additional theoretical considerations must be introduced here, however, before undertaking a careful analysis of So homeorhetic responses to such progressive and recursive change in their environment.

TABLE 3.1 ECOLOGICAL AND ENVIRONMENTAL CHANGES AFFECTING
THE SO OF NORTHEASTERN UGANDA, 1880–1970

Progressive Change	Time Occurring	Recursive Change
↓ Wild game*	1880–1910	↓ Incidence of rainfall
↑ Availability of domestic animals	1880–1950	↓ Agricultural produce
↓ Wild flora	1920–present	↓ Well water
↑ Population (human)	1920–present	↓ Grazing
↑ Colonial intervention	1911–61	↑ Livestock death
↑ Intertribal communication	1880–present	↓ Wild flora
↓ Free-flowing water	1950–present	↓ Disease and epidemics
↓ Population (cattle)	1950–present	↓ Death rate
↑ Uganda government intervention	1961–present	↑ Infant mortality
↑ Raiding	1950–present	

SOURCE: Author's field notes, 1969–70.

*Arrows indicate increase (↑) or decrease (↓) of that particular variable. Direction of change of recursive variables is indicated for peak drought period.

A DIACHRONIC MODEL OF PRIMITIVE EXCHANGE

The So are by no means the only tribe in East Africa to face the sort of conditions described above. Colin Turnbull (article 2; see also Turnbull 1967, 1972) found the Ik in a state of advanced social disintegration due to food scarcity. He discovered the nuclear family no longer functioning as an economically corporate unit. Small children and old people were expected to find their own food. During extreme deprivation these two age strata were left to die of starvation while the young adults remained relatively healthy. Most surprising of all, perhaps, was the all but total acceptance of this condition as "the natural thing" (Turnbull 1967:68–69).

Viewed from the standpoint of economy, both the So and the Ik confront continuous fluctuations in basic resource availability. This condition has important consequences for modes of reciprocal exchange of goods and services in particular, and for the momentary state of social coordination in general. Although the conditions faced by So and Ik are to some measure extreme, it is important to understand that many societies in marginal environments confront significant fluctuations in resource availability. A number of studies are presented in this book that illustrate these conditions (see Bishop for the Ojibwa, Dirks for Caribbean slave populations, and Cawte for the Kaiadilt). The important factor in all these cases is that significant diaphasis has occurred; that is, adaptively significant fluctuations in basic resource availability are attended by shifts in social orientation, including changes in production or exchange priorities. I am principally concerned here with changes of exchange priorities.

Marshall Sahlins (1965a, 1965b, 1971a) characterizes three types of reciprocal exchange that may be operating, often simultaneously, in any particular primitive society. These he terms *generalized* (where the emphasis is upon the act of exchange and not upon immediate return or making a profit), *balanced* (where the emphasis is upon immediate exchange of goods or services of equivalent value), and *negative* reciprocity (where the emphasis is upon exchange for profit; see Sahlins 1965a:147–48; Brady 1972a:292–94). Reciprocity may be viewed as existing on a continuum of trust and affect from generalized at one ideal pole to negative at the other. Balanced reciprocity as a type characterizes a midpoint, an area of overlap in motivation lying between the extremes. According to Sahlins, generalized reciprocity is more or less characteristic of exchange between persons who share close kinship and residential proximity. Reciprocity tends to become more balanced between kinsmen or non-kinsmen who reside at a distance from one another and more negative in intertribal exchange sectors (Sahlins 1965a:151; cf. Brady 1972a). Among the So, for example, generalized reciprocity occurs when a household member gives a portion of butter to one of his kinsmen living in the same *eo* "residential compound."[6] Exchange of livestock among non-related So usually takes the form of balanced reciprocity, and cash purchases from Karamojong itinerant traders incline toward the negative end of the reciprocity continuum.

Explicitly excluding some of Sahlins' psychomotivational assumptions and concentrating upon his types of reciprocity, his model of exchange constitutes an extremely useful formulation. However, the model requires substantial reformulation in order to apply it to an explanation of dynamic patterns of reciprocity and the shifts in circuits of exchange that are likely to result from fluctuations in basic resource availability. For one thing, the boundaries of Sahlins' reciprocity types relative to kinship, ethnic and residential proximity must be redefined more flexibly so that they may shift along their continuum in order that the inherent advantages of each type of reciprocity may attain maximum mobile utility.[7] Incorporating flexible boundaries into the continuum transforms the model from an essentially synchronic descriptive instrument to a diachronic explanatory instrument.[8]

As originally formulated by Sahlins, the reciprocity model describes a correlation between modes of exchange and social relations. With certain modifications the model not only is capable of predicting shifts in this correlation that are due to extrinsic factors, but it also becomes deductively entailed by general maximization theory. The reformulated model of primitive exchange may now be stated as follows:

> *Theory:* Reciprocity in primitive society may be seen as existing on a continuum from generalized to negative at the poles. Gen-

eralized reciprocity is commonly correlated with long term maximization of payoffs having little or no immediate utility and
with exchange between individuals of close kinship and residential proximity. Negative reciprocity is commonly correlated
with short-term maximization of payoffs having relatively great
immediate utility and with exchange between individuals of relatively distant residential proximity. In any primitive society
which is confronted by a progressively deteriorating economic
situation so that payoffs of immediate utility become more limited in type and scarce in quantity, reciprocity between individuals of close kinship and residential proximity will increasingly
be marked by short-term maximization of payoffs of immediate
utility and will become either negative or non-existent.

The valence of reciprocity is determined by the momentary range
of possible payoffs as conceived by participants in the exchange, and
the range of payoffs is partially dependent upon factors extrinsic to
the exchange, such as season of the year, subsistence prospectus,
and so on. The payoffs potentially obtainable in exchange between
kinsmen and co-residents are, during "good times," essentially different from the payoffs obtainable from non-kin or between persons
of different tribes or economic sectors. Also when faced with ecological stress so that goods of greatest and immediate utility become
scarce for a prolonged period, people will change the decision strategies they employ in exchange with close kinsmen. The shift is from
concern with long term maximization of such payoffs as children,
lineage solidarity, enhanced prestige, and the like, to concern for immediate survival. People now desire to maximize goods, especially
foodstuffs, of the most immediate utility. With the return to relative
affluence, people again become concerned with long-term maximization.

Thus, the total picture of reciprocal exchange in such a group
should include the periodic, inward movement of the bounds of negative reciprocity. Furthermore, when a society confronts periodic deprivation—that is, is affected by such conditions as drought, tidal
waves, hurricanes, or earthquakes—then there should occur a periodic centrifugal-centripetal fluctuation of the inner bounds of negative reciprocity. This process may be called the "accordion effect" of
negative reciprocity and is an example of adaptive diaphasis. It will

be argued later that the centripetal extension of negative reciprocity is not an aberrant byproduct of deprivation occurring in an otherwise "adequately functioning" system of exchange, but rather is part of a total effect—the accordion effect—which forms a constantly fluctuating and systematic adaptation of a society to shifting ecological conditions.

ADAPTIVE DIAPHASIS IN SO

As was argued in article 1, the infrastructure of any organic system must not only be amenable to change in response to environmental change, but must also remain flexible in response to rhythmic, ecological fluctuations. So infrastructure incorporates a diaphatic quality that has thus far proved adaptive, although for how long it will remain adaptive is a moot question. Diaphasis of the So adaptive infrastructure is most evident in two complementary changes that occur with the onset and that recede with the waning of deprivation conditions: (1) a decline in generalized reciprocity within and between residential compounds and a corresponding increase in the incidence of negative reciprocity; (2) an increase in the activity of, and social orientation toward, central authority.

During the period of my field research among the So, I carried out a statistical study of patterns of reciprocity among a random sample of So households. This study examined the differences in patterns of reciprocity occurring as a result of drought-related deprivation. The quantitative data relative to this study have been presented elsewhere (Laughlin 1974b) and the reader interested in statistical support for my conclusions is invited to consult that source. Specifically, a number of hypotheses drawn deductively from the diachronic model of primitive exchange were tested utilizing data from the two periods, one of drought and another of relative plenty. The hypotheses were for the most part confirmed, thereby giving the model empirical support.

In less formal terms, the picture of change in patterns of reciprocity appears as follows: A considerable decrement in exchange interactions between people is likely to occur during a period of deprivation, especially a decrement in generalized reciprocity, even among close kinsmen living in the same compound. Decline in generalized reciprocity is accompanied by an increment in the frequency of negative reciprocity, and represented by an enhanced articulation with the cash market sector, including the Moroto township commercial center. Production shifts to the manufacture or collection of goods that can be sold in the town for cash (such as charcoal, honey, herbs, building poles, etc.). The money, in turn, is used to buy both food and non-food commodities (see Laughlin 1972 for details). Agricultural production always appears to be ordered in anticipation of drought. A "surplus" is generally produced if the year is a "normal" one and no drought ensues. During a drought period, young men may occasionally elect to make lengthy journeys in search of wild game in order to supplement food resources. If game is found, a ˎmajor proportion of it (perhaps all of it) will be consumed by the hunter in the bush.

In general, the impression one has during a period of deprivation is of the household involuting on itself at the expense of generalized relations beyond the household or compound.[9] This is evidenced by a decline in the frequency of meal sharing (Laughlin 1974b:386) and in enhanced balanced alternation in giving and receiving among "friends." If generalized reciprocity were the sole medium of interaction between people, deprivation might easily resolve the social fabric beyond any possibility of reclaimable solidarity. However, deprivation for the So is also accompanied by an orientation toward central authority and an increase in politico-religious compensatory activity on the part of those in power. Drought-related deprivation exacerbates scarcities already present due to progressive decline in basic resource availability. Graze, for example, becomes scarce in a gradient approaching centers of population density. Disputes over grazing rights thereby become more frequent and require a greater number of adjudications by the elders. The elders will set aside choice grazing areas close to population centers as "off limits" until they are needed to feed young calves at the height of the drought. Violations of such restrictions require action by the elders. Also, the frequency of disputes over past debts increases and control of water sources requires much greater attention than during the "normal" dry season.

Perhaps most importantly, the ritual activity undertaken by the elders, especially by the members of a select ancestor cult comprised of the oldest males in the tribe (Laughlin and Laughlin 1972), is greatly accelerated. The ritual cycle during a drought year might include ceremonies for rainmaking, for the blessing of the crops, for exorcising of spirits causing epidemic, and for burial of dead. During their early phases most of these rituals require the participation of a major proportion of the population. Rituals thus bring the people together and emphasize the importance, the indispensability, the power, and the wisdom of corporate authority. It has been argued elsewhere that ritual is a major power resource (see article 1) available to social leaders in societies confronting ecological stress—a resource that allows the leader to initiate, coalesce, and lead a set of social actions that are perceived by participants as reasonable and effective coping behavior (Burns and Laughlin 1977; d'Aquili et al. 1978). The pattern of involution evident in reciprocal economic exchange is thus counterbalanced by the picture of enhanced politico-religious compensatory action, action that allows tribal members to maximize payoffs of immediate utility while actively underscoring the solidarity of the So people. Table 3.2 is a summary of these and other diaphatic responses to deprivation by the So.

TABLE 3.2   DIAPHATIC RESPONSES BY THE SO TO RECURSIVE FLUCTUATIONS OF BASIC RESOURCES DURING A TIME OF SEVERE DROUGHT

↑ Ritual activity♂ (rainmaking, crop blessing, death rites, banishment of spirits responsible for epidemics)*
↑ Control of grazing resources ♂
↑ Centralization of authority ♂
↑ Production of surplus ♀
↑ Fission of herds ♂
↑ Control of water resources ♂
↑ Adjudication ♂
↑ Articulation with cash market sector (production and exchange) ♀ and ♂
↑ Reliance on government welfare
↑ Hunting ♂
↓ Generalized exchange ♂ and ♀
↑ Hoarding ♂ and ♀

SOURCE: Author's field notes, 1969–70.

* Arrows indicate increase (↑) or decrease (↓) of a particular variable; ♂ and ♀ indicate predominance of sex-specific participation.

ADAPTATION TO PROGRESSIVE
CHANGE IN SO

Diaphatic structuring of So responses to deprivation has occurred simultaneously with their ongoing, homeorhetic responses to progressive changes in the environment. The latter changes have principally
been rendered at the level of surface structure—that is, at the level of
cultural content without fundamental change in underlying infrastructure. For example, whereas the So changed from reliance during drought upon big game to a reliance upon cattle for subsistence,
the structure of power relations determining allocation of these resources remained essentially the same. In other words, big game and
cattle are transformational equivalents in that either resource base
has precisely the same adaptive advantage, namely mobility. During
drought the big game would come to the mountain for water. Cattle
may also be moved to water. This is in contradistinction to the fact
that crops may not be transported to water, and in the absence of an
irrigation capability, water cannot be transported to crops. Everything
else being equal, hunting and pastoralism are differentially more
adaptive than agriculture in areas with marginal climates (see Leeds
and Vayda 1965).

Equilibratory responses by the So to progressive change are summarized in table 3.3. Some of these responses—such as the shift from
hunting to pastoralism, increase in agricultural production, decrease
in foraging activity, increased population density around administrative centers, recent decline of pastoralism—have already been described. Some of the remainder need further amplification.

A major result of So participation in the ivory trade and wife exchange was to bring them into intense contact with the Karamojong.
A network of kinship relations developed between the groups as well
as a network for exchange of goods and services. Cultural borrowing
began to emerge in the direction of So; the So ultimately incorporated
the Karamojong language, various aspects of the "cattle complex"
(Herskovits 1926), and the Karamojong version of the widespread
age generation system. The Karamojong language has nearly replaced traditional So, but the age generation system was modified by
the So in such a fashion that it coincided perfectly with, and provided

TABLE 3.3   SIMPLE EQUILIBRATORY RESPONSES BY THE SO,
             1880–PRESENT

Response:	*Time Occurring*
↑ Acculturative borrowing*	1880s(?)–present
↑ Pastoralism ♂	1880s–1950
↓ Pastoralism ♂	1950–present
↑ Agricultural production ♀	1900(?)–present
↓ Hunting ♂	1900(?)–present
↓ Gathering ♀	1930(?)–present
↑ Institution of age generations ♂	1920(?)–present
↑ Population	1920–present
↑ Population density	1950–present
↑ Control of water resources ♂	1960–present
↑ Reliance upon government protection	1920–present
↑ Reliance upon government services (employment, agricultural innovation, welfare, health) ♂ and ♀	1930s–present
↑ Articulation with cash market sector (jobs, trade)	1950–present
↑ Randomization of post-nuptial residence patterns	1950–present
↓ Full brideprice marriages	1950–present
↓ Mean brideprice paid	1950–present
↑ Institution of brideprice	1900(?)–present

SOURCE: Author's field notes, 1969–70.

*Arrows indicate increase (↑) or decrease (↓) of a particular variable. Question marks (?) indicate uncertainty in dating; ♂ and ♀ indicate predominance of sex-specific participation.

additional support for, their traditional politico-economic system (Laughlin and Laughlin 1974).

Along with the borrowing of other "cattle complex" attributes, the institution of brideprice emerged sometime around the turn of the century replacing minimal "token" brideprice. As I have argued elsewhere (Laughlin 1974a) the present tendency in So marriage patterns is toward fewer full brideprice marriages and for a decrease in the amount of brideprice paid. These changes primarily result from the increasing scarcity of cattle. Furthermore, insofar as raids strike herds more or less at random vis-à-vis descent groups, some lineages are left with intact herds while others have been left with few or no cattle. This has caused an increasing randomization of postnuptial residence patterns from the previous pattern of predominant patrilocality (Laughlin 1974a). Young couples today frequently decide to live in proximity to kinsmen (either the husband's or the wife's) controlling the greatest pastoral and agricultural resources.

Over the years there has been a growing reliance upon government services. First the colonial and then the Uganda governments imposed external law upon So affairs. A growing minority of So seek employment either from the government (as police officials, for example) or from civilians in the administrative center. There is also some ongoing trade with the townspeople in exchange for money and other items (Laughlin 1974b), as previously mentioned. An effect of increased reliance upon government protection and health care has been an increment in population in So.[10]

Finally, control of water resources by the elders is a recent response to the growing scarcity of that resource. Wells have been dug in stream beds, sometimes as deep as eight to ten feet, in order to obtain sufficient water for human and livestock needs. This has necessitated controls, both over the upkeep of wells (which otherwise fill with silt) and over access to wells. Unlike the Karamojong wells, which belong to the lineage that digs them (Dyson-Hudson 1966:25, 219), So wells belong to the entire population of the valley in which they are located. The elders in open council will direct the upkeep of wells and adjudicate access disputes as they arise.

I have thus far described a number of compensatory, adaptive responses on the part of the So to environmental adversity. Some of these (such as shifting from hunting to pastoralism and randomization of postnuptial residence patterns) are responses to progressive change and deterioration in the basic resource base of the tribe. Other responses, such as fluctuations in patterns of reciprocity and reliance upon corporate authority, are to recurrent ecological stress. Changes of the latter sort have been shown to be not fortuitous but predictable and thus explainable by a diachronic model of primitive exchange. These considerations have a number of wider ramifications for social theory. The remainder of this article will be devoted to exploring some of them.

ATOMIZATION AND ADAPTATION

Viewed from a synchronic and macrosocial level, the depression of generalized reciprocity during a period of stress appears as social "atomization"—the disruption of "traditional" social relations which were somehow more systematic and functional. The notion of "atomization," however, is value-laden and misleading. The concept assumes a time past when considerations governing modes of reciprocity were statistically balanced between long- and short-term returns. Analyses of this kind are more the byproduct of synchronic research than an accurate reflection of social reality. If I had entered the field during an exceptionally good year, or even an "average" year, I might well have missed the patterns characteristic of the centripetal phase of the "accordion effect." The point is that an accurate description of So society, or any society faced with a fluctuating resource base, must include a description of the entire cycle. So society does not disintegrate in the common sense of the term. Rather, socioeconomic relations change in a systematic and predictable fashion so that the society can adapt to shifting ecological and external social conditions. This process has been demonstrated as well among the Ojibwa (see Bishop, article 7).

ADAPTATION AND ECONOMY

The primary biological function of any social system is the maintenance of a genetically viable reproductive population which is capable of perpetuating itself through time. This may be called society's *adaptive* function. In order to fulfill its adaptive function, a society must assure the existence of modes of production and distribution of basic goods and services to at least the biologically critical fraction of its population. The "critical fraction" will usually consist of a sufficient number of its reproductively fertile young adults.

This may at first glance appear to be trivially true. Yet with reflection, one is struck by a number of important considerations. For one thing, economic anthropology has for too long emphasized the importance of the means of distribution to the exclusion of the means of production in primitive economic systems. One result of depressing the role of production is confusion about the exact operational boundaries of the study of economics. If, it has been argued, the study of economics is the study of exchange, then any social interaction may be seen as economic (see Homans 1958).

An adequate theory of primitive economics requires a reemphasis upon the roles of production and consumption, but one which does not commit the same error in reverse—a deemphasis of the role of exchange. The definitive referent in primitive economics is production. With production as prime referent, the study of primitive economics becomes the study of the relationship between a society and its ecological environment. I am arguing here, as Scott Cook has argued (1971), for a theoretical merger between economic and ecological anthropology. Production becomes the exploitative relationship between a population and its operational environment. Exchanges involving goods and services related to production are thus within the purview of the economic anthropologist. Cook (1971) has said that when the goods have been produced, "the economy has done its job." I would amend his comment to say that when the goods and services have been produced, distributed, and consumed, the economy has done its job.

Sahlins has discussed the problem of the allocation and intensity of labor in primitive and peasant societies (1971b). He centers his discussion on the Chayanov model which states that the intensity of labor exhibited in peasant households will be a probability function of the capacity for labor in the household. In other words, productive intensity will be inversely correlated with productive capacity as measured by the number of consumers per household divided by the number of producers (1971b:34). A critical point made by Sahlins is that in neither peasant nor primitive economics is the normative level of production intensity anywhere near the theoretical maximum potential (1971b:32). The norm of productive intensity, he says, will vary in relation to quantity produced depending upon the society one examines. The norm will always exceed, to some measurable extent, that necessary for the maintenance of minimal subsistence requirements. The production of a surplus in primitive economics is a social universal, not an exception. Sahlins concluded that patterns of production intensity are embedded in and determined by non-economic social variables. And, as men in primitive society ordinarily do not maximize wealth for its own sake, but rather maximize prestige and other non-material returns through the medium of wealth, men tend to produce only enough wealth to sustain these goals. There exists a

plethora of information in the literature in support of this proposition
(see Carneiro 1968:134; Woodburn 1968:51).

In emphasizing the social determinants of the upper limit of production output and intensity, Sahlins thereby *fails* to note the more
important fact—that the lower limits of production output and intensity are determined, not by social variables, but by limitations imposed upon the economy by the nature of ecological resources. It is
evident upon reflection that production cannot fall below a point
where a quantity of basic goods and services proves insufficient to
support a viable reproductive population. And, once production has
reached the point of sufficiency, *including surpluses produced to offset potential periods of deprivation,* then the amount of "cultural"
elaboration in production and distribution becomes *adaptively irrelevant* and may be established by social convention; that is, just so
long as social convention does not interfere with society's prime
adaptive function.

For my part, I contend that the lower limit is the more critical and
instructive for the development of a nomothetic anthropology; for
societies confronted with a radically shifting resource base must
maintain a marked flexibility in their modes of allocation of labor,
both in direction of utilization and in intensity. Flexibility in the
allocation of productive capabilities, like flexibility in modes of reciprocity, will necessitate a range of strategy alternatives, and, more
likely than not, any distinction we make between the goals of production and the goals of exchange will be purely analytic. As I have demonstrated here and elsewhere with the So data, a shift in the availability of resources will affect both direction of production and
patterns of exchange—and both to the same purpose, namely, continued survival. The inevitable result of this chain of reasoning is that
production, and *reciprocity* stemming from production, are only two
analytic aspects of the single process termed *economizing*—the allocation of scarce resources among alternative ends.

CONCLUSION

Returning once again to the discussion of the prime adaptive function of society, I have said that systems confronted with fluctuating

ecological resources must, in order to remain adaptive, provide a certain quality of flexibility in their structure. Such flexibility is required so that the modes of production and distribution may shift, often rapidly, to match a changing set of resource alternatives. Sometimes only the type of resource will change while the overall quantity of input remains the same. The social structure may need only to respond to such a situation by redirecting the mode of production and retaining the same distributional structure. However, if the ecological fluctuation involves alternating minimal/maximal resource availability such that during one phase in the cycle basic resources become both more limited in type and scarce in quantity, then we would expect to find more dramatic flexibility in the social structure.

Adaptive social systems of the latter sort will not incorporate strictly enforced, normative rules or structures during periods of peak resource availability which will impede change in modes of production and exchange required for survival during periods of ecological deprivation. The So are aware, for instance, that the next season's crops may fail and that they may be faced with starvation. Their socialization procedures inculate attitudes and institutions which make it possible to modify social interaction from that based upon long-range maximization strategies to that based upon relatively short-range strategies, and still retain the integrity of their ethnic boundaries. So social structure is capable at any time of cyclical disassociation and reassociation in response to the vicissitudes of ecological variables. It seems likely that this is the case with Turnbull's Ik as well.

One of the problems in testing the present theory is that the literature offers few cases of *non*-adaptive societies. Such a society is, by definition, one in which the population is either rapidly exterminated by ecological factors or is ultimately incapable of supporting a sufficiently large reproductive population and hence becomes slowly extinct.[11] The Ik do not constitute a non-adaptive society. Quite the contrary, they adapt remarkably well to the miserable conditions afforded them. Turnbull himself offers a clue to the effectiveness of Ik adaptation when he says that the young adult males and females remain relatively healthy while the very young and old die from starvation (1967:69). It is precisely the young breeding population which survives to establish the future population.

The present theoretical position argues, therefore, for closer analytical attention to marginally adaptive societies—in fact, the type of study represented by the present volume. Probably more important in terms of practical availability of data, it also argues for increased attention to societies which have adapted to extreme resource fluctuation. Studies of such societies must be diachronic in design. Despite a tradition of theory-building in anthropology based usually upon data from time-slice ethnography, valid social theory, capable of explaining social change, must be grounded upon studies which isolate and control for temporal variables. Let me emphasize this point—causal models *cannot,* in principle, be supported by synchronic data.

NOTES

1. A number of persons helped in the formulation of my field research. I thank Richard Chaney, Neville and Rada Dyson-Hudson, Vernon Dorjahn, Joseph Jorgensen, and Colin Turnbull. Elizabeth R. Allgeier helped immeasurably in collecting the data upon which the present description is based. My thanks also to Ivan Brady, Ron Cochran, Patricia Kolarik, Terry Morse, Iain Prattis, and Deborah West for their helpful suggestions in preparing this study. Research among the So was funded by a grant from the National Science Foundation and by a research assistantship from the Department of Anthropology, University of Oregon.

2. The population of So was approximately 4,800 in 1970, including 3,500 on Mount Moroto, 1,000 on Mount Kadam, and 300 on Mount Napak. Fieldwork was carried out during 1969–70. For a more complete description of So ecological history, as well as a list of relevant historical sources, see Laughlin (1972) and Laughlin and Laughlin (1972).

3. For detailed climatic data relevant to So subsistence see Laughlin (1972:39ff.).

4. Entebbe Archives 106/1910, DC Nimule-PC Hoima, 15 February 1911.

5. For demographic data relevant to lineage size, see Laughlin 1972.

6. The minimal patrilineage in So is usually localized and forms the genealogical core of the residential compound, a fenced area which may be located independently of others. The compound is extremely varied demographically (Laughlin 1974b:394; see also Laughlin 1972).

7. This modification of Sahlins' model was originally formulated in the field, prior to formal testing. It was published in Laughlin (1972, 1974b).

8. Although the factor of change has not been a central concern in the formulation of his model, Sahlins has clearly anticipated the need for flexibility in applying the model to individual instances in which stress is a factor (see Sahlins 1971a:55).

9. I found evidence of hoarding by the household, and even on the part of household members relative to other household members, although I at no time observed the extremes of hoarding reported for the Ik (Turnbull, article 2).

10. For more details about health care and family planning among the So, see Laughlin and Laughlin (1973).

11. Examples of the latter sort may be found in the demise of the Tasmanians (Kroeber 1944:819) and the near demise of the El Molo of Kenya (Dyson and Fuchs 1937).

Gross Stress in Small Islands:
A Study in Macropsychiatry

John Cawte

In John Cawte's description of the Kaiadilt, we have another instance of a society adapting to unremitting deprivation. Cawte's innovative application of transcultural psychiatry demonstrates that the intricate process of fit between cognized and operational environments may be confounded by reverberative psychopathology. As another psychological theorist, John McManus (1978), has argued elsewhere, ecological stress results in widespread psychological stress when institutionalized buffers fail under unremitting deprivation, that is, when the institutionalized coping responses cognized by individuals are no longer perceived as adequate. This condition is usually marked by a concomitant failure of the traditional myth-ritual complex and institutional authority. With failure of these buffers, unremitting deprivation and ecological stress may leave the cognitive systems of individuals in the society vulnerable to superoptimal noxity from the operational environment. Without some resurgence of authority and confidence, such as in the form of a millenarian movement (see Wallace 1956), prolonged superoptimal stress may lead to psychopathology of epidemic proportions, which, in turn, may decrease the flexibility of the adaptive infrastructure itself by undermining reproduction and sociability and thereby survival itself. Even the fine line of survivability clung to so tenaciously by groups like the Ik may disappear under such circumstances. The result is normally extinction. A major source of continuation for the Kaiadilt, however, has derived from cross-cultural interference. But, as will be seen in later articles, such intervention varies widely in scope and effect and does not necessarily enhance the population's survival chances.

This article directs attention to psychiatric aspects of extinction and survival, taking as examples two Aboriginal societies occupying small adjacent islands off the coast of Australia. The term "macropsychiatry" is proposed as a conceptual framework and also as a source of methodology for studies of this kind. The concept of "gross stress," in the sense of massive psychophysiological traumatization, is also proposed and subjected to conceptual analysis as a psychiatric category essential to the understanding of a survival-extinction situation.

Macropsychiatry is concerned with the *pathology* of adaptive processes employed by human groups. By focusing on group pathology, macropsychiatry reflects the customary medical orientation toward sickness rather than toward health. It studies the maladaptive responses which may be employed by groups under stress, including the stress produced by prolonged or extensive resource deprivation.

Macropsychiatry has to be distinguished from social and community psychiatry, which are terms for aspects of the public health movement concerned with the malaise of individuals in their relation to society. Macropsychiatrists study corporate groups which, when confronted by environmental stresses or cyclical privations, behave in ways that make matters worse—for example, by reducing rather than maximizing the production of resources.

The prefix *macro* in macropsychiatry signifies *large* as applied to a corporate group and *long* as applied to the duration of the process of stress or unfitness. It may be thought of as antithetical to micropsychiatry, which is examplified by images of a patient being interviewed in a doctor's office or of micropsychiatry on individual psychiatric illnesses. The task of macropsychiatry is to consider what effect these illnesses may have on corporate groups.

Macropsychiatric research is thus a joint psychiatric-anthropological venture. Its special value is to remind the student of "culture" and "society" that people are individuals, as well as members of society, who follow private ends and personal pathologies; and that these ends and pathologies may have adverse retroflexive effects on the functioning of the group.

Gross stress came into vogue as a medical category in World War II to refer to the illnesses of combat personnel which could not fairly be described in terms of existing psychiatric categories in use in civilian life. The syndrome was officially called "reaction to acute and special stress," "gross stress reaction," or "acute situational maladjustment."

Gross stress as a causal category is also applied to situations other than combat, especially to community disasters such as cyclones, floods, earthquakes, and tidal waves. Four phases are commonly described: anticipatory, impact, recoil, and post-traumatic. The post-traumatic phase has been depicted best by Eitinger and Strom (1973) in studies of concentration camp survivors; it may take the form of chronic—indeed lifelong—syndromes expressed by apathy, hostility, or turned-in hostility.

The social sciences, including anthropology and psychiatry, have until recently neglected the concept of gross stress from ecological privation. In Australia, for example, whole Aboriginal communities have been described in solemn detail without recognition that most of the members were suffering gross stress. Observers have failed to give the concept due weight in part because of their insensitivity to the power of physical factors of chronic ill-health, anemia, subnutrition, and overcrowding, and in part because of their insensitivity to the psychological features of high anxiety levels that are expressed in various ways. Accurate observation is also compounded by the responses of those inside the situation, who suffer from illnesses without clearly identifying them or perceiving them objectively.

In this article the macropsychiatry of two small island societies will be considered. Mornington and Bentinck are the two habitable islands of the Wellesley group in the southern reaches of the vast Gulf of Carpentaria in north Queensland (see map 4.1). In the period under consideration, the smaller and more ecologically marginal Bentinck Island was less able to withstand a series of prolonged droughts than the larger Mornington Island. The Kaiadilt of Bentinck Island underwent gross stress, while the Lardil of Mornington Island were less affected. The following psychiatric comparison of the two groups highlights the role of human ecological and bionomic factors in setting in motion a depressive pattern which afflicted the first group in a wholesale manner. It is suggested that in this "sick" group, ecological disturbance came first, interpersonal disturbances followed, and intrapsychic disturbances completed a psychopathological sequence which then reverberated throughout the society. While the ecological privation is not relieved, the psychosocial sequence is still reverberating.

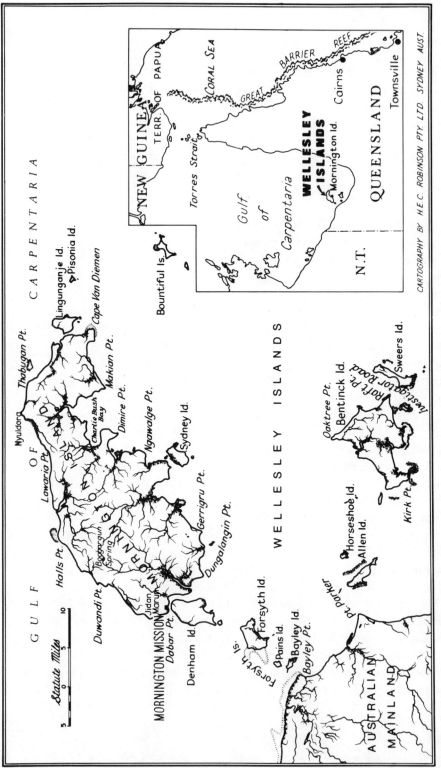

MAP 4.1 WELLESLEY ISLANDS, GULF OF CARPENTARIA

CARTOGRAPHY BY H.E.C. ROBINSON PTY. LTD. SYDNEY AUST.

I will describe here the ecological privation, the changes in inter-personal behaviors, and the psychiatric responses, in order to illuminate these basic processes of macropsychiatry.

FROM THE EDGE OF ANNIHILATION: BENTINCK ISLANDERS

Insofar as they survived as a physical population, the Kaiadilt may be said to have adapted biologically, though in surviving they tested the limits of human suffering and endurance. The macropsychiatric sequelae could be studied in the survivors. Bentinck Island lies in the relatively shallow southern reaches of the Gulf of Carpentaria, unreliably subject to rainfall from the summer monsoons. A flat, poorly covered island, it normally exposed its inhabitants to cyclical privations and to physiological stresses. For the past twenty years it has been a desert island: the survivors were evacuated, as a life-saving measure, to Mornington Island.

The Bentinck Islanders are among the world's most excluded and isolated people—isolated even from contact with other Aborigines.[1] They are probably the last group of coastal Aborigines to come into regular contact with white men. The American anthropologist Lauriston Sharp, noted for his work in Cape York (Sharp 1934), had hoped to visit them but could not arrange to do so. When they were studied initially in 1942 by the Australian anthropologist Norman Tindale (1962a, 1962b), their total number was recorded at 123. At that time they were gripped by Malthusian forces of famine, disease, and warfare, which by 1948 had reduced them to only 47 very sick survivors.[2] In order to arrest further decline, and to avert the total extinction which was feared, this population remnant was evacuated by the missionaries and some Aborigines of Mornington Island. There they were literally nursed, fed, and calmed into survival.[3]

The material basis of Kaiadilt insecurity may be gleaned from knowledge of their ecology. The small island is covered by sparse woodland and clay pan, with several reefs offshore. There are no hills or regularly filled watercourses. Lacking agriculture, the Kaiadilt were dependent on gathering the edible species from the land and the sea. In good seasons the land provided frogs, lizards, yams, berries, and waterlily roots; the runoff of rainwater into the sea was sufficient to ensure supplies of crabs, oysters, and shellfish. While the women and children gathered these species, the men speared the larger fish from the reef. Sometimes they paddled flimsy rafts in hunts for dugong and turtle or visited outlying sand bars to gather turtle eggs.

The wood and tools available for making a raft seem to have been critical factors in the human ecology of this island. There are no stones on Bentinck suitable for making knives; shells are available for scraping and cutting. The frail wedge-shaped platforms which were constructed from the stoutest wood available—dried stems of the mangrove—settled slightly below the surface of the water when straddled by a man so that they could not be stood upon. It is also hard to navigate when no land can be seen over the horizon. Voyage by raft to Mornington Island or to the mainland of Australia could not be accomplished without undue risk and probable loss of life. There was no visible land to steer by. Strong winds and currents prevailing in those waters made it hard to keep to a desired course. Tindale (1962b) calculated from his demographic work that a voyage of eight miles from the island was associated with a 50 percent chance of mortality.

Bentinck Island was thus a natural prison to which the Kaiadilt were confined, in uneasy equilibrium with their basic resources. Evidence that the Kaiadilt did not traffic much with other societies comes from another source: namely, genetic studies. Blood groups and fingerprints completely separate the genotype of the Kaiadilt from that of their nearest neighbors, the Lardil of Mornington Island, as well as from that of the mainland tribes. The Kaiadilt possess no blood group A gene from the ABO series. The converse is true for the Lardil: they are rich in blood group A, like other Aboriginal groups (Simmons et al. 1964). Fingerprint patterns as well show similar differences (Singh 1968).[4]

The distinctive genotypes of the Kaiadilt and Lardil are evidence of spatial confinement on Bentinck Island. In times of privation, emigration was not an option. A characteristic feature of this ecology is its fluctuating abundance. Periods of plenty and population growth were succeeded by drought and famine. At an estimate, the natural resources of Bentinck Island, exploited by the existing level of technology, could not safely have supported more than 100 people, certainly less than 150.

The Commonwealth Bureau of Meteorology assists our study by providing the annual rainfall records from the nearest "Met" Station, at Burketown. In order to specify the periods of moderate and severe rainfall deficiency in the Gulf country, the technique employed by Foley (1966) has been applied. The periods of rainfall deficiency, determined objectively by daily measurement, correspond approximately to periods of drought. Table 4.1 gives an idea of the conditions at Burketown. In the recorded period from 1925 to 1963, rarely do five years elapse without a moderate or serious drought of two or more years duration. In twenty years there are eight years of moderate drought and twelve years of severe drought.

TABLE 4.1   PERIODS OF DROUGHT,
BURKETOWN, QUEENSLAND

Period		Extent of Drought*
1925 April	–1926 November	moderate
1927 March	–1928 February	moderate
1931 February	–1936 January	severe
1937 February	–1938 December	severe
1941 December	–1944 January	moderate
1947 April	–1948 December	moderate
1951 February	–1952 December	moderate
1959 February	–1963 December	severe

SOURCE: Report, Commonwealth Bureau of Meteorology.

* After criteria of Foley 1966.

To the food privations affecting this part of Australia—with which all adult Kaiadilt were undoubtedly familiar—must be added the heat stresses of the environment. Social scientists err when they neglect to take into account the physiological tolerance limits of man as an aspect of his adaptation. These limits have obvious relevance to the sun-scorched island of the Kaiadilt. Data on heat and cold, protection, endurance, and tolerance limits have all been combined on a chart by environmental stress researchers (Webb and Blockley 1962). Key heat stresses include high air temperature, solar radiation, high water vapor pressures, and high work loads. These are exacerbated by internal stresses such as high metabolic rate, subclinical infection, and dehydration. Prime stressors on Bentinck Island are high air temperature, solar radiation, and high work load; secondary stressors include poor water supply, dehydration, lack of shade, high air movement, and infections. The multiple stress-strain relationships with the environment assume heightened significance during periods of ecological privation.

With these essential data on the stresses and privations facing the Kaiadilt, we may now examine what problem-solving was possible for them in the process of adptation. How did they handle the problem? Anticipating the somewhat unexpected conclusion, it may be noted that the Kaiadilt themselves defined their problem differently from the way outside observers saw it.[5]

The outsider's view is what an intelligent but uninvolved person might expect from a knowledge of these circumstances. The most important outsider for the Kaiadilt, and indeed my chief informant on this matter, is a Lardil elder called Gully Peters. In the years preceding the Kaiadilt collapse, Gully had been engaged in collecting trepang (bêche de mer) from Bentinck waters. Gully and his wife established a relationship with the Bentinck Islanders while camped ashore and had learned their language. He was impressed by their mental and physical distress. According to Gully, they were dying out because of killing among the bands. They were also suffering from famine because of the long drought. Gully reported that a man who came back at night from fishing on a reef might be killed for his catch. The band that killed him would then take his wife and eat his children.

In response to Gully's information, in 1947 the missionary from Mornington Island visited Bentinck and found the people suffering from starvation, dysentery, and chronic chest disease. Then came the final catastrophe. In 1948 there was a tidal wave or freak high tide in the Gulf. It salinated the water holes of Bentinck Island and made survival so precarious that Gully and the missionary decided to evacuate the Kaiadilt to the mission at Mornington Island. The era of sustained contact with other Aborigines began for this sick, frightened, and demoralized group.

Few people would question the ethics of this intervention. Since the drought continued, it seems that but for this intervention they could be as extinct as many other small Australian bands. Any altruistic outsider would feel impelled to define the situation as a disaster, calling for disaster relief. This is how the outsider observers, including Norman Tindale, defined the situation: it was one of great ecological stress, caused by food and water shortages after the prolonged drought. We now come to what is probably an essential problem in macropsychiatric situations. People on the inside and undergoing stress define the stress differently from the way outsiders define it (see article 1). The Kaiadilt defined their problem in a completely interpersonal manner, as one of warfare and revenge. Their viewpoint emerged most strongly when I knew some senior Kaiadilt sufficiently well to discuss it with him. They relate the high stress to persistent fighting *over women,* and to its complications. They dispute that hunger and sickness were important to them. They wanted women.

The distinction between the "ecological" and the "warfare" hypotheses fades somewhat if women are regarded as economic resources, as providers of food and services. However, when this is pointed out to the Kaiadilt men they disagree. They emphasize that by fighting over women they were concerned with the satisfaction of sexual needs, rather than economic security, social status, and children. Since sexual desire is a feature of all mankind, our problem concerns why the killing of men in order to steal their women became so intense among the Kaiadilt in the stress-torn years of which we have knowledge. We shall return to explain this response to gross stress after the psychiatric data have been presented.

MACROPSYCHIATRIC FINDINGS

Before summarizing the macropsychiatric patterns of the Kaiadilt, it might be prudent to state what precautions were taken to ensure that these data are reliable. Psychiatrists and psychoanalysts especially have been accused by anthropologists of psychiatric imperialism when they have attempted to apply, across a cultural boundary, concepts of psychiatry which were derived largely from Western neurotics. Non-Western people break down in their own way, that is, in a way that may not correspond with Western ways at all. Nor is the characteristic Western system of casefinding—if it consists of waiting for the more affluent sufferers to seek out the psychiatrist—appropriate. How then can a Western psychiatrist hope to obtain a fair and accurate estimate of the amount and kind of psychiatric disorders in societies such as the Kaiadilt and the Lardil?

The problem was tackled in this instance by devising two instruments, consisting of 20 questions that described in simple lay terms kinds of behavior commonly associated with psychiatric disorder. One instrument was designed for adults (over 15 years of age) and the other for children (under 15 years). The 20 questions were then administered to two separate committees, one Aboriginal and one European. The separate committees were used in order to avert a European or an Aboriginal bias as to what constitutes "disorderly" or "sick" behavior. The European committee consisted of the missionary, his wife, the trained nurse, the cattle overseer, the carpenter, and the schoolteacher. The Aboriginal committee was comprised of village men and women having seniority and status. Each committee was instructed that the individuals indicated by them would be examined by the visiting doctor, who would probably be able to help some of them by medical treatment. Experience at previously visited Aboriginal outposts suggested that this was a fair promise. Good cooperation was obtained, and each committee debated its answers with care and thoroughness.

The number of adults and children indicated by the Aboriginal and European informants is shown in tables 4.2 and 4.3. The Aborigines indicated more individuals, suggesting that they used a finer filter. They also employed a qualitatively different filter, though there is substantial concordance between the two committees in many of the behavioral categories. Psychiatric examinations were then carried out on the individuals indicated by the census. This involved physical medical examination, interviews with the aid of interpreters, and seeking additional information from family members. Under these procedures, many of the individuals indicated by the committees

TABLE 4.2 MORNINGTON ISLAND MORBIDITY CENSUS OF
INHABITANTS FIFTEEN YEARS AND OVER

Symptoms	Indicated by Aboriginal Informants	Indicated by European Informants
1. DULL, backward, slow learner	12	5
2. CONFUSED, forgetful, gets lost	5	2
3. EPILEPTIC, takes fits, has blackouts	5	4
4. OVERACTIVE, restless, interfering, noisy at night	3	2
5. CRIPPLED, paralyzed, many burns, blind, deaf, deformed	6	5
6. BATTERED, many fight cuts, sorry cuts	"Old Bentinck people"	"Old Bentinck people"
7. QUARRELSOME, abusive, destructive	14	7
8. MARKED DOMESTIC UNHAPPINESS	4 couples	6 couples
9. JEALOUS, markedly so of husband or wife	7	2
10. CRIMINAL, frequent clashes with the law	"Most people a bit"	1
11. CRUEL, to men, women, or children	7	none
12. OVERDEPENDENT, poorly occupied, unable to keep a job	9	3
13. SEX PROBLEMS	Reluctant to say	1
14. DEPRESSED, miserable, frequent crying, suicidal	5	4
15. SUSPICIOUS, blaming, twisted outlook	"Nearly everybody"	3
16. FEARFUL, anxious, very worried	"common"	1
17. COMPLAINING, makes a fuss about many aches and pains	1	10
18. MAGIC, claims command and use of	4	5
19. MAGIC, claims caught by *puripuri* or bad magic	3	1
20. WITHDRAWN, solitary, quiet, dumb	3	2
TOTAL	88*	64†

SOURCE: Cawte 1972:57, reprinted with permission of the publisher.

*49 males; 39 females.
†37 males; 27 females.

TABLE 4.3 CHILDHOOD (TO AGE 15) PSYCHIATRIC MORBIDITY CENSUS

Symptoms	Indicated by Aboriginal Informants	Indicated by European Informants
1. DULL, backward, slow learner	10	10
2. CONFUSED, forgetful, gets lost	—	—
3. EPILEPTIC, takes fits, has blackouts,	2	4
breath-holder	6	—
4. OVERACTIVE, restless	8	—
5. CRIPPLED, paralyzed, many burns, blind, deaf, deformed	4	2
6. SPEECH DIFFICULTIES, stammer, dumb, baby talk	4	6
7. QUARRELSOME, many fights with playmates, tantrums	8	7
8. DISOBEDIENT to parents or teachers, very cheeky	7	4
9. TRUANT, refuses to go to school	3	3
10. THIEF	7	8
11. RUNS AWAY, has to be found	2	—
12. BABYISH, won't compete, won't defend himself, cry baby	6	3
13. POOR CONTROL OF BLADDER OR BOWEL	5	6
14. CHILDISH HABITS, thumbsucking, nail biting, hair pulling	1	5
15. EATING PROBLEMS, too much, too little	2	1
16. FEARFUL, shy, timid, afraid	3	5
17. COMPLAINING, many aches and pains	1	4
18. SLEEP PROBLEMS, nightmares, sleep walking, insomnia	3	1
19. MAGIC, reputedly suffers from	2	2
20. WITHDRAWN, does not play with others	5	—
21. MISCELLANEOUS	—	3
TOTAL	64*	58†

SOURCE: Cawte 1972:116, reprinted with permission of the publisher.

*46 males; 18 females.
†36 males; 22 females.

were rated as not seriously disturbed. The number of adults finally determined to be showing the more serious disturbances, the diagnoses given, and the distribution among the three populations now occupying Mornington Island—Lardil, Mainland Aborigines, and Kaiadilt—is shown in table 4.4.

TABLE 4.4 MORNINGTON ISLAND ADULT PSYCHIATRIC MORBIDITY CENSUS BY DIAGNOSTIC CATEGORIES*

Primary Diagnosis	Lardil	Mainland	Kaiadilt	Total
Organic Disorder (with behavior disorder)	1	1		2
Mental Subnormality (mild)	1		1	2
Epilepsy (with behavior disorder)			1	1
Depression			7†	7
Schizophrenia			1	1
Transitory Delusional State	2			2
Personality Disorder	6	4	1	11
Neurosis	4			4
Psychosomatic Disorder	1	1		2
Total	15	6	11	32
Risk Population	142	76	60	276

SOURCE: Cawte 1972:60, reprinted with permission of the publisher.

* Note that no cases of mania or senile dementia were identified.

† Significant at the 0.01 level by chi-squared technique using the Yates (1934) correction factor for small numbers.

Psychiatric examinations of the child population were carried out in a similar manner by my colleague Dr. Barry Nurcombe, whose findings are shown in table 4.5. For details the reader must consult Cawte (1972). The broad outline may be sketched here.

In the census, the Kaiadilt showed the highest total incidence of serious mental disorders, as well as patterns that differ from those of the Lardil and the mainlanders. Out of the Kaiadilt population of 60 adults, 11 had psychiatric disorders, contrasted with 15 Lardil out of a total of 142, and 6 mainlanders out of a total of 76 (table 4.4.).

TABLE 4.5   CHILDHOOD (TO AGE 15) PSYCHIATRIC MORBIDITY
            CENSUS: DIAGNOSTIC CATEGORIES OF ASCERTAINED
            CASES

Primary Diagnosis	Lardil	Mainland	Kaiadilt	Total
Reactive Disorders	1	—	—	1
Developmental Deviations	4	1	—	5
Anxiety-Inhibition Syndrome	1	1	5*	7
Tension-Discharge Syndrome	2	9*	2	13
Aggressive	2	7	—	9
Acquisitive	—	2	2	4
Sexual	—	—	—	—
Personality Disorder	1	2	—	3
Psychoneurotic Disorder	—	2	—	2
Psychotic Disorder	—	—	—	—
Brain Syndromes (epilepsy)	2	—	—	2
Educational Retardation	14	—	—	14
Severe Mental Retardation	—	—	—	—
Traditional Disorders	—	—	—	2
Total	26	15	7	50
Risk Population	197	45	38	280

SOURCE: Cawte 1972:126, reprinted with permission of the publisher.

*Significant at the 0.01 level by chi-squared technique using the Yates (1934) correction factor for small numbers.

The most striking difference in the pattern of illness was that of the seven cases of severe depressive disorder in the entire population, all came from the Kaiadilt group—a difference significant at the 0.01 level of probability. In interpreting this, we were impressed with the role of human ecological and bionomic factors in setting the depressive pattern in motion. As suggested at the outset of this chapter, ecological disturbance came first, interactional disturbances followed, and intrapsychic disturbance completed the psychopathological sequence which then reverberated throughout society.

The high incidence of Kaiadilt mental disorder carried through into the new generation, as a separate census of the children under 15 years of age reveals (table 4.5). Of the 38 Kaiadilt children, 7 show a psychogenic disorder. The mainland children show a still higher incidence, 14 out of the total of 45, showing a psychogenic disorder. The adjustment of Lardil children is in striking contrast: only 6 out of 197 show a psychogenic disorder.

Although the Kaiadilt and mainland children are conspicuously maladjusted, their disorders are of different kinds (table 4.5). Children of the mainland group show predominantly a tension-discharge syndrome, characterized by chronic patterns expressing aggressive and acquisitive impulses at odds with the norms of society. The children act impulsively in frustrating circumstances and are repeatedly in conflict with authority. The Kaiadilt children, on the other hand, display an anxious-inhibition syndrome characterized by extreme shyness, inhibition of initiative, and apprehension in new situations. The children tend to remain dependent, clinging, and timid into school years. They are by no means among the duller scholars; if anything, dullness in school is the characteristic of the apparently emotionally adjusted Lardil child.

A comparison of the three populations by means of the census is reliable for the overtly disturbed members of society, but might overlook the neurotic individuals who suffer more privately and create little or no disturbance socially. To detect this group we adapted the Cornell Medical Inventory for use in the adult population, using questions relevant to Aboriginal culture.[6] The questions test whether individuals consider themselves to be suffering from symptoms in the main areas of physical and psychological functioning.

We next surveyed for individual symptom levels, using the modification of the Cornell Medical Inventory. Five peaks of personal discomfort were revealed which we would not have suspected if we had restricted ourselves to epidemiological techniques designed to measure overt disturbances. The strongest complaints were of musculoskeletal aches, of low energy and fatigue, of poor sleep, of social inadequacy, and of irritability. The complaint levels were high among the whole population, but highest among the Kaiadilt (see figures 4.1, 4.2, and 4.3).

It is not possible to describe the macropsychiatry of the Kaiadilt further here without going into cultural and social factors, cognitive-ideational structure, and the psychiatric findings in detail. The interested reader may refer to Cawte (1972) which presents these details.

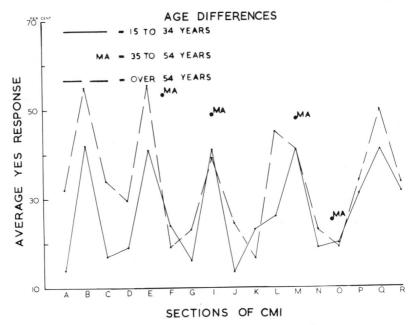

FIGURE 4.1   Sections of Cornell Medical Index

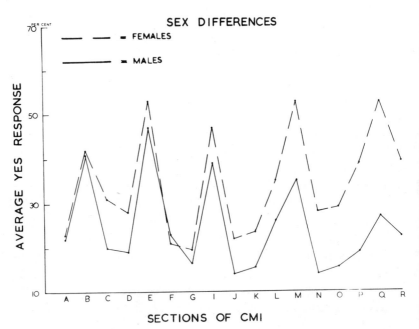

FIGURE 4.2   Sections of Cornell Medical Index

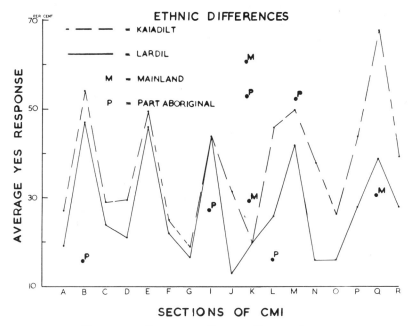

FIGURE 4.3   SECTIONS OF CORNELL MEDICAL INDEX

Nevertheless, one briefly cited case history may convey more about the Kaiadilt distress than a wealth of tabulated statistics; this case also illustrates the macropsychiatric principle that psychoses may have a seriously adverse and retroflexive effect upon the functioning of the group.

> I frequently encountered C, a strong Kaiadilt apparently in his mid-forties, sitting morosely outside his hut, looking at the ground and muttering to himself. His two wives, resigned in appearance, attended him from just within earshot. C was recovering from a self-inflicted blow in the face with a tomahawk. Some months previously he had tried to drown himself in the channel. Sometimes I observed him standing atop a sand-hill, shouting and cursing in his vernacular, too angry to be approached. He blamed his countrymen from Bentinck Island for his sickness, and believed that they were burning his feces and his fish bones. As the history of his disorder emerged, I grasped the implications that it had for his group. One of his wives was formerly (on Bentinck Island, before the exodus) married to a

man whom C killed. She had been taken by C as a co-wife.
After they moved to Mornington Island C had been expected to
give her up and to live with one wife in the Christian manner.
He had no wish to live monogamously but the second wife took
advantage of the situation to rebuff his sexual advances. Constant tension arose when C, dependent and regressed, insisted
on the attention of both wives. The family was terrorized by his
demands, complaints and accusations. Nobody in that family
worked.

THE SURVIVAL OF THE
MORNINGTON ISLANDERS

The Lardil of Mornington Island came through the period under consideration, if not without stress, without much damage to their collective health and morale. Although neighbors of the Kaiadilt, they are
hardly contemporaries because they have lived with a Presbyterian
Mission since 1917. After some initial tensions in which the first missionary was killed by them, they have had a fairly satisfactory relationship since. Not a great deal of information is available about their
pre-mission adaptation, but there is no indication that their survival
was ever threatened by the Malthusian forces which we have seen to
be overwhelming in other places.

It is easier to study sickness than health. We take health for
granted and ignore its dynamics: "Health is a crown that the well
man wears, which only the sick man sees." So it appears to the suf-
ferer. To the physician, health is not a static concept, an absence of
disease or stress. Since the world is full of disease and stress, health
should rather be defined as the ability to rally from noxious environmental input (Audy and Dunn 1973) or the ability to prevent such
input from occurring in the first place.

If we were to study the healthy adaptions of the Lardil, we should
consider by what means the population rallied when they encountered privations, and by what means they maintained their social integration and corporate harmony at times when each man felt the
pinch of his personal needs.

In what follows, I have selected just one aspect of the survival ma-

chinery of the Lardil in order to show how the medical beliefs of a
culture may help ensure the equitable distribution of the resources of
a small island. The set of medical beliefs comprises what has been
called the culture-bound syndrome *Malgri* and described in more detail, with illustrative cases, in a previous publication (Cawte 1974).
Enough should be said here to indicate how the fear of this condition
by the Lardil led to greater respect among the clans for one another's
resources. It provides a further example of the relevance of a macropsychiatric frame of reference for group adaptation and group pathology.

In the Lardil medical system, *Malgri* is a spirit-intrusion syndrome
linked with the totemic organization of the people and their territory.
The central theme in *Malgri* is the mutual antipathy between land
and sea. A person who enters the sea without washing his hands
after handling land food runs the risk of succumbing to *Malgri*.
Traces of land food are dangerous in the sea and must first be rubbed
off with sand and water; even body paint and grease must be removed. *Malgri* spirits can also operate in the reverse direction—from
the land—when, for example, a person who has been fishing in the
sea uses a freshwater rock pool or lagoon without first cleansing his
hands of traces of saltwater food. If these precautions are neglected,
the totemic spirit that is guardian of that particular littoral is believed
to invade the belly "like a bullet." The *Malgri* victim grows sick, tired,
and drowsy. His head aches, his belly distends, he writhes and
groans in pain and may vomit. Most islanders seemed to have at least
some anxiety about contracting the illness.

To appreciate this disorder one must know that a feature of Lardil
cosmology is the division of the coastline of Mornington Island into
upward of thirty littorals, each forming the sea frontage for a particular subsection of the tribe or class of totemites, each with its distinctive totem. In many cases, the totems, such as the shark, stingray,
coolibah tree, and rock cod, are obvious local natural species; in other
instances, such as with the moon and sea serpent, the legendary associations of the site are represented. *Malgri*, then, is a sickness of in-
truders. The social group occupying an estate enjoys immunity in its
home range. The Lardil's fear is directed toward the intruding spirits
that ring his island. A map has been prepared of Mornington Island

estates with the help of several islanders and mapmakers (see map 4.2).

Malgri belief thus helps regulate resource utilization, including the distinctiveness or exclusiveness of the local group's territorial boundaries, and the availability and the utilization patterns of the food and water resources to which the local group has access rights or ownership claims. The apparent distinctiveness and exclusiveness of the Lardil estates may be attributable to the fact that the Lardil occupy an island, limited in resources and capable of supporting only limited population, so that territorial rights might be jealously safeguarded. The *Malgri* syndrome itself appears connected with the fact that the territory is an island; it is not encountered in such a specific form among mainland tribes.

It seems reasonable to infer that ecological or subsistence tensions were factors leading to the etiology of this syndrome and its relationship to the island population units. The composition of the social units, after fifty years of Western contact, is not known with any precision, although map 4.2 provides an approximation with which to begin. It is in any case more a subject for the social anthropologist than for the clinician. Meanwhile, *Malgri* provides a clear example of the interweaving of ecological adaptation, social organization, and macropsychiatry.

CONCLUSIONS: THE MACROPSYCHIATRIC PROCESS

Small island societies, for which it is difficult to increase basic resources that fall into short supply, may react to the resultant stresses with conflicts of interest that threaten their survival. One of the chief purposes of this chapter is simply to document this fact. The failure of human groups to survive is no mere theoretical possibility. Instances of its occurrence can be found and even studied at the present time. By "failure to survive" we are referring in this chapter not to groups that have succumbed to the onslaught of outside enemies having superior strength, but to groups that, by reacting pathologically to gross stress, managed to eliminate themselves.

Thomas Hobbes in *The Leviathan* (1651) would have declared that

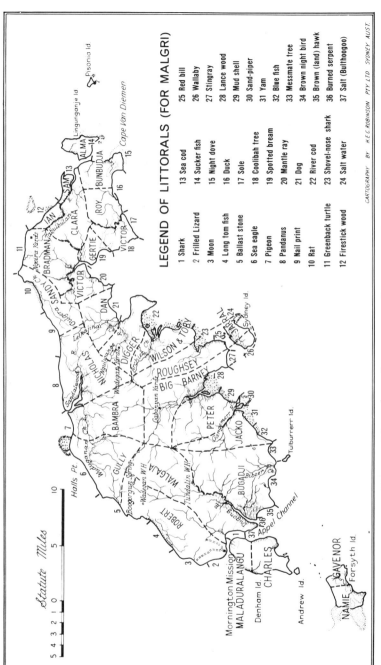

LEGEND OF LITTORALS (FOR MALGRI)

1 Shark	13 Sea cod	25 Red bill	
2 Frilled Lizard	14 Sucker fish	26 Wallaby	
3 Moon	15 Night dove	27 Stingray	
4 Long tom fish	16 Duck	28 Lance wood	
5 Ballast stone	17 Sole	29 Mud shell	
6 Sea eagle	18 Coolibah tree	30 Sand-piper	
7 Pigeon	19 Spotted bream	31 Yam	
8 Pandanus	20 Mantle ray	32 Blue fish	
9 Nail print	21 Dog	33 Messmate tree	
10 Rat	22 River cod	34 Brown night bird	
11 Greenback turtle	23 Shovel-nose shark	35 Brown (land) hawk	
12 Firestick wood	24 Salt water	36 Burned serpent	
		37 Salt (Bulthoogoo)	

MAP 4.2   MORNINGTON ISLAND AS THE INHABITANTS SAW IT

Wessel[7] and Bentinck Islands were *unsafe states* because their people broke "the fifth law of nature which is *complaisance:* that is to say, that every man strive to accommodate himself to the rest." Hobbes might be disappointed, although perhaps not surprised, to hear that the word "complaisance" has now atrophied through disuse from the English language. Social scientists, meanwhile, have intensified their quest for the rules of human survival. Some social scientists might care to think that we can specify the basic rules more clearly than Hobbes, concerned as he was with this issue.

The basic role of ecological privation in mental disorder has been neglected by the modern psychiatric sects, especially those drawing their data chiefly from the middle and upper socioeconomic strata of Western society. The Kaiadilt data highlight the role of ecology. They suggest that ecological privations, for which a group can find no escape or relief, set in motion severe interindividual conflicts and hostilities, sometimes to the point of madness. Ecological privation comes first, frustrating man's need to hold his place in the ecology; interpersonal disturbances follow, with man against man; then intrapsychic disturbances complete the pathological sequence as fears and suspicion reverberate around the society and down into the new generation. The concept of powerlessness, or perceived inability to cope, is thus a suitable place as the starting point of this macropsychiatric process.

The adverse retroflexive effect of an individual with a mental disorder on his group is also often overlooked by social scientists, including psychiatrists, who concentrate upon the effects of society upon the individual. This approach views only one side of the coin. Some clinicians, particularly non-psychiatric general practitioners, tend to be more sensitive to what Leighton (1972) calls the other side of the coin. An individual with a mental disorder can destroy the morale and purpose of his family or his group. Such an individual (perhaps meriting the label psychotic, paranoid, or sociopathic) cannot always be controlled by his group. An illustrative case history from Kaiadilt society has been cited. The history of the catastrophe suggests that one strong man, who was bent upon acquiring wives and who could not be controlled, set in train a sequence of killing and vendetta by lesser men trying to get women who were in short supply. In sum, these behaviors become a cumulative or "symmetrical" process, affecting the prevailing social character of the group. Bateson (1936) called this process "schismogenesis," or the cumulative effect of repetitive social interactions on personality. It is clear that one disturbed person, unrestrained by his group, can initiate a sequence of destruction, or as Berndt and Berndt (1954) put it, "warlike habits."

We must now examine the seeming paradox that while the Kaiadilt openly admit that they were heavily engaged in killing and wife-stealing, their recall of the situation plays down, or even overlooks, their subsistence problems. In the conceptual language of this volume, we have two bodies of facts, one pertaining to the cognized environment, the other pertaining to the operational environment, and they contradict each other. We know that the ecology of Bentinck Island was and is marginal, and that the Kaiadilt had meager means to cope with the cyclical vicissitudes of their operational environment. They must have faced serious hardship, yet they deny this hardship and rather say that they were killing each other off over women. How is one to reduce the dissonance between the "operational" and the "cognized" stress factors?

A partial explanation may come from a consideration of the social roles of Kaiadilt males, on the assumption that a satisfactory amount of role fulfillment is necessary for good mental health.[8] The main social roles available for Aboriginal men in this area are those of provider, family head, and protector (warrior). These roles overlap; for example, a man may wish to acquire a larger family to ensure better protection. Subsidiary roles also known to be important among the Lardil—we have scanty information for the Kaiadilt—were those of artist, craftsman, and ceremonial actor. Viewing the matter from the point of view of role deprivation, one may infer that the serious ecological deprivation faced by the Kaiadilt obstructed role fulfillment as providers; out of this frustration they displaced their energies into a role which was acceptable and accessible, namely aggression. "If I can't be a man by feeding my family, I will be a man by accumulating women!" This could only be done by decimating other men who stood as their role rivals. During their last years on Bentinck Island, they defined their situation in this way: "We were great providers, but we are such men that we were wanting women all the time; the more the better." Aggression and killing became the norms.

Evacuated to Mornington Island, Kaiadilt men found themselves further trammeled by events. It was no longer possible to kill other men, nor to steal their wives; indeed, they were expected to give up the plural wives they had before. Apathy, withdrawal, depression, and suicide became the prevailing norms. "There is no way I can be a man; I now give up." There is ample evidence from transcultural psychiatry that the incidence of depression is correlated with failure to cope. Wittkower (1969) has emphasized "role deprivation" and Leighton (1959) "interference with vital strivings." The Kaiadilt, when I first saw them on Mornington Island, illustrated this process. The men were found to be in an extensive state of apathy and depression, the women in a state of peevish disarray, and the children unusually inhibited and timid. They kept away from the sea's edge as though it were no place for them.

Posed against such eventualities in most primitive societies are the moral and religious belief systems and rituals of the group. The function of ritual in relation to stress has been examined by d'Aquili et al. (1978). Of the belief systems acting as a counterpose to stress, one of the most powerful resides in the medical set. Pain and suffering are "universal categories of culture"—in the sense suggested by Kluckhohn (1962). A fundamental motivating principle of intelligent man is that, having suffered, he wishes to reduce further suffering. Medical belief systems regularly exploit the occurrence of suffering—to induce "desired" or "healthy" conduct in the believers. An extensive study of Aboriginal medicine (Cawte 1974) reiterates the theme that suffering is a keystone, not only of the healing process, but of social control and conformity to the dominant cadres. It is a powerful inducement to every man to put aside individual ambitions and to conform to corporate rules. *Malgri* is a clear example of medicine functioning as the law and thereby as a factor in Lardil adaptation.

The search for macropsychiatric principles that may be derived from the study of the survival or extinction processes of small societies presents an exciting opportunity for the social sciences. How far may such principles be generalized to larger societies and to the modern populations in which we live? One anticipates antithetical interpretations of the data—by those seeking to generalize them into social laws and by those seeking to restrain these generalizations. No science is more familiar than is psychiatry with antithetical readings of the same phenomenon, as psychoanalytic interpretations often attest.

Microtheorists may claim that small island societies are fundamentally different, lacking as they do such alternative channels of maximization as full-blown market exchange and systems of resource acquisition through conquest and expansion (see Sahlins 1961). Insights derived from the behavior of small isolated communities such as these may have little application to more complex societies and to modern urban life.

Macrotheorists, on the other hand, in pursuit of basic structures of the mind and social interaction may be struck by some parallels. They may point out that a particularly common vicissitude of human life is the shortage of valued resources. In relation to this the psychiatrist Hamburg (1971:216) comments: "It may well be that millions of years of vertebrate and primate evolution have left us with many legacies—one of which is a readiness to react fearfully and aggressively toward strangers, especially if we are crowded in with them, competing for valued resources." Resources often perceived to be in short supply, in Hamburg's view, include valued objects, activities, and persons—anything from parking spaces to sexual partners. Going further, Calhoun (1972) finds parallels between the demise of crowded (though adequately fed) mouse populations in laboratories and human populations in cities.

Macropsychiatric generalizations deduced from observations of small island societies may or may not be supported in other field situations, but some may be offered here as hypotheses for further testing under appropriate conditions: (1) People are less disturbed when they perceive they have access to sufficient resources; (2) People are less disturbed if they have some social protection from the retroflexive effect of individuals with mental disorders of sociopathic or paranoid kinds; (3) People are less disturbed if physiological stresses related to shelter, sanitation, and nutrition are reduced; and, (4) People react to frustration in one aspect of role fulfillment by overactivity in another.

These generalizations strike one with varying degrees of salience, depending on one's past experience. Some seem mere commonplaces of clinical wisdom. One of the salient images conveyed by our data is that the male islanders, whose role was defined traditionally in terms of resource acquisition and possession of women, react to privation of the former by accentuating the latter. When access to basic resources was frustrated, they placed desperate emphasis on the acquisition and abuse of women, as well as aggressive display of prowess as warriors. Finally, when access to aggressive display and to women was frustrated, they reacted with apathy and depression.[9]

This has a familiar ring for the modern city dweller, whose mythical hero is Portnoy, struggling to tell his psychiatrist something similar. Frustrated in his quest for valued resources (and being unsure of what they consist) he turns to a desperate quest for sex. Frustrated in his quest for sex, he sees life through a mist of depression. When psychiatry and cognitive psychology approach the solution of this perceptual phenomenon, around which the promise of relief might be organized, we might reasonably expect to see Hobbes's visionary word "complaisance" return to our vocabulary.

NOTES

1. The history of gross stress reviewed here is recorded in more detail in Cawte (1972).

2. Birdsell (1970) in his historical review emphasizes that the Kaiadilt remained in an essentially precontact position until 1948.

3. The credit for this rescue operation of a unique aboriginal stock must go to the Presbyterian mission and a distinguished leader of the Lardil tribe, Gully Peters, who had made contact with the Kaiadilt while fishing in their waters. This contact will be described later in this article.

4. Before we consider the implications of these extraordinary gene frequencies, we might consider their cause. The kind of explanation that might suggest itself to a social scientist is the "founder" effect (see Dobzhansky 1965): the Kaiadilt descended from ancestors who lacked the A gene. Another explanation, that might be suggested by a medical geneticist, concerns differential genetic susceptibility to disease. Smallpox is a case in point. Indian village studies by Chakravarti and Haurav (1966) show that the incidence is higher among blood group A people than in other groups of the ABO series. Did smallpox come to Bentinck Island in the person of a chance visitor or castaway?

5. This is predictable from the distinction between the "cognized" and "operational" environments made in article 1.

6. For discussion of methodology involved in transposing Western teaching procedures to non-Western societies, see Cawte (1972).

7. The Wessel Islanders, off the coast of Arnhem Land, became extinct just after the turn of this century. Their history is being reconstructed by the author in a separate study.

8. I am indebted to Charles D. Laughlin, Jr., for discussion on this point.

9. The latest news from the Gulf of Carpentaria is that an unlikely little band of Bentinck Islanders has recently revisited their island. They made a camp to catch turtles and they built an airstrip. The outcome of their initiative is doubtful but at least the Kaiadilt are experiencing an upsurge of morale and well-being. This late rally of a unique people from the edge of annihilation will gladden all who are concerned for humanity.

5

Resource Fluctuations and Competitive Transformations in West Indian Slave Societies

Robert Dirks

In contrast to some of the other articles in this volume, the West Indian slave society described by Robert Dirks represents an instance of increased availability of resources from external sources that does not in fact expand the viability of the population's life chances. The emerging system of access to the pool of traditional and imported resources under transcultural circumstances can be especially important in determining the outcome from the standpoint of adaptation and change. Dirks isolates some critical patterns of behavior, such as scramble strategies and rituals of rebellion, that function both to offset differential access to strategic resources under the unequal politics of an authoritarian colonial system and to relieve some of the physiological, psychological, and sociological stress that otherwise might debilitate the system from the perspective of both slavers and slaves. The dominant society in this instance has a vested interest in keeping the slave population both alive and subordinate, for it is from such arrangements that the dominant group draws energy and has engineered a transcultural adaptive infrastructure of its own. The political disposition of resource management and allocation (including people) is the critical management function of the dominant society. The primary field for survival of the slaves depends on resource maximization within the pool of constraints structured by their own psychobiological welfare as played off against their freedom to maneuver in the dominant political and economic system. One could argue that the plight of the West Indian slaves, that is, the environment to which they must adapt, is structured less by a scarcity of resources than by a scarcity of power to determine the use of those resources.

This article presents an analysis of a body of ethnohistorical data that describe an intense struggle for scarce resources against the backdrop of nearly two hundred years of regular and dramatic fluctuations in food availability.[1] The data are drawn from a variety of accounts of plantation societies in the British West Indies during the era of slavery. They are used to explore certain aspects of the interaction pattern that linked sugar planters and their praedial slaves, two of the major strata in plantation society. Attention will focus most sharply on the competitive dimension of planter-slave interaction. Within this framework, empirical relationships among ecology, nutrition, and levels of interaction are discussed. In addition, tentative hypotheses are offered concerning both the dynamic process linking fluctuations in food supply to modes of competitive behavior and the adaptive aspects of competitive transformation in the face of recurrent change in nutritional state.

BACKGROUND TO THE SLAVE ERA: HISTORY AND THEORY

British settlement of the West Indies began in the third decade of the seventeenth century. Colonies of Englishmen were established first on the island of St. Kitts and soon afterward on the islands of Barbados, Nevis, Montserrat, and Antigua. These colonies were primarily commercial ventures organized by individuals interested in exporting tobacco and other tropical produce to the markets of Britain and Europe. The promoters of these enterprises initially had little difficulty in securing agricultural laborers. Emigrants were recruited from the ranks of the poor, their passage guaranteed by an indenture that fixed a period of plantation servitude lasting up to seven years. After the term of indenture, emigrants were provided with a small parcel of land suitable for "own-account" agriculture. Island societies commenced their development on this basis in a direction that was soon to be altered completely.

The introduction of sugar manufacture in the 1640s radically transformed the technoenvironmental foundation of society in the islands and with it the entire social order. Unlike the mode of farming employed by the islands' "ten-acre men," sugar production called for a considerable capital investment. The sugar planter not only required a quantity of land; he also needed an expensive factory. An economically viable investment in a mill and other manufacturing apparatus demanded their efficient utilization over an extended period of time. To be certain that their factories would receive sufficiently large and steady inputs of cane during each annual crop, planters sought to acquire tracts of land encompassing several hundred acres. The consolidation of land holdings that followed was achieved at the expense of smallholders, many of whom were without clear legal title to their land. Thousands of yeomen were dispossessed of property but soon proved instrumental in the British takeover of a number of additional islands, including Jamaica. The ability of British yeomen to retreat to open frontiers beyond the sphere of the labor-hungry sugar plantations quickly reduced the attractiveness of short-term indentures from the planters' point of view and contributed to the institutionalization of African slavery. The shift from indenture to enslavement allowed the recruitment of a work force of otherwise unobtainable size and without the escape route afforded by a short-term contract.

The social structure of any slave-holding society ordinarily is thought of in terms of a stratification model. Generally, theoreticians take slavery to be a form of social stratification in which some members of the society are held as property by the others and thereby are constrained to their exclusive service (e.g., Nieboer 1900; Landtmann 1938). As a system of bondage, slavery appears to be a political response to conditions that include underpopulation relative to the availability of land and other strategic resources (Nieboer 1900; Domar 1970). Such conditions promote an open resource situation in which all members of a resident population have full access to strategic resources, which undermines the ability to concentrate and to control labor for large-scale undertakings. The introduction of slavery or feudalism effectively terminates an open resource condition. In feudalism, elites establish political domain over most available resources and thereafter are in an excellent position to acquire servitors through the negotiation of favorable personal contracts with individuals who are economically dispossessed. Bilateral contracts are non-existent between master and servitor in a system of true slavery; in contrast to feudalism and indentured servitude, slave bondage is established and maintained unilaterally. In the British West Indies, the constraints of slavery had a profound ecological effect. The enslavement of Africans and their subsequent geographic immobility set up a situation in which two distinct sociocultural units with overlapping resource needs and conflicting survival requirements were so juxtaposed within a single environment as to take continuous competition between them unavoidable.

Competition is a process that has been defined in a number of ways. In ecology, its meaning is relatively unambiguous. Competition is a resource-centered, density-dependent interaction process that takes place in two basic situations: (1) when organisms on the same trophic level seek to utilize a resource which is in short supply; or, (2) when organisms utilizing a plentiful resource interfere with one another's access to it (Birch 1957). In both situations, competition occurs between taxonomic units that can be defined at any useful point along a continuum ranging from the level of single individuals to large populations. Whatever the scale, each unit is associated with a fundamental niche.

Although originally thought of as a "profession" or "status" (Elton 1927:63–64), today a niche is viewed from a less anthropocentric perspective. It is defined on multiple dimensions as a hyper-volume: the sum of all environmental variables that bear on the life-chances of an organism (Hutchinson 1957:416; Vandermeer 1972). A niche is distinguished from a habitat, the location in which an organism lives. All the variable dimensions that affect the survival capacity of an organism need not originate from within its immediate habitat. Relevant niche variables may emanate from extra-local sources. This is often the case whether one employs the niche concept in strictly biological terms or uses it with reference to sociocultural identities.

At times, anthropologists have used the niche concept to better understand the ascription of sociocultural identities (Bennett 1969:95). In such instances, the taxonomic unit is an emically defined population category, and an attempt is made to delineate the set of environmental variables relevant to categorical placement. The understanding is that a given identity can be ascribed and maintained only under certain conditions. Thus, anthropology's biocultural use of the niche concept implies a concern with identity survival in addition to the purely biological question of survival (cf. Barth 1969).

THE PLANTER NICHE

British West Indian sugar planters comprised a highly generalized social category in which membership depended upon the skillful management and successful integration of a broad range of specific niche dimensions. The proprietor of a small plantation filled many roles. He was at once a landlord, farmer, manufacturer, and politician; his daily activities often included such diverse assignments as overseeing labor, buying and selling commodities, rendering medical care, hiring shipping space, keeping account books, attending legislative sessions, and serving militia duty (Sheridan 1970:57). On large plantations, many of these tasks are allocated to agents and hirelings. But, regardless of the division of labor, the planter niche constituted a whole, defined by variables that gave rise to several critical adaptive problems, including environmental pressures that continually threatened the economic survival of island planters and the maintenance of their identities. More specifically, the problems confronting planters included: (1) securing capital in quantities large enough to employ the most advanced planting and manufacturing technologies available; (2) utilizing land in ways that ensured maximum short-term profits; (3) obtaining laborers in sufficient numbers and managing their work at peak efficiency; (4) enforcing the subordination of laborers and maintaining the general political order; and (5) assuring the viability of import and export markets.[2]

Securing Capital: Founding a sugar plantation required either a substantial cash investment or a well-established line of credit. In addition to land, the planter needed slaves, livestock, mills, boiling vessels, crystalizing pots, stills, lumber, and hundreds of miscellaneous fittings and tools. The quest for capital led the planters without independent means to seek the support of a merchant-capitalist. Most planters financed their enterprises with long-term credit secured from either a colonial or a metropolitan merchant. Mercantile interests were attracted to sugar investments by the prospect of quick and sizable profits. The planter consigned his crop to his creditor who disposed of it in the British market. If the planter experienced a succession of bad crops or other losses, he soon found his credit exhausted. Because losses due to hurricanes, droughts, fires, diseases, and other disasters were sustained with great frequency, financial ruination was not uncommon (see Ligon 1657:117; Beckford 1790:142; Caines 1801:274; Edwards 1819 ii:18). Sooner or later, most British West Indian sugar estates fell into the hands of creditors. These properties and those of successful proprietors who retired to Britain were managed by colonial attorneys through resident overseers.

Utilizing Land: In their efforts to maximize production, sugar planters totally transformed island ecologies. Competing vegetation was eliminated from all areas favorable to the growth of cane. Moreover, estate managers on various islands sometimes pushed their fields up mountainsides and into other marginal growing areas, using massive inputs of slave labor. These practices excluded food crops from many areas and forced reliance on imports. Generally, cane was planted with such intensity that serious soil depletion resulted. Proprietors with sufficient capital were able to abandon degraded plantations and migrate to the comparatively rich soils of colonies newly annexed to the British Caribbean by conquest. For those that remained behind, economic survival meant a constant struggle to restore exhausted lands.

Obtaining and Organizing Labor: Planters sought to keep slave markets operational through organized political efforts aimed at creating positive metropolitan policies toward this trade. The task of organizing slave labor was carried out according to a quasi-military model. Plantation slaves were organized into two major categories: praedials and non-praedials. The latter included tradesmen and domestics; the former were mostly field laborers. Field slaves were sorted according to their size and strength into three gangs. The first gang consisted of the strongest and healthiest adults, regardless of sex. The members of this gang engaged in a multiplicity of tasks, depending upon the nature of the estate's lands and the season of the year. At various times, the first gang felled timber, built and repaired roadways, holed and manured fields, and cropped mature canes. The second gang performed somewhat less strenuous labor such as weeding and gathering cut canes. It was made up of youths, pregnant women, the ill, and convalescents. A third gang consisted of children between the ages of about four to ten. Sometimes referred to as the "small gang" or the "hogmeat gang," this group was supervised by an elderly woman who directed the gathering of "greenmeat" for cattle, pigs, and other livestock. The chain of command on British West Indian sugar estates was invariably pyramidal: highly segmented in the lower ranks while ultimately converging on the office of the proprietor. Senior "head people" were positioned at the free-slave interface of the organizational ladder in every segment of the work force. Head tradesmen and drivers reported to the plantation overseer for daily work orders. His orders were relayed to junior heads and specific task assignments were given out. Head slaves were held responsible for maintaining discipline and an acceptable work pace among their subordinates; white bookkeepers kept close watch on drivers and other personnel to see that they they were properly employed and to guard against theft or the misuse of estate resources and equipment. The daily and weekly schedule for slave gangs in the British islands varied throughout their history, but for the most part a six day workweek was standard. A workday usually extended from dawn to dusk but was lengthened during crop-time when slaves were assigned to shifts that lasted up to eighteen hours. Able-bodied fieldhands typically comprised from 35 to 50 percent of the total complement of slaves on a plantation. Other praedials were either temporarily or permanently detached from the main gangs because of special labor requirements or sickness, injury, or old age. Detached slaves served as watchmen, stockmen, firemen, stable hands, cartmen, cooks, fishermen, and in numerous other capacities.

Enforcing Subordination and Maintaining Order: From the very beginning of large-scale sugar cultivation in the British Caribbean, the resources that supported the planter were under continual threat from a host of potential usurpers. These originated from within and from outside the various island societies. To protect the vulnerable dimensions of their niche, planters participated actively in their colonial governments and saw to the organization and upkeep of substantial military units. Through the domination of island assemblies and councils, planters wrote laws that described a society in which they alone retained full access to government and the means for capital formation. The passage of statutes that excluded non-whites from complete civil rights meant that manumitted offspring of planter-slave unions were consigned to a residual ethno-legal category that precluded effective entry into the ranks of sugar planters. Direct competition was curtailed further by prohibiting slaves from own-account commercial production that overlapped with planter interests. Such legal barriers were enforced by white plantation personnel and civil authorities backed by military garrisons. Military forces constituted a heavy financial burden on planters. However, they offered basic protection from European enemies as well as from Caribs, Maroons, and rebellious slaves. In general, direct threats issuing from these sources were managed without great difficulty. The most difficult opponents of the British West Indian sugar planter emerged from the ranks of the British citizenry and threatened the market organization on which the planters relied.

Assuring the Viability of Markets: Most important in the defense of the planter niche was the so-called "absentee planter," a resident of Britain with plantation holdings in the West Indies. In the course of their dealings, many absentee planters worked to maintain the flow of capital, labor, and supplies to the islands at favorable rates. Some used their influence to maintain a profitable market for the sale of sugar in metropolitan exchanges. These activities drew planters into the metropolitan political arena. From an early date, members of the planter category attempted to direct the course of British governmental policy. Power was brought to bear on executive decisions at all levels of government, including important administrative agencies such as the Council for Trade and Plantations. Each West Indian colony retained an agent in London to represent local interests. Furthermore, proprietors of estates formed various London-based associations in order to coordinate their political efforts. The struggle for influence escalated to the point where by the middle of the eighteenth century, wealthy planters were willing to pay up to 5,000 pounds for a seat in the House of Commons (Ragatz 1928:39). By 1766, as many as forty members of the planter category reportedly sat in Parliament (Burns 1965:491). Their political opponents at one time or another included mercantilists, industrialists, militarists, abolitionists, and other colonists, both from the West Indies and elsewhere. From the third quarter of the eighteenth century onward, the power and influence of the West Indian plantocracy in metropolitan government affairs began to wane. Increasingly, the markets and resources controlled by the remaining members of the planter category were absorbed by others for whom sugar production was but one aspect of far more extensive financial interests, and for whom the social identity "planter" no longer held any meaning.

THE PRAEDIAL SLAVE NICHE

In contrast to that of the planter, the ecological amplitude afforded the praedial was extremely narrow. That is to say, the slaves' niche contained fewer dimensions than their masters'. While the survival of the planter as a social entity depended upon access to capital, land, labor, markets, and government, the minimal requirement for survival as a slave extended no further than basic subsistence needs. Survival depended upon acquiring and maintaining access to food resources sufficient to sustain life under the pressure of severe labor. The subsistence activities called for by slave populations varied somewhat from island to island. But, from an overall perspective, the niche of praedials demanded three sorts of activity: (1) the exchange of labor for food allowances or subsistence garden plots; (2) own-account provision horticulture; and, (3) food-market trade. By and large, the relative importance of these dimensions depended on the sugar-growing capacity of particular island microenvironments.

While all of the British West Indian colonies were equally dependent on Britain for their manufactured imports, the situation was less homogeneous with regard to bulk food imports, particularly those provisions consumed by slaves. Basically, there were two main methods for feeding slaves in the British islands. The first method was specific to entire islands and estates where land unfit for commercial cultivation was relatively plentiful. In these habitats, provision plots were assigned to adult slaves who were obliged to feed themselves. This method of feeding was common in Jamaica and the Windward Islands. Planters on self-feeding estates were not absolved entirely of the need to import provisions, but their provisioning expenses were reduced considerably. A second method of provisioning slaves was common to Barbados, the Leeward Islands, and other areas where little land was diverted from sugar. In these places, the planter bore most of the expense of providing his laborers with foodstuffs. Some estate lands were gang-cultivated in provisions to cut food costs and to protect against famine in the event that transoceanic supply lines failed. Furthermore, scattered and distant patches of waste land were eligible for use by slave horticulturalists. But, in the main, such islands and estates were reliant on off-island sources of food supply. The chief provisioners of these plantations were England, Ireland, and the North American colonies. A brief description of the specifics regarding subsistence on some islands will prove useful in subsequent discussion.

On the island of Barbados, slaves were fed mainly from estate stores. Praedials were issued a combination of imported and locally grown foodstuffs (Stephen 1824 ii:260). Guinea corn, yams, eddoes, and sweet potatoes were cultivated by estate gangs and distributed by overseers. Imported provisions consisted chiefly of rice and maize.[3]

When Ligon (1657:37) first arrived on Barbados in the mid-seventeenth century, he reported that plantation Negroes seldom received any "bone meat." Island slaves did get an occasional portion of "God's killing"; dead cattle were divided between white servants and blacks, the latter receiving the skin, head, and entrails. Regular allotments of mackerel were distributed as well. Nearly a century later, each Barbadian slave was entitled to a pound of salt fish or a smaller amount of salt beef or pork each week (see H.C.A.P. 1790b:349; Bennett 1958:38). Small domestic animals—pigs, goats, and chickens—were raised by slaves in the early nineteenth century, and some of this meat found its way into the island's weekly markets (see Pinkard 1816:200).

Like Barbados, Antigua was extensively cultivated in cane and plantation slaves were provisioned mostly at the expense of proprietors. Much of the slave diet was based on imported foods, primarily horsebeans, rice, and maize.[4] There were no legal standards for the distribution of provisions on Antigua prior to 1798 and allowances appear to have varied widely from one estate to the next.[5] In that year, however, a statute regulating the feeding of slaves was put into effect under pressure from British humanitarians (Southey 1827 III:144; Pares 1960:39).[6] Unfortunately, the new legal standards prescribed diets that in some cases fell short of those previously described as custom.

Some Antiguan plantations included plots of gang-cultivated crops such as Guinea corn, maize, yams, and potatoes with the aim of reducing feeding costs (Sheridan 1957:18–20). Beyond this, a number of overseers allocated individual "Negro grounds" and allowed their laborers to raise pigs, goats, chickens, turkeys, geese, and ducks (see Colonial Office 1788a; Wentworth 1834 II:203). Much of this own-account produce was channeled into St. John's Sunday market (see Luffman 1789:94–95, 138–40; H.C.A.P. 1790a:307).[7]

On the island of St. Kitts, slaves were mostly foreign-fed. Some were provided with plots of ground on which to raise provisions but many times this land was located a great distance from the slaves' residence (H.C.A.P. 1790a:271). In the last quarter of the eighteenth century, the weekly food allowance on St. Kitts ranged from 6 to 8 pints of maize, beans, or flour, and from 6 to 8 herrings (H.C.A.P. 1790a:29). Caines (1801:156) observed that salt provisions (fish and other meats) were the most coveted part of the negro diet.[8]

In 1745, Smith (1745:232) reported from Nevis that the local slave population subsisted chiefly on sweet potatoes and salt herrings and that, "Besides Indian Corn or Maiz, I have known some of them to be fond of eating Grasshoppers, or Locusts; others will wrap up Cane Rats in Bonano-Leaves, and roast them in Wood Embers." Later in the same century, this diet seems to have undergone some change, with grains and legumes assuming the status of staples. During the planting season, workers received more rations than during harvest plus a bonus in the form of a regular breakfast of biscuits and a beverage concocted of molasses and water which was spiked with rum in wet weather (H.C.A.P. 1790a:277).[9] As compensation for the short rations issued during harvest, field hands were "supplied with hot syrup, and a liberty of eating as many canes as they chuse" (H.C.A.P. 1790a:258).

On Montserrat, plantation slaves were provisioned partly at their own expense, partly at their masters' expense. An anonymous correspondent writing in 1788 on behalf of the Council and Assembly of the island indicated that: "Food consists of Beans, Corn-flour, Rye-meal, Herrings and Salt fish of which their allowance consists of from four to eight pints per week of the grain and from four to eight Herrings tho' this varies according to Circumstances . . ." (Colonial Office 1788b). The same writer pointed out that many planters put in quantities of plantains, potatoes, and cassava for the benefit of their laborers and that most overseers prepared a mess twice each day for the juvenile and elderly residents of their estates. For extraordinary work, Montserratian planters distributed rum and biscuits.

Jamaica was considered a home-fed island. As early as 1696, a law called for Jamaican planters to cultivate one acre of food crops for every five slaves on their estate (Southey 1827 ii:108). In addition, Jamaican slaves, like those on Nevis, usually received an allocation of land for their own use.[10] Most of this was located in hilly terrain a considerable distance from the slaves' quarters (see Beckford 1790 i:152–53; Senior 1835:41). For many, the necessity of walking distances on the order of seven miles meant that horticulture on this parcel was limited to Sundays and other days specifically set aside for that purpose (see Beckford 1790 i:152–53; Edwards 1819 ii:199–200). Nevertheless, in the time set aside for them, estate praedials raised quantities of maize, plantains, yams, sweet potatoes, lima beans, callalou, eddoes, tanias, and numerous other fruits and vegetables (Edwards 1819 II:163).[11] Cocoa, yams, and other gang-raised provisions were used to feed incapacitated slaves and to augment the diet of able-bodied laborers.[12]

Although Beckford (1788:91) believed that "most negroes in Jamaica have either fowls, hogs, or cattle," earlier writers did not find island slaves so well provided with meat. According to Blome, "as for meat, they are seldom troubled with it, except at Christmas, Easter, and Whitsontide, and then they have Hoggs flesh . . ." (1678:37). Sloane (1707:xlvii) observed that this scarcity selected against certain ethnics: "Those from the East Indies or Madagascins, are reckoned good enough, but too choice in their Diet, being accustomed in their own Countries to Fleash Meat, &c. and do not well here, but very often die."

The range of animal species hunted by praedials was rather impressive.[13] On estates near the sea, fishing was a common occupation outside the field regimen (see Hibbert: 1825:76). Nonetheless, as in the case of other islands, the animal portion of the slaves' diet on Jamaica consisted mainly of imported salt fish. Just prior to abolition, adults were receiving 7 to 8 salt herrings per week (Cooper 1824:6) with some variation in this ration determined by rank.[14]

Jamaican slaves conducted markets in Kingston and throughout the countryside. These markets supplied townsmen and planters with a large portion of their diet (see Stewart 1808:207; Sells 1823:11–12; Kelly 1838:17). As in the case of Antigua, reports describe Jamaican slaves going to market with loads of wood, fodder, ground provisions, fruits, and fresh meat while returning with salt provisions such as herring, mackerel, pork, and beef (see Foulkes 1833:31; Kelly 1838:17; Phillippo 1843:274–75).

The slaves of St. Vincent subsisted mainly on the produce of their own provision grounds and house gardens. Slaves were allowed one day each fortnight or every Saturday afternoon to work their land, except during crop-time (Carmichael 1833 I:174). Provision plots varied in fertility, with those near Kingstown being less productive than those located in more remote areas of the island (Carmichael 1833 I:194).[15]

Unlike Leeward Island praedials, those of St. Vincent received no fixed ration of grain, although mothers might receive an allowance of grain for their children (H.C.A.P. 1790a:104). Estate workers did receive salt provisions, however. This allowance came to about 2 pounds of salt fish per week (Carmichael 1833 I:161). Salt pork was also issued at times (Young, in Edwards 1819 III;273).

Slaves were able to supplement their salt provisions to some extent by fishing, by purchase, and by raising domestic animals. Since most plantations on St. Vincent were proximate to rivers, slaves had some access to fresh fish (Carmichael 1833 I:179).[16] Eggs, watermelons, peas, cabbages, and the other commodities disposed of in the markets of St. Vincent were exchanged for "bread, salt pork, salt beef, mackerel, corned fish, cakes, or other nice things" (Carmichael 1833 I:136, 176, 180–85).

Because 90 percent of Dominica was too mountainous for any sugar cultivation, fieldhands appear to have been active hunters and gatherers. Atwood provides a clear indication of this: "They [slaves] have many opportunities on the plantations to procure things to sell, or make use of themselves, which are not to be had in many other islands, as plenty of fish in the rivers, Crapaux, wild yams, and other articles in the woods . . ." (1791:254–55). Dominican slaves gathered honey in the forests (Coke 1808 II:345). They hunted grubs, iguanas, crabs, and frogs (Atwood 1791:57). Other game included wild pigeons, doves, mackaws, and parrots (Atwood 1791:27–32). Fishing was also important; two or three times each year, the island's rivers were filled with migrating fish that were caught and consumed in great numbers by Negroes (Atwood 1791:38–40). The pattern of provision raising and rationing varied.[17]

On Grenada, estate negroes were thought to have sufficient provision ground available to them and therefore received imported grains only during spells of dry weather (H.C.A.P. 1790a:103).[18]

COMPETITION BETWEEN PLANTER AND SLAVE

Since competition is a resource-centered relationship, when the niches of two taxonomic units are completely discrete, no competition can occur between them. On the other hand, when two niches intersect, competition is bound to take place in the presence of resource scarcity or behavioral interference.

For the purposes of this analysis, it is important to distinguish between two ways in which niches can intersect. One is a simple overlap configuration (Hutchinson 1957). In this case, the boundaries associated with the niches of two discrete taxonomic units cut across one another, delimiting an area in common. In other words, one or more dimensions of the first niche are identical to one or more dimensions of the second, although neither niche is completely incorporated within the other. Given that the efficiency of any two units is not likely to be precisely equal with respect to the survival capabilities demanded within the shared niche dimension(s), Gause's Law predicts that one or the other unit will be excluded from it. If the two units are closely matched in terms of their ability to cope with the variable, competition may last for a considerable length of time, but it cannot go on forever.

Indefinitely sustained competition is a distinct possibility, however, given another type of niche intersection and some additional considerations. Two niches can intersect in an included pattern (Hutchinson 1957). In the case of inclusion, one taxonomic unit has greater ecological amplitude than the other; the former's niche contains more variable dimensions. The unit associated with such a niche must be relatively generalized in terms of its coping behaviors. Its competitor stands as a comparative specialist. All of the specialist's niche overlaps with some dimensions of its competitor's niche; the specialist's niche is completely a subset of the generalist's niche. In such a case, two outcomes are possible (Hutchinson 1957; Miller 1967). If the unit with the smaller niche is an inferior competitor, then it will be eliminated totally from competition. However, if the specialist unit is a superior competitor, then it can continue to compete from its included position for an indefinite period of time. The unit with greater niche amplitude will simply retain a realized niche that is somewhat smaller than the fundamental niche that it would occupy if no competition existed. A situation is set up in which neither competitor is able to eliminate the other. Because of the pressure exerted by the encompassing generalist, the included unit cannot expand beyond its relatively narrow domain. At the same time, the generalist unit will not be able to eliminate the included unit from contested dimension(s) of its fundamental niche. Even if the included unit is competitively inferior—if it suffers losses in excess of its ability to replace them through reproduction—continual immigration into the included domain has the same result as more efficient competition (MacArthur & Wilson 1967). Replacements from external sources enable the included competitor to resist exclusion, and competitive interaction can go on for an indefinite length of time (as long as immigration continues at a replacement rate).

These theoretical considerations bear directly on the relationship between planters and slaves in the British West Indies. Having defined the respective niches of British West Indian planters and their praedial slaves independent of any presumed competition, one can see that their mutual alignment conformed to an included configuration. While not all the variables pertinent to the planters' survival were relevant to the survival of the praedial slave, all the dimensions of the slaves' niche fell within the planter's domain of control. Virtually all the slave's behaviors and some of the planter's behaviors centered on the acquisition and control of the same scarce resources. Thus, the activities of slaves that were directed toward securing a subsistence and the activities of planters that were directed toward production economies brought their respective niches into an included alignment. It can be demonstrated that this inclusion constituted an immense pressure on the slave niche—a pressure that severely limited the capacity of praedial slaves to survive in plantation environments. In this connection, data bearing on the quantity and quality of the rationed slave diet, the presence of specific hungers among plantation laborers, and the inability of field slaves to maintain their numbers comprise conclusive evidence.

RATIONED DIET

An attempt to assess the nutritional value to the rationed portion of the praedial diet is aided by a number of surviving records and accounts. A notable source is the *House of Commons Accounts and Papers* for the year 1790.[19] In this and other scattered sources, the prescribed or actual allocation of weekly provisions given to slaves is recorded with attention to quantities. On the basis of these data, I was able to calculate the average caloric value of plantation allowances at various times and places in the islands. My figures were compiled from standard food tables and are exclusive of occasional rations such as the molasses and alcoholic drinks that were sometimes served to field gangs. Where records revealed the existence of alternative foodstuffs in a ration, I arrived at the separate total values of the various combinations of grains, pulses, roots, and animal foods that made up the allowance. These were averaged. Averages could not be weighted since the frequency with which separate combinations of foodstuffs were issued is nowhere noted. In some cases, the caloric value of the alternative rations distributed on one island during a single period varied quite markedly. This variation arose from the tendency of planters to reckon equivalencies in terms of volume rather than food value. For example, in the late 1700s a slave on Montserrat might receive 4 to 8 pints of either corn flour, rye meal, or dried beans each week. If one takes 6 pints to be the average allowance, then the daily energy yield of these foods ranged from about 267 calories per day in the case of beans to about 788 calories per day in the case of corn flour.

The rationing schedules for several islands at various times during the slave era, as previously outlined, show considerable variation. Over the years, the amount of food granted to slaves generally increased; but from one locale to another the rationed diet showed little uniformity. In 1790, for example, the rationed diet of slaves residing on St. Kitts provided at best around 1,000 calories per day. At the same time, on Dominican estates that had little provision ground, allocated foodstuffs in some instances had an energy value on the order of 3,000 calories per day. This latter allowance was extraordinarily liberal. Discounting such anomalies, it is clear that the rationed foods accorded to slaves in the British West Indies at any time during their history did not provide the total energy required by the average field laborer.

The chief factors that determine energy requirements are body size and the sort of work that an individual performs. I am not aware of a historical source for British West Indian slave weights. It is possible, however, to make a rough estimate of average weights from Patterson's (1969:138) compilation of slave statures from Jamaican documents.[20]

Taking these weights as a basis and *conservatively* estimating a slave's daily work load at about 8 hours of heavy farm labor, the average energy demand placed on a young man in a first gang must have been in excess of 3,500 calories per day, perhaps 150 calories per day less for a woman.[21] These requirements are far beyond the energy available through the average estate ration which, considering all sources, was some 1,500 to 2,000 calories per day.[22]

As in the case of caloric content, the protein content of rations seems to have been inadequate to the needs of praedial slaves. The quantity of protein contained in the foodstuffs received by plantation laborers can be estimated from the same data used in calculating caloric contents. Once again, I used standard nutritional tables. Considering all the rationing schedules available to me, the average daily allowance of protein for an adult field slave seems to have been about 62 grams. I suspect that this figure is unrealistically high and that for several reasons it does not represent a completely acceptable estimate of the protein available through rations. First, if one omits the information on food allowances provided to the British House of Commons, the remaining sources describe rations with an average protein content amounting to an average of only 41 grams per day. Thus, there is reason to believe that the statements made to the House were inflated. This suspicion gains added credibility when official and unofficial sources are compared on a one-to-one basis. Comparing Luffman's (1789:94) observations, for example, to official testimony concerning the feeding of slaves on late eighteenth-century Antiguan plantations reveals a discrepancy of nearly 30 grams per day in the protein content of the diets described. A second basis for caution regarding average figures for protein allowance is introduced by Stephen (1824 II:286). His check of fish imports into Jamaica between the years 1783 and 1787 showed that if slaves were the only consumers of salt herrings on the island they would have received only one-half of their alleged allowance.[23]

In attempting to assess the adequacy of the protein content of plantation rations, I based my calculation on the Food and Agriculture Organization's estimates. According to the FAO (1957), the average minimum requirement needed to maintain nitrogen balance in a young adult is .35 grams of ideal reference protein per kilogram of body weight per day. Applied to a population, this figure needs to be adjusted upward by 50 percent to allow for individual variation. Further adjustment is needed to compensate for the quality of the protein available as compared to the FAO's reference protein (egg).[24] Allowing for these adjustments, the slaves' daily requirement for protein can be placed at approximately 45 grams per day. It should be realized that this is probably an underestimate; the heavy nature of plantation work, the prevalance of injury and disease, including the rampant intestinal disorders that plagued slaves, must have increased this requirement by a considerable quantity.

It seems reasonable to conclude that under ideal conditions the proteins available through plantation rations were marginal at best and more likely inadequate to the extraordinary demands of life and labor on a West Indian estate. With reference to the diet of British West Indian slaves as a whole, Collins, a physician and a planter, urged his colleagues not to judge the dietary requirements of praedials by their own needs. Citing the prevailing standards of slave alimentation in the islands, Collins (using the pen name, "Professional Planter") wrote: "With so scanty a pittance, it is indeed possible for soul and body to be held together . . . provided a man's business is to live . . . but if motion short of labor, much more labor itself, and that too intense, be extracted from him, how is the body to support itself?" (Professional Planter 1811:75). The evidence available provides a revealing answer to Collins's query.

EVIDENCE OF MALNUTRITION

The degree to which slaves on the various islands of the British Caribbean relied on estate rations for their total diet varied a great deal. As pointed out previously, there seem to have been few instances in which plantation allowances comprised the only source of subsistence. Gardening, trade activities, and, to a lesser degree, hunting, fishing, and gathering appear to have offered individuals an opportunity to improve their diets. Whether these production and exchange activities were rewarded with an overall level of nutritional adequacy is another question. In this area, there are no quantitative data to provide answers, but there exist in the literature numerous medical observations pertaining to the health of slave populations.

Hunger leaves both physical and behavioral marks on its victims. These symptoms are rarely clear-cut. Even among modern-day populations, the detection of specific hungers is a complex diagnostic problem. For historic populations, the positive identification of cases of hunger, short of outright famine, is next to impossible. An attempt to assess the nutritional state of British West Indian slaves must rest on the reports of physicians, planters, and other observers whose medical knowledge is now some 200 years or more out of date. While the symptoms of severe and chronic hunger hardly could have escaped the notice of these individuals, their descriptions of these symptoms cannot be expected to lend themselves to unambiguous interpretations. Yet, without underestimating the diagnostic difficulties introduced by historical distance, and certainly without pretending to offer a clinically acceptable picture of malnutrition, the records and descriptions of slave society in the British West Indies strongly suggest the presence of several types of hunger on plantations, including caloric starvation and protein deficiency.

Many of the hungers that troubled plantations visited the islands seasonally. This seasonality was regulated by environmental factors which in turn governed the agricultural cycle and the general availability of food resources. The agricultural calendar for sugar estates was divided roughly in half. Crop-time (harvest) extended from December or January through the spring and occasionally into summer. During this time of year, the dry season, canes were cut and most ground provisions were harvested (see Belgrove 1755:10–19; H.C.A.P. 1790a:138–39; Orderson 1800:31–37; Roughley 1823: 241–49; Hibbert 1825:57–59). A wide variety of fruits important in local diets also ripened with the onset of this season (see Carmichael 1833 II:65). In contrast, the months of July through November marked a wet spell, the time for cultivating, planting, and weeding canefields. This was the season of the year that the slaves of

Barbados referred to as the "hard-time" or the "hungry-time" (Dickson 1814:308–09). It was the annual period during which the visible signs of hunger were most acute among plantation praedials.

Throughout the islands, the hungry months often meant outright starvation—a caloric deficit among field slaves. On islands almost exclusively devoted to the production of a low-cost, high-energy food such as sugar, the presence of caloric starvation at first seems incredible. Nevertheless, evidence suggests that slaves were victims of starvation on a consistent basis, stemming from the fact that no abatement in the demand for labor accompanied the seasonal decrease in the availability of locally produced foodstuffs. With little ripe cane on hand and with subsistence plots yielding relatively few harvestable species, the physical toll that the preparation of the canefields took on praedials was tremendous. In fact, it so alarmed planters that some preferred to hire jobbing gangs to prepare their fields rather than risk depleting the ranks of their own slaves. For those who could not afford this measure, other steps were taken. The field slaves' diet was bolstered with extra doles of grain or with twice daily rations of high-calorie supplements—drinks concocted of rum and molasses (see Beckford 1788:64; Colonial Office 1789; Roughley 1823:278; Carmichael 1833 i:98–100). Despite such steps, observers were stuck with the diseased and emaciated condition of slaves during the planting season (see Belgrove 1755:19; H.C.A.P. 1789; H.C.A.P. 1790a:185; Orderson 1800:36). Marasmus, a disorder brought on in children through gross starvation, was reported in one Jamaican district by Dr. Sells (1823:20–21), along with numerous cases of "cachexies," a general wasting condition among adults. The impression that slow starvation was rampant among field gangs driven to expend more energy than they could consume is heightened by the numerous reports of the sudden physical and behavioral transformations that occurred as soon as such slaves had access to ripened canefields at the end of the rainy season. With the approach of crop-time, behavior suddenly became more animated; wasted physiques were quickly restored to a far more healthy appearance (see Luffman 1789:90–91; H.C.A.P. 1790a:86, 341; H.C.A.P. 1791:185; Anon. 1828:73; Senior 1835:51; Wentworth 1834 ii:65). Moseley (1799:142) is most graphic in his description; "I have seen old, scabby, wasted negroes crawl from the *hot-houses* (infirmaries), apparently half-dead, in crop-time; and by sucking cane all day long, they have become strong, fat, and sleaky." One might allow for some exaggeration on the part of Moseley but Edwards (1819 ɪɪ:259) confirms his general observation: "The meager and sickly among the negroes exhibit a surprising alteration in a few weeks after the [sugar] mill is set in action."

Seasonal access to an energy-rich diet of cane was not a cure-all for the plantation slave. "Sugar disease" or "plantation sickness," a form of beriberi or a beriberi-pellagra syndrome, seems to have been common. This syndrome has been described in some of the areas of the Caribbean in recent times (Scott 1939 ɪɪ:915–17; de Castro 1952:93). Experimentally, a heavy diet of sugar has been shown to induce pellagra or pellagra-like symptoms in animals (Scott 1939 ɪɪ:929). In the early part of this century, Scott's Palsy, a probable variant of pellagra, was described among Jamaican plantation workers. Symptoms included conjunctivitis, redness and swelling of the eyelids, small ulcers and abrasions on the eyelids, photophobia, stomatitis, and a burning sensation around the mouth and lips. In some cases, these symptoms were accompanied by diarrhea; in others, by a numbness in the legs. In all cases, death was common (Scott 1939 ɪɪ:916). Similar symptoms were described in earlier times. "Sore-eyes" was a frequent complaint among the slaves of the British West Indian sugar estates (see Professional Planter 1811:287). Cutaneous symptoms were also widespread. Such symptoms typically were labeled "leprosy," a term applied throughout most of Western medical history to almost any kind of scaly eruption or skin ulcer (cf. Scott 1939 ɪ:579–80; Copeman 1960:124, 132). The particular form of leprosy most frequently reported among plantation slaves was "coco-bea" (or "caca-bay"), sometimes called "leprosy of the Arabs" (see Stewart 1808:266; Professional Planter 1811:331–32; Dancer 1819:233; Edwards, 1819 ɪɪ:166–67; also, Caines 1801:165; Chisholm 1801:24–26; Gurney 1840:65). This was probably a manifestation of pellagra.

Various bowel disorders, so-called fluxes, were extremely prevalent in slave communities and were ranked as a major cause of slave mortality by island residents. Diarrhea, in fact, accompanies many forms

of undernutrition, including protein-calorie malnutrition (PCM). The
suspicion that the lethal fluxes experienced by plantation slaves were
related to undernourishment is supported by the periodicity and specificity of their occurrence. Praedials suffered from epidemics on both
a seasonal and an irregular basis. With respect to Antigua, Grenada,
Jamaica, and Nevis, observers reported fluxes most commonplace
during the hungry-months (see H.C.A.P. 1790a:256, 344; Chisholm
1801:33; Stewart 1808:266; Madden 1835 ı:117). Some writers attributed epidemics to wet weather, while others placed the blame on
the consumption of unripe canes. In view of the numerous descriptions of flux encountered in connection with famine, these explanations lose credibility. A physician on Barbados carefully noted that
"bloody flux" struck only ill-fed slaves and that few well-fed people
ever died from the complaint (H.C.A.P. 1791:96). Dr. Collins (Professional Planter 1811:247) did not regard bloody flux as contagious,
noting that it was not transmitted between sick-house confinees.
Whenever a flux swept through a black community the death toll
was staggering. According to one source, 4,500 slaves died of flux between the months of August and November on Antigua in 1779
(H.C.A.P. 1790a:344). A Grenadian proprietor reported the loss of 47
slaves in just two months (H.C.A.P. 1790a:184); another recounted
the loss of 25 laborers in a matter of a few weeks (H.C.A.P.
1790a:157).

Another frequent symptom of hunger is edema, a condition that accompanies a number of disorders, including beriberi, ancylostomiasis, and PCM. Referred to as "dropsy" by the writers of the day,
edema appears to have been commonplace among field gangs. It was
associated with a high mortality rate (see Schaw 1923:128; Roberts
1952:175; Bennett 1958:58).

Wet beriberi, a disease caused by thiamine deficiency, appears to
have been endemic in some of the colonies. Beriberi typically mani-
fests itself among populations that are overly dependent on decor-
ticated grains for their subsistence. It is found mostly where rice is
the dominant staple. Slaves were observed to suffer from "dropiscal
swellings" on those plantations where rice was the main ration (Professional Planter 1811:85). The extensively cultivated islands of the
Eastern Caribbean relied most heavily on rice and, significantly, the

term "Barbados leg"—apparently a reference to the lower-extremity edema found in some cases of beriberi—made its way into the English medical jargon. Severe swellings of this sort were seen in Jamaica typically in association with coco-bea (Dancer 1819:233).

Parasitic worms apparently plagued field slaves (see H.C.A.P. 1790a:110; Chisholm 1801:34). West Indian canefields are ideal for the development of hookworm larvae. In humans, these parasites can cause anemia and hypoproteinemia. In severe cases of infestation, edema appears. Among the poorly nourished, infestations may be fatal, and indeed infested slaves often died (see Sells 1823:20–21). The impact of hookworms was particularly acute during the hungry months when slaves were especially dependent on rationed food allowances. The worst effects of ancylostomiasis may have been alleviated to some extent whenever foods became more abundant. With respect to children, at least, observers indicated that edema and worm infestations were relieved by sucking the juices of canes (see Moseley 1799:141; Joseph 1836:90).

Deaths accompanied by hookworm and edema were often attributed by planters to "dirt-eating," or geophagia (see Renny 1807:208: Professional Planter 1811:295; Edwards 1819 ii:167). Pellagra-like symptoms accompanied by edema were associated with dirt-eating as well (see Williamson 1817:268–69). Actually, dirt-eating seems to accompany several deficiencies, with victims seeking to relieve their hunger by consuming earth. The wide distribution of this particular evidence of hunger on Jamaica is attested to by Stewart (1808:273–74), who professed to find dirt-eaters on almost every estate (cf. Dancer 1819). Similarly, Chisholm (1801:22) discovered that Grenadian slaves, especially women, ate dirt with "astonishing avidity." Greg (H.C.A.P. 1790a:227) believed geophagia to be the principal cause of mortality among the slaves of Dominica.

In addition to the regularly occurring hungers among praedial slaves, the destructive effects of irregularly occurring droughts and hurricanes produced severe famines. Hurricanes were a frequent menace to some islands in the British Caribbean. The winds destroyed many food-producing plants that required several months to recover their productivity. Between 1780 and 1787, Jamaica was struck by five hurricanes. Planters estimated that 15,000 slaves died in the wake of these storms—more specifically, from the diseases that they contracted on account of the "scanty and unwholesome diet" (Edwards 1819 II:512). If this prolonged famine was typical, then most of the deaths were probably attributable to fluxes (see H.C.A.P. 1790a:157, 363). Disastrous outbreaks of malnutritive diseases were sometimes averted in the case of droughts by the timely arrival of relief supplies (see Colonial Office 1726:269; Edwards 1819 I:484–85), an occurrence that was impossible after most hurricanes, since shipping was at a standstill during the hurricane season. Even so, droughts caused severe hardships, particularly in the Leeward Islands and most notably on Antigua. As one writer described the recurring situation: "The Drought is generally followed by an Army of Worms, Flies, and other Insects which eat up what little green things are left on the Earth; then comes a scarcity of Indian provisions, and a proportionable Dearth of those from England, Ireland, and the North Continent; then a most dreadful Mortality among the Negroes and the Live-Stock" (Anon. 1732:49).

In the midst of a drought in 1779, Antiguan slaves were rationed one pint of horsebeans per day and "the stock and Negroes perished in the greatest agony . . ." (Coke 1808 II:429; Southey 1827 II:459; Flannigan 1844 I:114). Similar situations have been described for the years 1792 (Young, in Edwards 1819 III:265–66) and 1804 (Coke 1808 II:456). In 1718, the distress resulting from drought was so intense that planters were forced to sell slaves to other islands to avert their deaths (Colonial Office 1718).

At this point, I stress that I am not implying that all disease and mortality among British West Indian slaves was due to malnutrition. Yellow fever, smallpox, influenzas, yaws, numerous other infectious diseases, accidents, and suicides contributed to the death tolls. But, from the evidence that can be gleaned from the historical accounts, there is a strong suggestion that lethal disorders related to malnutrition were at various times and places both endemic and epidemic in the sugar islands. In addition, it seems likely that the severity of many infectious diseases was enhanced by poor nutrition.

In general, the available evidence seems to indicate that the praedial slaves' efforts to feed themselves were not as successful as many accounts of vigorous gardening, hunting, gathering, and trading activities might lead one to believe. If such activities were general among field slaves and if they were uniformly rewarding in nutritional terms, then it is hard to understand the reports of planters such as Leslie, Coor, Edwards, Collins, and Lewis. Leslie (1740:306), for example, describes slaves as "scraping the Dunghils at every Gentleman's door for bones." Coor (H.C.A.P. 1791:94) tells of the need to burn dead livestock in order to prevent slaves from digging up their putrid remains and eating them. Edwards (1819 II:167) and Collins (Professional Planter 1811:295, 325) report the cure of dropsy, geophagia, and suspended ovulation through prescriptions of animal meats, while Lewis (1845:77, 111) similarly details the curative powers of such basic foods as egg, milk, fish, and pork. Among the inhabitants of an adequately fed community, such observations would seem most unlikely. They suggest the nature of the pressures impinging on praedial slaves. The severity and outcome of these pressures can be appraised with reference to their transgenerational effect.

MORTALITY AND FERTILITY

Following a visit to his Jamaican estate, M. G. Lewis wrote: "Whether it be the climate not agreeing with their African blood . . . , or whether it be from some defect in their general formation, certainly negroes seem to hold their lives upon a very precarious tenure" (Lewis 1845:145).

One might well take issue with Lewis's sense of causality, but his feeling about the precariousness of slave existence finds strong support. Few communities of praedial slaves were successful in reproductive terms; few formed self-renewing populations. High mortality and low natality combined to create a situation in which numbers were maintained or increased only through the continuous arrival of newly enslaved Africans.

The natural decline of Negro populations was nearly universal in the sugar islands before and after the abolition of the British slave trade (Craton 1971). The depletion of slave gangs began early, most likely before 1698 when Littleton (1689:18) instructed the planter on Barbados who "hath but a hundred Negroes . . . [to] buy half a dozen every year to keep up the stock." For some planters, a 6 percent replacement probably would not have sufficed. Ten years after Littleton's instructions, Crew (in Southey 1827 II:200–01) indicated that Barbados as a whole required an annual replacement purchase of Africans amounting to 7 percent of its total slave population. The records of the Codrington plantation show that between 1712 and 1748 there was only one live birth for every six deaths among its slaves (Bennett 1958:53). Sheridan's (1973:247) demographic study documents the annual decrease among Caribbean blacks between 1627 and 1775 to have been in the range of 2.7 to 4.9 percent annually. Some years later, Leeward Island slave populations evinced a less drastic decline. In 1788, Adair and Spooner estimated an annual decline of about 2 percent for the slaves of Antigua and St. Kitts, respectively (Pitman 1926:638, 646). At approximately the same time, Jamaican slaves experienced 2 to 2.5 percent more deaths than births (H.C.A.P. 1790a:368; Edwards 1819 II:135; Craton 1971). Campbell (H.C.A.P. 1790a:160) reported a 3 percent annual decline for his estate in Grenada.

Not all categories of plantation slaves were subject to the same mortality rate. Mortality was by far the greatest among the native Africans, especially during their first two or three years in the West Indies (see Long 1774 II:433). Many newly arrived Africans were lost to diseases imported with them, 4.5 percent dying within two weeks after their arrival in Jamaica (Professional Planter 1811:47–48). In 1740, Leslie figured that about 50 percent of the immigrated Africans died in Jamaica during "seasoning," the one- to three- year acculturative period following their purchase (1740:312). This compares with a 40 percent loss in the Leewards (Anon. 1732:44). By the end of the century, mortality among new slaves during seasoning had been reduced to around 25 percent (see Beckford 1790 II:343; Professional Planter 1811:44). According to some estimates, the purchased African had a laboring life that probably did not exceed seven years (McNeill 1788:4; Dickson 1814:453–57).

Infants and juveniles had an especially precarious hold on life. According to Renny (1807:207), up to 25 percent of the infant slaves on Jamaica died between the fifth and the fourteenth day after birth. On Grenada, the mortality among infants was even higher. Castles (H.C.A.P. 1790a:210–11) reported that one-third died before they were one month old. Only one-third survived childhood to reach puberty (H.C.A.P. 1790a:210–11). On Montserrat, this figure was put at 50 percent (Colonial Office 1788b). Roberts' (1952) life table for British West Indian slaves, derived from Guianese historical sources, lends credence to these estimates. Throughout the islands, "lockjaw" (or "jawful") contracted in severing the umbilical cord was blamed for most infant deaths (see Moseley 1787:508–10; Professional Planter 1811:139; Lewis 1845:50). Worms and yaws killed many more during the post-weaning years (see H.C.A.P. 1790a:110).

In evaluating accounts of slave mortality, it must be kept in mind that among non-praedial slaves mortality rates were far lower than among field gangs. Domestics were immune to many of the disorders experienced by praedials. This, combined with the fact that domestics were probably far more fertile than laborers, gives reason to believe that estimates of natural decrease would be far greater if presented with reference to field slaves alone.

Explanations offered by whites to account for the infertility of their field gangs were varied. One popular belief held that female praedials were infertile because of their supposed promiscuity (e.g., Edwards 1819 ii:176–77; De La Beche 1825:18; Carmichael 1833 ii:19). Other factors seem more relevant, especially the widely recognized fact that many planters did nothing to encourage births, believing it cheaper to purchase new slaves than to invest in the careful nurture of a new generation (see Anon 1732:44–45; Beckford 1788:24–25). Early in the nineteenth century, particularly after the slave trade had been terminated, female praedials were encouraged to bear children by offers of cash bonuses, gifts, extra food allowances, and remission from duties (see Young in Edwards 1819 iii: 253, 278; Flannigan 1844 i:Lewis 1845:66). Under these circumstances, scattered natural increases did occur. But, for the most part, the physically demanding and unrelenting schedule of field labor continued right through pregnancy without any increment in diet (see Anon 1732:44–45; H.C.A.P. 1790a:208, 252, 262; 1791:186–87; Professional Planter 1811:131–32). Even prior to pregnancy, the plantation regimen seems to have been detrimental to the reproductive process. Collins (Professional Planter 1811:325) reported that the cessation of ovulation (amenorrhea) was common among women unless care was taken to feed them a substantial diet, including animal flesh. No problem appears to have existed for reasonably well-cared-for women. Significantly, both Long (1774 II:437) and Jeffreys (H.C.A.P. 1790b:236) attested to seeing a great number of children among domestics and others unconnected with field labor.

Evidence suggests that the array of pressures exerted by planters were the cause underlying the inability of slave populations to reproduce themselves. It seems curious that the very men who were most dependent on slaves for their own economic success were responsible for their natural decrease. However, this paradox is resolved easily. Planters were interested mainly in short-term maximization, not transgenerational outcomes. Where short-term interests were most vital to the planters' financial survival, slave populations suffered their greatest declines. During the early years in Jamaica, for example, before soils were depleted to the point that the potential for vast profits had largely disappeared, the natural decrease among island slaves was in the range of 3 or 4 percent annually (Roberts 1957:37; Craton 1971). By the beginning of the nineteenth century, this figure was down to about 2 percent (Beckford 1788:74; Craton 1971). Lest this be attributed to increased knowledge and the capacity to care for the health and well-being of slaves, it should be noted that at the same time Trinidadian slaves were being exhausted at the rate of 14 percent per year (Southey 1827 III:521). Examples of this nature led Riland (1827 III:521) to believe that there was a strong negative correlation between soil fertility and slave natality. Provided with fertile soils, "over-anxious planters" aimed for immediate profits and pressed both seasoned and unseasoned slaves to "sudden and unremitted exertion" (Professional Planter 1811:18, 52). For these planters, every pint of grain, every pound of fish, every acre of provision land, every hour spent in provision gardening was seen ultimately to be at the expense of sugar production and in conflict with their immediate economic interests. Especially for those small proprietors on the frontier sugar estates, "the pressure of mortgages and personal need" was so intense that slaves were scanted and overworked far beyond the limits at which a population might remain self-replicating (Young, in Southey 1827 III: 506).

Faced by debts and a great number of environmental uncertainties, planters were not encouraged to adopt a conservative style of management. The risks attached to their niche made strategies aimed at the maximization of short-term payoffs far more attractive than those involving long-term planning. The fact that the planting profession was seen as a hazardous gamble fostered an intensive and almost crisis-like approach to production year after year. Stemming from this approach, the standards applied to the working and provisioning of slaves clearly constituted a threat to their survival. Certainly these standards were not applied with the conscious aim of undermining the health and vitality of the slave population; the writings of planters exhibit too much concern with the physical condition of their slaves to accept any such conclusion. It seems more reasonable to conclude that the regimen applied to field slaves was simply a consistent part of the planters' overall efforts to maximize short-term economic gains. These efforts produced deadly effects when cost-cutting focused on preventive health care and nutrition. Given inadequate knowledge of human needs in these areas, the effects of plantation practices were not always immediately apparent to overseers who tended to blame the decline of praedials on defects inherent in their race. Discounting this view, it is clear that the failure of black populations was rooted fundamentally in prevailing levels of morbidity and mortality (Roberts 1957:223), levels that in large part were directly or indirectly the result of undernutrition. The end product of estate management was a system that used labor as an expendable input and drew upon Africa's seemingly inexhaustible populations as opposed to allocating potentially productive resources to the local propagation of laborers. With an eye toward their account books, planters sought to restrict local means of subsistence to a minimum. Their restrictions actually delimited a sub-minimal niche as far as maintaining viable slave populations on a transgenerational basis was concerned. Slaves struggled to expand their subsistence beyond these lethal bounds. The net result of this struggle and the planters' unrelenting efforts to contain slave activities was a sustained ecological competition that endured some two hundred years.

A competition model seems to fit the situation that prevailed in the islands for two reasons. First, the data present us with two distinct ethno-legal units in an environment where the unchecked utilization of commonly required resources by one unit necessarily had the effect of harming the viability of the other unit. Second, the degree of harm entailed by this fundamental antagonism proved density-dependent, as evidenced both by the stimulation of heightened levels of violence and brutality in areas that sustained a net growth in slave populations (see H.C.A.P. 1790b;264–69) and by the increased rates of natural decline experienced by praedials wherever the sugar sector expanded. The actual lopsidedness of planter-slave competition in island history does not upset the usefulness of the model. Competition is not absent just because the outcome is one-sided. Results that consistently favor one group over another may be indicative of competitive superiority, not necessarily passive submission on the part of one of the groups. The superior might of members of the planter category usually enabled the plantocracy to work its will against resisters; but, regardless of this asymmetry, counter-efforts were always forthcoming from the slave community, and masters were never so secure that they could relax their restrictions. Given the vast power imbalance that differentiated master from slave, there is little question that the former could have eliminated the latter. But here an additional aspect of the planter-slave relationship becomes pertinent— the counter-force that prevented the process of competition from moving to its conclusion.

Because slaves were essential to sugar production, the behaviors that excluded them from the acquisition of sufficient subsistence resources could not result in competitive exclusion. The constant immigration of Africans into the British islands added to the ranks of slaves, swelling their numbers despite a natural decline. It really made no difference that this immigration was involuntary. Migration is always the outcome of one pressure or another. The important point is that the ecological effect of this movement of Africans was the same as a natural increase among the slaves. It allowed uninterrupted competition by setting up a situation in which included populations could continue to exert pressure on the niche dimensions of competitors despite the latters' competitive superiority. In essence, the newly arrived Africans represented replacements for those slaves who fell victim to the management practices of planters. These replacements provided the basis for a population that could continue efforts aimed at circumventing or overcoming the barriers to creating a viable human niche that planters continued to erect and maintain.

ELEMENTS IN THE COMPETITIVE PROCESS

The competitive process consists of two elementary forms of activity: *interference* and *exploitation* (Park 1954:180; Nicholson 1957:165). These elements have distinctive properties (see Miller 1967:8–12).

Interference is the restrictive element in competition. It involves a *contest* for resources (Nicholson 1957:165). This contest may be direct or indirect but includes by definition behaviors that hinder a competitor's access to needed materials or conditions. In effect, contestants place various sorts of barriers in the way of their competitors and may thereby restrict the full realization of their fundamental niche. A territorial animal typically has a repertory of behaviors that interfere with entry into its domain. The modes of military, police, and industrial control that were aimed at the containment of slave activities were clear manifestations of competitive interference.

Exploitation involves activities that are indirectly competitive. It is well-suited to the acquisition of resources that can be readily consumed or utilized. In competition characterized by exploitative activity, the most successful unit is typically the one able to consume the largest quantity of resources in the shortest span of time (Miller 1967:12). Exploitation often is characterized by what Nicholson (1957:165) terms a "scramble." Resource consumption evinces a minimum amount of coordination between organisms as they race to utilize available supplies while they are still available. In this sort of competition, A exerts pressure on B simply by reducing B's supply of strategic resources (MacArthur 1972:21). There need be neither agonistic display nor any confrontation whatsoever.

The relationship between scramble and contest is complex. In most species, including our own, neither element often appears as a pure form (Miller 1967:12). However, my research indicates that the respective *emphasis* and *deemphasis* of these two elements in human competition is in part causally dependent on the level of food supply available to a population. For the chronically hungry slaves of the

British West Indies, exploitative scrambles were particularly appropriate strategies.[25]

EXPLOITATION STRATEGIES

Among slave populations, exploitation took the form of several sorts of activities. These included escape, dereliction of duty, sabotage, and theft. I classify these as exploitation because their implementation resulted in the consumption, utilization, or expenditure of estate resources, including the slaves' own energies, in ways that deprived planters of their benefit (A reduces B's resources without direct confrontation).

Escape, dereliction, and sabotage had the common effect of reducing individual work loads relative to nutritional levels for at least a brief duration. My study of surviving records from Hanover Parish, Jamaica, showed escape to be the most frequently tried offense in slave court during the 1820s. However, escape offered a respite from labor that must have been difficult to sustain, especially in areas without extensive wilderness or Maroon villages. The evasion of work was a strategy more readily sustained than escape. It was a strategy that all slaves pursued to some extent but one at which some individuals enjoyed more success than others.[26] Those with well-placed personal ties derived certain clear-cut benefits. For example, a friendship with the slave in charge of the estate hospital allowed frequent malingering (see Madden 1835 I:117) and a favored relationship with a driver eased the application of discipline (see Kelly 1838:33). Like escape and the evasion of work, the destruction of estate property sometimes provided a short-term remission from duties. The firing of canefields is cited as one kind of repeated sabotage (see Littleton 1689:19).

From the slaves' viewpoint, perhaps the most rewarding exploitative activities involved theft. The theft of plantation goods was not only a challenge to the planters' control over estate resources and a continual pressure on local dimensions of their niche; it was also a source of material benefit to the slaves. Because of this, stealing was relentless. Much of it was petty but its total effect was nothing short of massive. In testimony to its frequency and pervasiveness, planters saw theft as a kind of cultural focus among the slaves of various islands (see Edwards 1819 II:185).

Slaves were enculturated in the behaviors and ideologies surrounding theft from a very early age. Sloane was told by Jamaican whites that theft was a physiologically transmitted behavior: "[Black wet nurses] are not coveted by Planters, for fear of infecting their Children with some of their ill Customs, as thieving, &c." (1707:cxlviii). Although the empirically minded Sloane confessed that he "never saw such consequences," transmission obviously took some other means. Based on her residence on St. Vincent and Trinidad, Carmichael reported the following: "The elder negros teach theft to their children as the most necessary of accomplishments, and to steal cleverly, is as much esteemed by them as it was by the Spartans of old" (1833 I:264).[27]

The main object of theft, as one might expect in the case of a hungry population, was food (see H.C.A.P. 1791:108; Moreton 1793:161). From all indications, quality protein products were most liable to be stolen. The theft of milk seems to have been extraordinarily frequent (see Caines 1801:126; Carmichael 1833 I:263; Flannigan 1844 II:33). Eggs likewise were subject to depredation, as were plantation livestock (see Carmichael 1833 I:263). Madden (1835 I:107) found "hen-roosts and goat-pens" the ruling passion of island Negroes. Cattle, horses, mules, and asses were butchered as well, despite death penalties for such exploits. In addition to animal products, slaves exploited all available grains, including stores intended for livestock and seed grains already planted in fields (see Orderson 1800:365; Carmichael 1833 I:117–18). Cane, sugar, and molasses also were taken in great quantities. These were applied to direct consumption, animal feed, and sale (see H.C.A.P. 1790a:315; Professional Planter 1811:76–77; Flannigan 1844 II:70–71). On St. Kitts, Wentworth (1834 II:46–47) estimated the annual loss of sugar to be in the vicinity of 15 to 20 percent of the crop. Fields other than cane were subject to loss, too. One planter on Grenada found his grass field plundered by hungry slaves who presumably sold their spoils to purchase food (H.C.A.P. 1790b:303–04). Plantation provision grounds were continually under attack by slaves, despite the fact that planters placed watchmen on these grounds and employed whites to monitor these guards (see Long 1774 ii:436; Coke 1808 ii:286; Stewart 1803:133, 140; Professional Planter 1811:165; Roughley 1823:88, 113). A lack of watchfulness was an open invitation to expropriation. The slaves of one Jamaican estate actually began to cultivate the neglected lands of a neighboring plantation until discovered by the proprietor (Roughley 1823:25–26). From his experiences on St. Kitts, Caines summarized the situation confronted by planters on every estate in the West Indies: "every article of plantation consumption, coarse or fine, cumbersome or easy of removal, will be stolen by the slaves if the neglect of the master leaves it in their way" (1801:208). From the slaves' position, such boundless exploitation was unavoidable and necessary; as Madden reflected: "I would pause for a moment to inquire what weapons beside falsehood, cunning, and duplicity, has the slave to oppose to oppression" (1835 i:104).

Planters were not the only ones to suffer the consequences of ceaseless exploitation. Slaves also preyed upon one another's gardens. Drivers expropriated the labor of subordinates to cultivate their own provision grounds (see Kelly 1838:19–20). Experienced slaves lightened their own burden by working unseasoned Africans far beyond their endurance (see Long 1774 ii:435). These actions created antagonisms that were compounded by other factors. For those threatened by want, the differential treatment accorded ranking slaves and the continual arrival of new field hands set up basic categorical distinctions marked by enmity. Domestic slaves remained apart from praedials and were not trusted by those assigned to the fields. Creole slaves held Africans in contempt. Africans not only attempted to segregate themselves from Creoles but also from one another according to various intertribal animosities. Intracommunity exploitation and tensions seem to have created immense pressures, manifested in accusations of malevolent sorcery and a heavy traffic in magical paraphernalia that were supposed to curb theft and incapacitate enemies. The same wants that aligned slaves against their masters also proved divisive within slave communities.

By drawing attention to the existence of divisive tendencies within slave communities, I do not wish to give the impression that they were disorganized. The historical literature reveals something of the nature of slave social organization all too infrequently, but the glimpses that exist suggest an organization based on several kinds of interpersonal bonds. A type of clientage seems to have been important among slaves. Drivers and other principal Negroes apparently established themselves as protectors of certain subordinates. These protectors arbitrated conflicts and received tribute for their services (see Stewart 1808:258–59; Phillippo 1843:190–91). So powerful was their patronage that Beckford (1788:12) saw the maintenance of "proper connections" as absolutely essential for the adjustment and contentment of newly purchased field laborers.

Among Africans, "shipmate" bonds were valued highly (see Renny 1807:172; Sells 1823:28). The shipmate relationship pertained among those who had sailed to the West Indies together and it persisted throughout life. Sexual intercourse was proscribed between shipmates, indicating a kind of fictive kinship and the likelihood of reciprocal obligations of various sorts. The data are ambiguous here but fosterage and perhaps some kind of co-parenthood also seem to have provided fictive kin (see Carmichael 1833 I:101, 198). Whatever these arrangements, it is clear that kinship terminology was applied generally among all individuals who maintained amicable ties (see Luffman 1789:111; Renny 1807:167; Wentworth 1834 II:201; Flannigan 1844 II:152).[28] Surprisingly little was recorded regarding mating and domestic bonds other than the standard denunciations of promiscuity. However, there is some evidence from late sources indicating that about 10 or 15 percent of regularized mating relationships were confirmed by some kind of public contract (see Moreton 1793:159; Dirks and Kerns 1976). In addition, one gains the impression from the literature that once established, the slave household constituted a relatively stable domestic unit.

In general, outside of work situations, households, and the mission congregations of the late eighteenth century, organized groups were not regularly in evidence among slaves. Rather, dyadic relationships uncircumscribed by fixed memberships seem to have predominated. Indeed, planters actively discouraged their servitors from forming groups or congregating in other than specified task performance. Unsupervised assemblies, particularly at night, were banned. These legal prohibitions were not always rigorously enforced, but groups detected under suspicious circumstances were disbanded promptly (Goveia 1970:23).

INTERFERENCE STRATEGIES

Although they occupied a prominent place in the daily life of the slave, exploitative means were not his only weapons. As an element in the struggle to secure subsistence resources, interference played a less constant but nonetheless important part in the competitive efforts of plantation praedials. Interference manifested itself mostly in the form of sporadic violence directed at whites. This violence was perpetrated by individuals and small coalitions as well as by large groups.

Individual violence consisted mainly of acts of vengeance. These were aimed at the elimination of specific whites: persons who were conspicuous in their demands for excessive labor, who were unusually brutal, or who otherwise excited personal animosity. Poisoning seems to have been a common way to deal with such individuals (see Atwood 1791:271; Flannigan 1844 II:78; Lewis 1845:76, 145, 158–59).

What interests me most in this context are examples of occasional group violence. These stand in clear contrast to the furtiveness of the scramble and seem to have offered the slaves their only real chance for actually expanding their realized niche to what might have proved viable limits.

The masses required for concerted actions were recruited in various ways. One fascinating account from Antigua details the performance of a military ritual (termed "Ikem-dance"), said to be West African, in which a king and his subjects symbolically pledged loyalty before battle (Colonial Office 1737a:313–17). Perhaps more typical were clandestine assemblies where plans were laid and recruits were asked to swear an oath of allegiance. This oath often was accompanied by an ingestion of rum or water mixed with grave dirt as if to symbolize ancestral involvement in the pact (see Colonial Office 1737b:11; Long 1774 II:423; Phillippo 1843:249). Here is evidence of otherwise informally related conspirators incorporating themselves

into a body encompassed by a social boundary and subjecting themselves to a common sanctioning device.

Rebellious slaves were mobilized both to defend and to expand the
existing boundaries of the praedial niche. A good example of a "defensive" uprising occurred in 1831 when Antiguan planters abolished
the Sunday market held at St. John (see Flannigan 1844 I:146). At
first, slaves muttered threats; later, violence and incendiarism began.
These outbreaks are easy to understand: the disruption of the Sunday
market was a distinct threat to praedial slaves who depended on it for
the exchange of relatively plentiful vegetable foods, perishable meats,
and dairy products for quantities of cheap salt fish. Hence, the
planters' interference with this dimension of the slave niche yielded
counter-interference, violence which even though suppressed succeeded in bringing about the reestablishment of the weekly market.

"Expansive" outbreaks were of a more revolutionary character. Jamaican slaves rebelled in 1826 in an attempt to acquire the status of
free wage earners (Phillippo 1843:164–65). Even more radical was
an incident in Demerara where in 1823 insurgents sought to establish an independent state (St. Clair 1834:141ff.).[29] After the initial
battles, a round of negotiations gave the Negroes a chance to articu-
late their basic demands. In exchange for surrender, they were willing to settle for individual parcels of land and three days out of each
week to farm on their own behalf (Bryant 1824:29, 33). These demands, of course, were rejected but they remain interesting insofar
as they state a goal that seems intrinsic to many other mass uprisings. The desire for an adequate subsistence base appears to have
been a motivation that drove many slaves to undertake concerted efforts at interference.

While mass violence on the part of slaves was occasionally aimed at
the defense of a previously established niche and at other times at the
acquisition of a niche of greater amplitude, such categorization certainly does not exhaust the complexities of the slave rebellion. Whatever their objective, rebellions were organized according to a complex
assortment of principles. Sorting out all of these is clearly beyond the
scope of this contribution. However, since my concern in this chapter
is with the relationship between accessible food supplies and competitive strategies, the patterned incidence of attempts at interference is

pertinent. With this in mind, it may be useful to inquire if there was any temporal coincidence between slave uprisings and the cyclic pattern of fluctuating food availability that accompanied the passage of the seasons in the British West Indies.

CHRISTMAS IN THE ISLANDS

An annual pattern is discernible in the incidence of mass interference on the part of slaves. In the course of my research, I have accumulated references to 70 documented instances of concerted actions against whites, both planned and spontaneous; all occurred in the British Caribbean between 1649 and 1833. These include small-scale actions limited to single estates as well as large-scale insurrections encompassing entire islands. It is important to stress that this compilation in not an exhaustive one. To my knowledge, no such collection has been published. I should also note that my compilation contains 32 conspiracies that failed to materialize as open rebellions due to premature discovery or betrayal.[30] I include these acknowledging the peril that some may be spurious, more a product of planters' paranoia than a genuine plot (though all incidents to which I have reference appear to be well documented). Of the 70 incidents for which I have records, 37 have at least a month-specific date associated with them.[31] As shown in figure 5.1, December was far and away the peak month for concerted interference, 35 percent of the actions having taken place or having been scheduled to take place during that month. This seasonal clustering is rather pronounced. By chance, one would expect only about 8 percent to have occurred during a one-month period; so, something extraordinary must have been at work here. But lest my compilation be seen as subject to bias inherent either in the historical record or in my sample, some discussion is called for before moving on to an inquiry regarding annual distribution.

Island planters throughout the Caribbean stood ready and waiting to respond to mass interference at year's end. Whites on all the islands were well aware that December, and particularly the Christmas holidays, presented the immediate danger of insurrection. Any inquiry into this seasonally high incidence of mass violence cannot lead

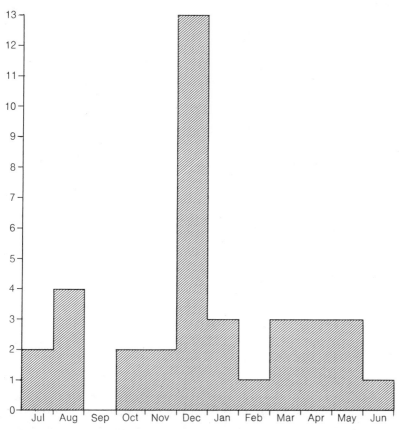

FIGURE 5.1   THIRTY-SEVEN PLOTS AND REBELLIONS, ORDERED BY MONTH

to the conclusion that slaves hoped to catch their masters unaware or in the midst of a holiday spirit filled with unrequited goodwill. Planters looked forward to Christmas with dread and apprehension. As the holiday approached, scattered violence often erupted, a herald to what might be expected in ensuing days. Exploitation in the form of theft increased dramatically (see Luffman 1789:38). Throughout the islands, forewarned but nonetheless worried planters took steps to ensure their own safety and the protection of their properties (see Edwards 1819 II:223). Those residing in towns hurried to their estates (see Ragatz 1928:143). Others were mobilized as island militias took up their posts to guard against anticipated attacks (see Atwood 1791:177; Senior 1835:175–76). As Wentworth (1834 ii:39) explained:

> At an early period after the colonization of these islands, it became necessary to adopt precautionary measures aginst the spirit of rebellion on the part of negroes, which has too frequently been manifest at this particular season, whence it has been deemed expedient to put martial law in force during the holidays.

Furthermore:

> It is worthy of remark that most of the insurrectionary movements on the part of negroes in these islands have taken place about Christmas. The first instance of revolt occurred on the estate of Don Diego Columbus, in Hispaniola, on the 27th of December 1522.

Wentworth's statements regarding the incidence of Christmas insurgence stands confirmed by numerous observers (e.g., Williams 1826:243; Thome and Kimball 1838:37–38, 122; Flannigan 1844 i:115; Bleby 1854:40; Schaw 1923:108–09), among them an anonymous author (1828:82–83):

> It has long been the practice of the colonies to proclaim martial law, and to put the different regiments and companies of militia on permanent duty, on the 24th of December, and during the holidays. This is a measure of necessary precaution; attempts having, at times, been made at this season, to excite rebellion amongst the slave population.

On the basis of such statements and descriptions of the defensive steps taken by planters, it seems patent that the Christmas season was hardly the most strategic time to plan an insurrection, at least in terms of gaining any advantage from surprise. Furthermore, it is likely that the counter-measures adopted by planters must have defused much of the potential for organizing attempts at rebellion during this particular season of the year. The relatively high incidence of planned and executed uprisings by slaves in late December is therefore all the more extraordinary and suggests that they were stimulated by forces inherently seasonal in nature.

The underlying cause for the marked rise in concerted interference seems to lie in the remarkable series of coincidental changes that profoundly altered the British West Indian environment at year's end. Just prior to Christmas, praedials were physically at their low point. From all reports, they were fatigued and wasted. As previously noted, for some months before the onset of dry weather only minor yields of local produce were available. The threat of hurricanes cut the islands off from outside supply; both British and Yankee merchantmen departed the Caribbean by midsummer and did not risk a return for some months. As a consequence, provisions often ran short. Even the all-pervasive sugar cane was unfit for consumption. In December, the situation changed drastically. The pace of plantation work slackened; December was the least busy month in the annual round of tasks, falling between the end of planting and the beginning of croptime (see Orderson 1800:36). Canes were nearly ripened, as were numerous other species of local cultigens. Maize, yams, plantains, bananas, sweet potatoes, and several other fruits and vegetables matured during the months of December and January. Hence, at one stroke the most obvious symptoms of the hungers that plagued slaves in the previous months began to fade and, on top of this, with the cessation of the hurricane season, hundreds of vessels from both Britain and North America began to arrive in the islands laden with provisions and other stores. Much of these first cargoes was distributed to plantation slaves.

Not counting their newly available garden provisions, the nutritional increment experienced by island slaves during the latter part of December was tremendous. Barrels of salt pork, beef, and herring were distributed by the planters (see H.C.A.P. 1790a:103; Flannigan 1844 II:31; Craton and Walvin 1970:135–36). Many butchered cattle for their laborers, providing several pounds of meat for each (see Atwood 1791:206–61; Pinkard 1816 II:140–41; Hibbert 1825:68; Carmichael 1833 I:192–93; Wentworth 1834:37; Phillips 1926:445). On St. Vincent, Carmichael's (1833 I:192) slaves were also given four pounds of salt pork, four pounds of flour, two quarts of sugar, and a bottle of rum. On Jamaica, De La Beche (1825:10) gave each of his slaves eight pounds of salt cod, two pints of sugar, two pints of rum, and slaughtered an ox to be divided among all residents of the estate.

Disregarding the ox, De La Beche supplied each adult slave with about 10,350 calories of food energy and about 1,052 grams of high-quality protein. Compared with the normal ration issued on his estate, each received ten times his usual daily allowance of caloric energy and twenty times his usual daily allowance of protein. Typically, such bonuses were consumed immediately in holiday feasting (see Belgrove 1755:10–11; Carmichael 1833 I:65). The effect of this nutritional boost and the other freshly available sources of nourishment on slave behavior and social patterns was nothing short of explosive.

Even in the absence of violence, Christmas was filled with extraordinary behaviors. During the holidays, slaves became immune to punishment. Runaways who returned to their masters were granted amnesty. The passes usually required for travel were not called for and individuals took this opportunity to visit relatives, friends, and shipmates throughout the countryside. Slaves feasted one another and numerous ritual performances were held, including various ancestral rites and the John Canoe dance (see Long 1774 II:424; Atwood 1791:261–63; Williams 1826:25; Carmichael 1833 II:289; Lewis 1834:51; Belisario 1838; Phillippo 1843:242–43). Slaves donned their finest garments, adopted an approximation of their masters' English, and entered their dwellings. There, masters and slaves danced together, drank together, and dined together. Slaves openly sang satirical songs at their master's expense. Stewart (1808:626), writing about early nineteenth-century Jamaica, summed up the tone and content of reports from the various islands:

> On this occasion, these poor people appear as if they were quite another race. They shew themselves off to great advantage, by fine clothes, and a profusion of trinkets; . . . they address the whites with greater familiarity; they come into their masters' houses and drink with them—the distance between them appears to be annihilated for the moment; . . . they seem as a people recreated and renewed. (cf. Anon. 1828:81)[32]

The white residents of the islands often attributed slave rebelliousness at Christmas to drunkenness, the grant of license, and free time. Yet, if the slaves' behavior was simply a response to the liberal-ity of their masters, then why, in view of the obvious fears suffered by planters, was such license not retracted? Why did the slaves' holiday celebrations go unsuppressed even to the point of violent uprisings?

From all indications in the literature, British planters seem to have been quite unwilling and perhaps quite incapable of completely restraining their slaves during the Christmas season. The data on this point are sketchy. In any case, it is clear that very early in the history of the islands slaves had come to expect Christmas holidays and gifts as rightful entitlements. Any attempt to withhold them appears to have presented the strong possibility of "unpleasant consequences" (Williamson 1817:130)—apparently more certain and more dreadful than might occur without such provocation. One possible consequence of restrictive action was recognized on Antigua by the beginning of the eighteenth century after Samuel Martin tried to interfere with the celebrations of his slaves. Martin's outraged slaves invaded his bedroom and set upon him with cutlasses, chopping him to death before the eyes of his horrified wife (Colonial Office 1701a:720; Thome and Kimball 1838:14). This incident received publicity throughout the islands. Years later, Williams (1826:29) reported that he was informed that any prohibitions on Jamaican slaves at Christmas would surely incite a riot. This proved to be more than idle speculation, for only a few years later an uprising did occur on the island when slaves were deprived of one of their holidays (Bleby 1854:22). It is not certain whether the denial of Christmas food allowances provoked a similar response. On the basis of his experience in Jamaica, Lewis (1845:146) was convinced it would. Planters did display a great deal of anxiety regarding the timely arrival of December's first convoys with their shipments of salt provisions; as one correspondent put it: "a Deprivation of this Addition of their customary domestic Comfort during their Holidays would be more sensibly felt by them than any other Disappointment which could befall them" (Colonial Office 1806; cf. Young 1807:138–39, 201). From such accounts, it might be inferred that the very threat of violence posed by the slaves during the Christmas period constituted a kind of interference with the otherwise normal treatment that they were accorded. However one interprets the planters' reluctance to restrain their slaves, it seems that British West Indian slave populations presented a particularly powerful threat to their masters during this season of the year, a threat that did not arise solely from the planters' bestowal of behavioral license and free time.

DISCUSSION

The foregoing data allow generalization only within strict limits. They do not allow comment on the relative docility or rebelliousness of slaves from one island to the next. The data shed no light on the ideological issues involved in planter-slave relations nor on the personalities, leadership, or decision-making processes that were associated with the resistance forthcoming from slave communities. The data reveal nothing of the immediate causes that provoked hostile reactions on the part of slaves, and they do not bear on the probabilities of success or failure connected with insurrection. In other words, the materials considered here provide inadequate grounds to draw conclusions about many of the favorite issues that have engaged scholars concerned with New World slavery. What the data do support is analysis showing a competitive relationship rooted in ecological conditions and responsive to some form of dynamic process. Before examining this process, however, a brief recapitulation is in order.

The stage for planter-slave competition was set by the containment of praedials in environments devoted to the commercial production of sugar without adequate allowance for worker subsistence. Within these environments, the behaviors pursued by planters to ensure their own economic survival and the subsistence activities of slaves delimited a pair of niches aligned in an included configuration. The efforts of planters to exert complete control over land and other resources so that they might maximize short-term gains on their enterprise had lethal repercussions on the biological viability of slave populations and caused them to enter into a struggle to circumvent or expand the boundaries of their niche. Hence, it is perfectly proper to conceive of the members of these two categories as competitors.

The competition between planters and slaves was an ongoing process, but one liable to change. While the pattern of competitive behavior displayed by planters was fairly uniform and was typically founded on direct interference with resource acquisition by their servitors, the pattern emerging from field gangs was less homogeneous. Praedials usually sought to sidestep the interference of their masters by using their own energies and other estate resources in ways that were self-beneficial but at odds with the designs of plantership. Slaves thereby competed mostly on the basis of strategies that contained a strong element of exploitation. However, on occasion, the competitive behaviors of slaves took another turn: one in which the typical scramble for resources was transformed into a coordinated confrontation, one in which slaves sought to interfere directly with their masters' activities on a mass basis. The occasional transformation to this latter pattern from the more pervasive pattern of exploitation shows a degree of annual regularity. This can be apprehended from two sorts of evidence: (1) a "sample" of thirty-seven historical references to plots and rebellions dated with sufficient precision to place them on an annual calendar; and (2) the writings of numerous participants in and observers of British West Indian slave society. In combination, these data indicate that attempts at mass interference emanating from slave communities often coincided with seasonal increases in the availability of foodstuffs over and above the subminimal level of subsistence usually accorded plantation praedials. This gives reason to suspect that nutritional factors lie at the base of many of the transformations from exploitation to interference among these populations. Is there any theoretical basis for making this connection?

It is widely recognized that hunger and starvation have an atomizing effect on groups (see Dirks 1976). The evidence for this comes from both ethnography and human experimentation. In the ethnographic annals, Holmberg's (1950) monograph on the Siriono represents an important document. Undertaken with the specific intention of discovering the effects of sustained hunger on Siriono life, Holmberg describes a people whose range of support relationships was limited almost totally to the relatively narrow sphere of the nuclear and extended family. It was within these bounds that foodsharing occurred. Beyond these limits, the Siriono consistently displayed an apathetic or uncooperative attitude—"crypto-stinginess" to use Sahlins' (1965a:158) word. Holmberg's interpretation of Siriono atomism is cultural in its orientation. The isolation of the individual and his close kinsmen from the wider social field is viewed as a learned tradition, a stable adjustment to persistent hunger and food scarcity and to the competition such conditions engender. In this respect, Holmberg's view of Siriono society anc culture shares much with Turnbull's (1972) work on the Ik as well as several of the studies represented in this volume.

Subsequent to Holmberg's work, ethnographic evidence has shown that periodic food deprivation can entail organizational adjustments that are quite distinct from traditional cultural patterns. This is aptly demonstrated in Firth's (1959) restudy of Tikopia. In this work, Firth reported the consequences of an island-wide famine brought on by successive hurricanes (cf. Spillius 1957). In their aftermath, society on Tikopia did not lose its corporate identity. According to Firth, it did not collapse into a mass of competing individuals struggling to obtain a share of the dwindling food supplies. However, remote kinship ties atrophied, theft became rampant, and transactions between affinal kinsmen became intermittent. In effect, sets of close kinsmen tended to become somewhat isolated from one another because of the shortage of foodstuffs normally exchanged in traditional ritual contexts. Such organizational changes, from Firth's perspective, were not of a structural nature but rather a product of situationally specific economizing. Similar deviations from otherwise stable patterns have been observed in response to situational hunger by social scientists working outside the ethnographic framework.

The studies directed by Keys (et al. 1950) at the University of Minnesota and Seaton (1962) in the snowfields of Greenland are noteworthy contributions to the experimental literature on the social effects of hunger and starvation. Although the starvation studies conducted by Keys were not designed to test the reaction of a community to food deprivation, the behavior of his subjects, in broad terms, was like that of the Siriono. Individuals became alternatively irritable and apathetic (Keys et al. 1950 ii:90). They sought solitary entertainments rather than their previously accustomed social interactions (Guetzkow and Bowman 1946:31). For the subjects of the Minnesota experiments, hunger clearly reduced sociality (Franklin et al. 1948).

Carefully observing soldiers marching on subminimal rations, Seaton discovered that hunger led to a measurably attenuated social range (cf. Leyton 1946). As deprivation continued, Seaton's subjects decreased the number of interpersonal relationships maintained through voluntary interaction.

> The onset of hunger . . . attacked group integrity by depriving members both of energy and of willingness to interact on group problems. The effect was equivalent to that one might produce in a laboratory by progressively breaking down communication links between members of a group until only an aggregate of diads remained. (Seaton 1962:116)

Seaton interpreted his observations by attributing them to de-energization and subsequent economizing.

> The hungry teams tended to become collective confederations rather than organic federations. In this sense, the absolute level of member's energy can be the prime asset, the fundamental resource of groups which enables them to function other than as aggregates . . . With very little interaction energy to supply, they (subjects) find it more economic to restrict reciprocity to just one or two co-members. This would be a matter of necessity, not of choice. (1962:117; cf. Franklin et al. 1948:39)

While there seems to be consensus regarding the fact that hunger has a constricting effect on social interaction and the range of altruistic, ego-centered social relations, there is less agreement as to the cause of this constriction. This may be because several determinants function as simultaneous constraints on wide-ranging sociality in such circumstances. If this is true, then one might profitably summate thinking along these lines by allowing that the reduced physical capacity of the human organism for interaction, the want of resources for reciprocal exchange, and the amount of interpersonal hostility generated by increased competition for scarce foodstuffs all serve to attentuate the strength and extent of an individual's supportive relations under the stress of hunger. To put this in another way, hunger engenders physical, economic, and political conditions that impose social isolation on individuals to a degree not experienced with nutrition and food supplies at more generous levels. Apparently, the hungry economize closely in all domains of action and transaction with parsimonious behavior capable of being carried to great extremes; witness the decimation of the elementary domestic group among the Ik (Turnbull 1972). On the basis of available evidence, it seems to me legitimate at this point to hypothesize generally that the scope, range, and intensity of interaction in human communities is directly related to certain thresholds in food supply and nutritional state. In any case, I submit that the competitive activity emanating from a community subjected to the stress of hunger conforms to a pattern that is reflective of its internal organizational state (see Brady, article 9).

Hunger divests a community of much of its political power. This divestiture occurs at two critical points. In the first place, a hungry community is crippled in its ability to unleash force. It incurs a loss of manpower in the sense that each of its members suffers some reduction in the ability to do work (FAO 1962). Thus, the capacity for exerting sustained force, especially that involving much physical expenditure, is curtailed. Second, under the impact of hunger, physical inertia, restricted reciprocity, and intragroup competition combine to inhibit the formation of a broad base of interpersonal alliances. By imposing relatively narrow limits on the size of coalitions, hunger robs a community of its potential for organizing externally directed competitive efforts across the widest possible spectrum of its constituent units. In a plural society where the stress of hunger is not uniformly felt by competing segments—where one or the other unit absorbs the greater want—any existing power differential can only be amplified at the expense of the most severely deprived segment. In other words, hunger can increase the political imbalance that presumably contributed to its differential impact in the first place by atomizing the deprived group, by effectively reducing its potential for intragroup alliance and thereby reducing its ability to organize available manpower for the purposes of concerted and direct competition. Hunger, therefore, appears to create a pattern of intragroup relations that promotes exploitative competition in the context of intergroup relations. Hunger sets up a pattern within a community that provides more chance of success in the face of a powerful external competitor through strategies incorporating independent action, indirection, and circumvention. Clearly, this was true for British West Indian slaves among whom malnutrition, poverty, and intracommunity antagonisms appear to have been correlated with strategies calling for theft and the evasion of labor as the principal means for escaping the constraints of the praedial niche.

The social consequences following relief from hunger are not nearly as well described as those entailed by its presence. However, there are suggestions that the cessation of want has the effect of rapidly reversing the social attenuation set in motion by food deprivation. Gluckman (1954:26), for example, has described such a reversal with reference to the tribes of Southeast Africa.

> As food supplies are drawn on in these subsistence economies, each household tends to withdraw into itself. After first fruits and harvest wider social activities are resumed: weddings, dances, beer-drinks become daily occurrences and attract whole neighborhoods.

Concomitant with this turnabout, the rise of violent interference is also in evidence.

> In all these tribes the first fruits come after a period of hunger. Quarrels may arise because of the sudden access of energy from the new food, for it is after harvest that wars are waged and internecine fighting breaks out. . . . (Gluckman 1954:26)

In connection with the tendencies observed by Gluckman, experimental science offers what on a very general level might be considered cognate findings. Again I refer to the experiments of Keys and his associates. Their work revealed that, while semi-starved men are relatively tractable, the progressive recovery from hunger may have quite the opposite effect. During the rehabilitation phase of Keys's experiments, it was found that the previously emaciated and introverted subjects became very difficult to manage. Irritability increased rather than decreased as the men returned to normal. Subjects displayed a greater environmental awareness and annoyance with the experimental regimen. Strikingly similar observations were made at Belsen, a concentration camp where previously weary complaints from starving inmates suddenly became more aggressive with the arrival of relief (Franklin et al. 1948:40). In Keys's experiment, increased food allowances seemed to nurture such pronounced hostility that "at times the experimenters felt as though they were watching an over-heated boiler, the capacity of the safety valves remaining an unknown variable" (Keys et al. 1950 II:917).

Keys and his co-workers explained their observations in terms similar to those used by Gluckman (Franklin et al. 1948:37), although a psychological explanation was put forth as well. Here reference was made to a frustrating disjunction between the subjects' expectations of a rapid return to a normal physical state and their actual slow progress (Keys et al. 1950 II:918). Whether this latter explanation is deemed adequate or not, the fact remains that the recovery of starvation subjects worked a remarkable change on social relations and was accompanied by behavioral manifestation not previously encountered.

How are the aggressive tendencies associated wtih the relief from hunger to be explained? Does a sudden boost in available food energy necessarily stimulate rebellious attitudes or fuel behavior appropriate to aggressive contest?

The response to these questions must remain rather circumspect. Yet, there exists some basis for cautiously suggesting that the link between aggressive excitation and relief from hunger is far more general and far more complex than either Gluckman or Keys indicate. Indeed, there is a preliminary basis for arguing that the relationship in question is rooted deeply in the psychophysiology of higher animals. At least this idea might be put forth tentatively as a reasonable hypothesis (see also Laughlin and Brady, article 1). The hypothesis relies on comparative observations of animal behavior and the assumption that severe and prolonged hunger engenders stimulus deprivation in humans as surely as physical isolation.

Animal experiments give no reason to believe that the introduction of food to previously deprived individuals is a stimulus to contest. Clark (1965) noted, for example, that starving predatory mice trained to fight and kept in pairs exhibited little aggressive behavior. When food was introduced into their cages, they were even less agonistic. Neither the presence of the food nor the nutritional increment excited contest. However, by isolating individuals of the same species under conditions of perceptual deprivation or monotony, Clark was able to excite an agonistic response to virtually any change in environment. King (et al. 1955) has made similar observations regarding laboratory mice. There appears to be a direct relationship between excitability as measured by aggression and the length of time mice are kept in isolation (Welch 1965:52). It is entirely possible that symptoms of hyperexcitability, including aggression, may occur in other higher animals following the interruption of a relatively asocial regimen. This possibility emerges from a consideration of Welch's (1965) synthesis relating to environmental stimulation and psychophysiological response.

Pointing out that animals respond in a continuous manner to their environments, Welch argues that certain of these responses tend to stabilize over time. Specifically, the activities of the brain stem reticular formation and the autonomic neuroendocrine system fix at basal levels under relatively stable environmental conditions. These levels are determined by what Welch refers to as the "mean level of environmental stimulation" (MLES). Marked environmental change, particularly an increase in the MLES, has the effect of altering the basal response level of psychophysiological systems in the direction of hyperactivity. Perturbations of this sort are stressful to the organism. In some species, aggression may result.

Welch notes that species differ with respect to the environmental dimensions that contribute to a specific MLES. These differences have to do with variances in sensory modalities. For gregarious species, the level of social interaction experienced by individual organisms seems to be an important environmental component, and this leads Welch to the position that interaction is a major factor determining the MLES for such species. Here, elevated levels of interaction stimulate increased central activation as well as enhanced levels of emotional involvement which in turn increase the rate of adrenal-steroid secretions. A social animal, such as *Homo sapiens,* habituated to relative isolation (a low MLES) is liable to considerable hyperactivation if suddenly thrust into an intensely social situation.

Welch's model is pertinent to this discussion insofar as hunger imposes social isolation on an otherwise gregarious species. In this connection, it is noteworthy that, when humans experience a food decrement and either voluntarily or involuntarily curtail their social contacts, they experience some of the same sensations felt by non-hungry isolates: apathy and torpor alternating with pronounced irritability. Similarly, the hyperexcitability observed subsequent to relief from hunger is to be expected—probably as much (or more) as a reaction to the heightened interaction level made possible by increased food supplies than as a direct response to the nutritional increment itself. Of course, there is no way to verify these suspicions in the present context, and my thoughts on this must remain speculative. However, I do find it curious that, when one looks at cases of aggression following relief from hunger from a comparative perspective, the objects of aggression seem indiscriminate, sometimes including individuals who might be considered benevolent, such as relief officers, and at other times including individuals who might be seen as oppressors, such as slave masters. For me, this adds to the suspicion that such aggression is an inevitable response emanating from a psychophysiological level that is quite beyond conscious control.

Returning to the problem of slave unrest, it seems plausible to propose that the transformation from scramble to contest that tended to accompany the passage of seasons rested on a series of relationships that linked (1) environmental states, (2) nutritional levels, (3) patterns of interaction, and (4) levels of psychophysiological activity. From all accounts, the increment in food supplies that began with the end of the hunger-ridden wet months increased animation and interaction among the members of slave populations. The large quantities of foodstuffs that became available in December provided the material basis for an intensive round of conjoint feasting and ritual, which brought together and incorporated into a common body slaves of diverse social rank, separate estates, and various ethnic memberships. Given this intensified pattern of interaction against the background of relative confinement, an increased level of environmental stimulation can be presumed, and, if Welch's model holds, subsequent behaviors at least in part may be explained in terms of a stress response. Indeed, the ritualized audacity displayed during the Christmas season may have functioned as a type of traditional and relatively certain safety valve that was missing from the rehabilitation phase of Keys's experiment. In this light, the planters' reluctance to tamper with the slaves' celebrations seems rational; the examples of violence that followed attempts at constraint appear predictable.

Thus, slave conspirators who seized upon the unrestricted chance to congregate during the final days of December also seem to have been taking advantage of a certain amount of volatility in island populations, applying this to political ends. In any case, at the socio-political level of analysis, situational plenty and the power derived from the formation or reaffirmation of alliances allowed members of slave communities the chance to redirect their attention away from the immediate scramble for food supplies and to attack those who stood in the way of less restrictive alimentation.

CONCLUSION

I have attempted to outline a model in the area of intergroup competition that delineates the principal pathways via which persons "sense" and respond to major fluctuation in food supply. I have argued that environmental changes relating to food availablilty affect interaction and interpersonal organization which in turn cause the emphasis or deemphasis of complementary competitive elements. In conclusion, I will remark briefly on some of the adaptive aspects of this competitive transformation at the level of social organization.

Interference and exploitation may be inherently more successful in association with different forms of social organization.

Miller (1967:12) has asserted as much from the study of animal ecology. He has drawn attention to the fact that, although elements of interference and exploitation are combined in the competitive interactions of most organisms, the latter element is more characteristic of simple metazoans among whom social interactions lack complexity. Conversely, exploitation is poorly developed among vertebrates whose sociality is more pronounced. For Miller, this indicates an evolutionary trend in which exploitation is the most primitive element in competitive interaction. Although Miller's comments stem from an interspecific viewpoint, they suggest to me the thought that exploitation can be conceived of as the more primitive element in the human repertoire. My thinking in this regard is not based entirely on the idea of temporal priority but instead upon the logic of organizational requisites.

Energetically, scramble is more efficient than interference (Mac-

Arthur 1972). It requires less elaborate social patterning than interference. In the most general terms, an egocentric form of social organization—a form that Boissevain (1968) argues is both temporarily
and logically prior to the development of a closed group—seems to
offer a social matrix sufficient to support exploitative activity. Organization beyond the level of the simple open network does not appear to
be essential to the success of scramble strategies. Certainly this
seems true regarding the slaves of the British Caribbean. Their inces-
sant exploitation was coincidental with what data suggest was a prevailing pattern of intracommunity organization conforming to the
network model. Indeed, looking over various accounts of the exploits
of slaves as irrepressible thieves, it seems to me possible that the association between exploitation and egocentric organizational forms
may be positively advantageous since speed and independence can
be essential to success in such a scramble. After all, the personal
network is eminently malleable. Its interpersonal bonds can be initiated and terminated quickly, allowing for instant entry into and
withdrawal from alliances that may or may not be suited to the
plunder of a particular resource domain (cf. Whitten and Szwed
1970:44–45). In contrast, the solitary group is not such a flexible
social form (Dirks 1972). Yet, this structurally more elaborate entity
holds greater potential for effective interference than the uncoor-
dinated activities of individuals or ad hoc coalitions.

Of course, this is not to say that interference is absent from the
competitive interactions of individuals acting on their own or in loose
alliances. What I am saying is that interference is likely to become
more effective with every increment in numbers and coordination
that is applied to a situation. Under deteriorating conditions, once a
critical level of deprivation is reached and substantial group solidarity
collapses, it seems logical to abandon all efforts to interfere with competitors and to concentrate remaining energy directly on the quest for
resources. This is precisely what appears to have happened in the
case of the Ik. In Turnbull's (1972) account, one is presented with a
society in which even the elementary domestic group is nearly
demolished by the pressure of hunger. Only bond friendship ramified
into tenuous networks tends to resist erosion. The sort of competition
accompanying this social order is a remarkable scramble of sometimes grotesque proportions.

For members of industrial societies exposed to a continuous stream of competitive encounters featuring a strong note of interference, the Icien scramble seems somewhat bestial, especially since it is essentially asocial and it is the small and the weak who lose. On the other hand, if the scramble is turned against the more powerful, as when an enslaved people seek to escape their lot, it can assume heroic proportions. In fact, exploitation is neither bestial nor heroic. It is simply acquisitive behavior that occurs without the preliminary steps involved in the delimitation of an exclusive domain and the marshaling of support needed to establish or defend that domain. Such support may be effective but it is also costly. It requires what Wolf (1966:7) aptly refers to in another context as "ceremonial expenditures." It requires energy and other resources that go into the ritual expression of a group's existence and solidarity. In the British West Indies, accounts of slave assemblies often make reference to feasting and drinking, the implication being that commensality was important to the symbolics of group existence and that boundedness, centrality, and other properties of group life were purchased at the cost of food-sharing. During the closing days of the year, extra supplies of foodstuffs bolstered the ceremonial funds of British slaves, giving rise to extensified and intensified solidarity and, as the evidence indicates, a concomitant increase in the propensity for rebellion. At the level of bare subsistence and below, it is questionable whether society can afford rebellion or, for that matter, any other actions dependent on groups. It is thus that hungry and starving peoples are essentially depoliticized.

NOTES

1. Financial support for this research was provided by the National Endowment for the Humanities and Illinois State University. I wish to express special thanks to Virginia Kerns, who as colleague, friend, and wife contributed much to this work. I found her own unpublished paper on hunger among British West Indian slaves extremely useful (Kerns n.d.). Gratitude is also due to Kathe Baker who helped assemble much of the data presented in this chapter into usable forms.

2. Note the similarity between these dimensions of the planter niche in the British West Indies during the slave era and the preconditions for the establishment of plantations as described by Wolf and Mintz (1957; see also Mintz 1959).

3. In 1741, 7 pints of maize comprised the weekly grain allowance for an adult field slave on the Codrington plantation; by 1760, this allotment had doubled (Bennett 1958:38).

4. Because they stored well, horsebeans were kept by managers for emergency situations (HCAP 1790a:335). Rice seems to have declined in popularity in favor of maize, probably because of the high incidence of beriberi on rice-fed estates.

5. Luffman (1789:94) recorded a rationing schedule in 1789 that included the weekly distribution of 6 to 10 pints of horsebeans, rice, or Indian corn and 3 to 4 pounds of salt herring or 2 pounds of salt beef or pork to praedials on estates without provision grounds. One year later, Willock (HCAP 1790a:353) told of 12 to 14 pints of corn and 5 herrings being distributed to working slaves each week, and 8 to 10 pints of corn and 4 herrings being distributed to non-workers.

6. The law required planters to provide their slaves with either: (1) 9 pints of beans, oatmeal, or corn; or (2) 8 pints of peas, wheat flour, rye flour, cassava flour, or farina; or (3) 8 pounds of biscuits; or (4) 20 pounds of yams or potatoes; or (5) 16 pounds of eddoes or tanias; or (6) 30 pounds of bananas; and (7) 1 and ¼ pounds of salt fish or 2 and ½ pounds of fresh fish or meat per week (Flannigan 1844 I:2).

7. Livestock must have been quite scarce in the market since it seems to have fetched rather high prices (see Wentworth 1834 II:208). Luffman (1789:138–40) noted that the slaves who traded at St. John were especially desirous of purchasing imported salt fish.

8. Caines (1801:138–39) stated that when these rations were distributed on a weekly basis they usually were devoured long before the week was out. He also noted that his slaves prized occasional allowances of superfine flour and white rice but that these invariably were sold rather than consumed.

9. In planting season, laborers were given 7 to 9 pints of maize, rice, peas, beans, wheat flour, or rye meal and 6 to 9 herrings each week (HCAP 1790a:249–50). The crop-time allowance consisted of only 4 to 6 pints of grain per week (Colonial Office 1789).

10. Individuals often cultivated two provision plots, a small kitchen garden and a larger tract of land between ¼ and 1 and ½ acres in size (see Beckford 1790 I:256; Senior 1835:41).

11. Renny (1807:178) found that Jamaican slaves were most eager to put in plots of maize and plantains but were not so fond of raising root crops such as yams. Perhaps these preferences related to the planters' reluctance to cultivate either maize or plantains. The former was regarded as damaging to the soil, while plantains were liable to wind damage. Above all, plantation managers favored cocoa, a species of yam that was given high priority on corporately cultivated provision grounds because of its capacity for prolonged storage (see Hibbert 1825:80; Lewis 1845:54).

12. On the De La Beche (1825:8–9) estate, all slaves were given 6 pints of Guinea corn each week. Beyond this, the head driver received 4 pints of rum and 4 pints of sugar. Other heads received 2 pints of rum during crop, 1 pint out of crop. In addition, they were offered 2 pints of sugar during crop and 1 pint between crops. Nursing mothers received an increment of 2 pints of oatmeal or wheat flour and 2 pints of sugar.

13. At various times, Jamaican slaves were reported to hunt snakes, worms, cats, rats, iguana, armadillo, wild pigs, racoon, pigeons, and turtles (see Sloane 1707:xvi–xvii, xx; Coke 1808 I:384; Kelly 1838:28; Phillippo 1843:218).

14. For example, De La Beche (1825:8–9) gave his head driver 18 herrings; other head people were issued 9 herrings, while most adults were provided with 6 and children with 4 or 5 (cf. Craton and Walvin 1970:141).

15. The produce of St. Vincent was quite varied. In their kitchen gardens, slaves grew sweet cassava, watermelons, grenadines, "vines" (?), lima beans, kidney beans, cucumbers, tomatoes, callalou, tanias, "gub-a-gub" (black-eyed peas), pigeon peas; and cabbages (Carmichael 1833 I:136–37, 164–67). Slaves also had access to various fruits including pineapple, plum, sappadillo, and alligator pear (avocado) (Carmichael 1833 I:170–71). Yams, maize, plantains, bananas, and breadfruit were raised on the slaves' main provision grounds. Some planters employed a "pot gang." This group worked to

feed individuals who were unwilling or unable to feed themselves. Among the latter were newly arrived Africans who had yet to learn the techniques of West Indian farming and food preparation (HCAP 1790a:104).

16. Fish and turtlemeat also were available in local markets and were occasionally purchased by slaves (Carmichael 1833 I:179). With the possible exception of poultry, other fresh meat products seem to have been scarce.

17. Orde (HCAP 1790a:460) described three principal subsistence systems in operation on Dominica toward the end of the eighteenth century. On estates containing a great deal of rugged land and forests, slaves were allowed to cultivate (and presumably forage) as much as they liked. No provisions were issued. On estates with little uncultivated land, slaves were provided with small provision patches and were rationed 7 or 8 quarts of farina per week as well as 7 or 8 herrings or 2 pounds of some other salt fish. Planters who had a moderate amount of provision land available gave their slaves a salt fish allowance only.

18. There were some exceptions: French planters allowed their hands 6 to 10 quarts of cassava meal per week and some of the British gave out like quantities of maize, Guinea corn, or wheat flour (see HCAP 1970a:83, 103; 1790b:314). Salt provisions, 8 to 12 herrings per week, were doled out to each adult slave; children were given half this amount (HCAP 1790a:144).

19. While this source provides quantitative information regarding the rations doled out on several islands during the 1780s, it should not be considered completely trustworthy. As I indicate elsewhere in this article, the quantities taken in testimony seem to be inflated.

20. If it is assumed that the average weight-height ratio of contemporary West Africans—about .349 kilograms per centimeter (see Hiernaux 1968)—also held for Jamaican slaves, then it is possible to infer average weights for Patterson's sample: about 56.6 kilograms for males, about 53.9 kilograms for females. There is no reason to suppose that these figures, as rough and ready as they are, cannot be applied to other islands in the British Caribbean.

21. These figures are based on calculations following the formula provided by the Canadian Council on Nutrition (1963). Canadian dietary standards, insofar as they are specific to a general climatic region and a biocultural sphere quite unlike the one considered in this study, cannot be applied with a great deal of rigor. However, since body size and work load are the principal determinants of caloric needs, the calculations used should provide a fair approximation of requirements, regardless of other variables (cf. FAO 1962).

22. Since it has been estimated that the measure of volume used by West Indian planters was nearly one-half of the British standard (Stephen 1824 II:280), it is likely that this estimated average is in reality somewhat greater than the actual energy value of the allowance issued on most plantations.

23. Herring was a major source of high-quality portein for slaves on Jamaica in the late 1700s.

24. In order to estimate this adjustment, I relied on a recently conducted nutritional survey of Barbados (Gov. of Barbados 1972). Contemporary rural residents subsist on a diet that has a protein score of 66 (as compared to 100 for reference protein). As in the case of many of their ancestors, rural Barbadians rely heavily on cereals, roots, sugar, and pulses. Relatively small portions of meat, fish, milk, and other animal foods are consumed. It seems unquestionable that contemporary diets in rural Barbados are nutritionally superior to those of 200 years ago. The use of a protein score of 66 in calculating the safe practical allowance of protein for the slaves of Barbados and elsewhere must therefore be viewed as conservative.

25. For an analysis of exploitative competition in a contemporary society and its relationship to ethnicity and political subordination, see my discussion of the "garrot" in the Virgin Islands (Dirks 1975a).

26. The tendency for slaves to evade work and to perform tasks at an extremely slow

pace probably was not entirely voluntary. Genovese (1967:298) has suggested that aspects of the Sambo personality among North American slaves, particularly their supposed laziness, may be attributable to undernutrition. The laziness of Quashee, the British West Indian counterpart to Sambo, was proverbial (Patterson 1969: 174–81). Here, too, physical inertia no doubt was due in part to nutritional deficiencies.

27. These enculturative efforts were not hampered by any moral ambiguities. Judging from an interrogation of a slave apprehended stealing sugar, the rationale and rules connected with stealing were quite straightforward. Since both sugar and slave belonged to master, a slave taking sugar caused his master no loss in overall terms. However, to take from another slave was reckoned as stealing (Phillippo 1843:252; cf. Long 1774 II:416; Atwood 1791:272; Pinkard 1816:302; Carmichael 1833 I:257–59; Wentworth 1834 II:206; Thome and Kimball 1838:56).

28. For some interesting comparative material on these matters, see Brady (1976e).

29. Geographically, Demerara's position on the South American mainland excludes it from the British West Indies proper. But from a cultural standpoint, in the years following its seizure by the British, it clearly falls within the scope of this article. The same holds true for Berbice.

30. In the British West Indies, open rebellions by slaves were preceded by a conspiratorial period during which recruitment and mobilization took place. These massing activities seem to have been integral to the process of concerted interference. Often such activities were highly visible. In cases where conspirators were discovered, the interference process was thwarted by planters at an early stage in its development. However, since interference is an element of process—not an outcome—early termination of the process does not warrant dismissal from consideration.

31. My compilation of concerted interference (riots, rebellions, revolutions, group-action murders, and conspiracies) datable to the month includes the following: Barbados (plot), 11/15/1649 (Coke 1808 II:108; Poyer 1801:47); Barbados (plot), 6/?/1676 (Schomburgk 1848:296); Jamaica (violence), 4/28/1678 (Dunn 1972:260); Jamaica (violence), 8/?/1685 (Dunn 1972:260); Antigua (violence), 12/27/1701 (Colonial Office 1701:701); Jamaica (violence), 7/?/1704 (Dunn 1972:261); Anguilla (plot), 12/26/1736 (C.O. 152/22 1737a:307); Antigua (plot), 10/11/1736 (Colonial Office 1737a:302); Antigua (plot), 1/15/1737 (Southey 1827 II:264); Antigua (plot), 10/30/1737 (Colonial Office 1737a; 1737c); Jamaica (violence) 5/25/1760 (Long 1774 II:447); Berbice (violence), 2/?/1763 (Southey 1827 II:366); Jamaica (violence), 11/?/1765 (Long 1774 II:447); Montserrat (plot), 3/?/1768 (Colonial Office 1768); Jamaica (violence), 12/24/1774 (Scot's Magazine 1775:105); Jamaica (plot), 5/?/1777 (Scot's Magazine 1777:449); St. Kitts (plot), 4/1/1778 (Colonial Office 1778); Jamaica (plot), 7/?/1784 (Scot's Magazine 1784:545); Jamaica (violence), 8/28/1784 (Scot's Magazine 1784:545–46); Tortola (.violence), 5/?/1790 (Goveia 1965:95); Dominica (violence), 1/?/1791 (Ragatz 1931:74; Tobago (plot), 12/25/1801 (Williamson 1817:301; Edwards 1819 V:92); Trinidad (plot), 12/?/1805 (Edwards 1819 V:96); Jamaica (plot), 12/?/1806 (Patterson 1969:272); Demerara (plot), 12/23/1807 (St. Clair 1834:141ff.); Jamaica (violence), 8/?/1808 (Edwards 1819 V:97); Jamaica (plot), 3/?/1809 (Bridges 1828 II:292); Jamaica (violence), 12/25/1815 (Lewis 1845:89); Jamaica (plot), 3/16/1816 (Lewis 1845:113); Barbados (violence), 4/14/1816 (Edwards 1819 V: 104); Jamaica (plot), 12/17/1823 (Jamaican Archival Collection 1823); Demerara (violence), 8/18/1823 (Bryant 1824); Jamaica (violence), 12/?/1824 (Anon. 1824; Kelly 1838:35 ff.); Jamaica (violence), 12/26/1826 (Philippo 1843:164); Jamaica (violence), 12/27/1831 (Senior 1835:272; Bleby 1854:22); Jamaica (violence), 1/1/1832 (Eclectic Review 1832:245); Jamaica (violence), 12/27/1833 (Senior 1835:178).

32. I have described the playful rituals and festivities associated with the Christmas holidays at greater length in a previous publication (Dirks 1975b).

Survival and Reciprocity: The Case of Urban Marginality in Mexico

Larissa Lomnitz

The following article by Larissa Lomnitz carries the study of adaptive dia-phasis and tandem exploitation cycles into a modern urban setting. The so-ciety studied is a shantytown in Mexico whose boundaries are mediated more by scarce access to resources outside the immediate area than by over-lordship and close integration with the society that dominates the environ-ment politically. In contrast to the previous case of West Indian slaves, the pattern of dominance that engulfs the shantytown of Cerrada del Cóndor is grounded more in the politics and economics of exclusion as a means of sub-ordination rather than in the strict authoritarian patterns of inclusion that characterize slavery systems generally. Either way, however, the subordinate population must adapt to an environment of apparent but relatively inacces-sible resource abundance. Lomnitz shows how social engineering through reciprocity and exchange in interpersonal networks provides adaptive flexi-bility in the form of a "spontaneous social security system" for the shanty-town dwellers. The principle of adaptation employed in tailoring behavior in the reciprocity and exchange networks to match the stress in the environ-ment is one of adaptive diaphasis, and the particulars involved reveal much of the kinds of complex interrelationships that are likely to develop between a population's cognized and operational environments in such highly strat-ified cultural contexts.

During the last two decades Latin America has witnessed the emergence of a new social stratum: urban marginality. It is charac-terized by dislodgment or exclusion from the dominant urban industrial economy and by chronic economic insecurity. It includes millions of unemployed and underemployed who live in the poverty belts around Latin American cities.

Economic development and the adoption of adequate welfare measures in Latin America have not kept pace with the population explosion and increases in the rate of rural-urban migration.[1] The livelihood of marginals depends entirely on their devalued manual skills in a glutted labor market. Lacking official protection and finding access to industrial jobs denied to them, they nevertheless manage to exist at a level which, however squalid, attracts a steady flow of new migrants to the cities.

In the Mexican shantytown of Cerrada del Cóndor, on which the present study is based, survival depends primarily on the reciprocal exchange of goods, services, and information in social networks (see also Lomnitz 1971:146–54; 1973). This article provides a description of these networks and of the nature of reciprocal exchange within them. The conditions for establishing reciprocal relationships are analyzed with particular regard to the concept of *confianza*, a psychosocial variable that has no exact equivalent in English, but is comparable to "trust" and "confidence." *Confianza* essentially measures the effective social distance between two partners in exchange in intervals that determine the difference between expected and actual behavior. It is therefore an important concept for understanding the quality of urban life, and, more specifically, for understanding the importance of reciprocal exchange in urban groups such as Cerrada del Cóndor.

The fact that large segments of urban strata in modern complex societies use reciprocity as an informal mode of exchange has certain theoretical implications for the present thesis. These implications are discussed in terms of the "substantivist-versus-formalist" debate in economic anthropology, and a middle-ground position is outlined. It is suggested that the use of reciprocal exchange among marginal populations does not contradict the economic law of maximization of utilities; rather, such use reflects a lack of economic options that forces marginals to convert a wide range of social resources into a system of mutual assistance, thereby providing economic security for themselves at a basic level of survival.

Underlying this study is an ecological model. Marginality is viewed as the result of an imbalance in the national socioeconomic system. Such imbalances frequently derive from a rapid introduction of industrialization in traditional agrarian economies. Rapid industrialization tends to concentrate resources and jobs in urban areas rather than distributing them equally throughout the agrarian hinterlands. A common ecological response to such imbalances by growing rural populations is to migrate into the cities in large numbers, which inevitably results in saturation of urban facilities and forces subsequent migrants to find an ecological niche of their own.

Latin American marginals appear to have found such niches with considerable success, considering the odds. Rural immigrants have not only managed to survive physically in the cities; they have also evolved into a visible new social stratum that can be identified formally as urban marginality. The ecological niche of urban marginality may be defined by the following characteristics: (1) it is interstitial to the expanding urban ecosystem; (2) it processes the leftovers of that system; (3) it extracts basic survival values directly from its system of social organization, and particularly from the mechanism of reciprocal exchange, which has acquired a crucial role. The survival of the group is ensured largely through reciprocity.

AN ECOLOGICAL APPROACH

The problem of marginality has been approached from several perspectives (see Parra 1972:221–47). But some investigators have failed to recognize the existence of marginality altogether; they interpret the growth of shantytowns around Latin American cities as a transitional phase in the process of modernization which, it is presumed, may lead to a socioeconomic structure not unlike that of the major industrial nations of Europe and North America.

The fact that marginals are not being absorbed into the national industrial economies belies such a point of view. Furthermore, the approaches of other social scientists also fall short of integrating the different facets of the new process into a systematic model. The best-known among such approaches is perhaps that of Lewis (1966; 1969), who saw the marginal stratum as that of the "poor" and endowed "poverty" with a culture of its own. This point of view has been critically discussed by other authors (see, for example, Valentine 1972).

The present paper attempts to integrate a number of heretofore disparate concepts into a more comprehensive and systematic matrix.[2] Human ecology is a branch of anthropology which deals with the adaptation of human societies to their environment. Every population adapts to its environment, not merely in terms of food, shelter, and defense, but also in terms of social organization; they attempt to adapt their biological, economic, and social needs to the requirements of their ecological niche, and, in doing so, they select for modes of social interaction that provide an acceptable level of orderliness, regularity, and predictability in their patterns of competition and cooperation (Cohen 1968:1–2).

In the broadest sense, an ecosystem includes the total operational environment of a society or nation—the global system of resources and living conditions which affects the inhabitants of a geographical domain. (see article 1). An ecosystem is successfully equilibrated in part when the population transfer between its various niches, and with neighboring ecosystems, is balanced and homeorhetic. One way to perturb an otherwise successfully equilibrated ecosystem is to dislodge individuals from their ecological niche. These individuals then become *migrants* in search of a more favorable niche. This process of migration can be divided into five stages:

1. *Imbalance:* In this stage the ecosystem is subjected to some local or regional perturbation (for example, by the accelerated industrialization of urban centers which generates economic pressures on the rural population).
2. *Population transfer:* This is the stage of actual migration for individuals or groups in search of a better niche. It may be described in terms of distance, time, and a wide range of accompanying circumstances (number of stages, size of migrant group, transgenerational continuity, and so on).
3. *Settlement:* As the migrants find a new niche they initiate a series of adaptive processes. The evolution of the settlement stage depends on the specific reaction (assimilation, rejection) of organisms in the

niche and on the resources the migrants are able to muster and use in achieving satisfactory integration in the new environment.

4. *Modification:* By integrating into the new environment, the former migrants modify the niche to some degree, depending on the size and characteristics of the migrant group and on the nature of their pre-migration environment. They may displace other groups in the process. If the migrant group must adapt to a situation of rejection in the new environment, it may create a subordinated niche of its own (marginality), which then interacts with other niches in the system in specific ways.

5. *Feedback:* Where there is communication between the migrant group and its place of origin, the success or failure of the migration process affects the original niche. Such information may determine the direction and intensity of future migrations, as well as influence the economy of the original niche through the feedback of resources and technology from the city to the countryside.

About 1950, a dramatic increase in the rate of rural-urban migration occurred in most Latin American nations. For some reason, the rural ecological niches had lost their capacity to retain an increasing proportion of their population. The following is an attempt to analyze this phenomenon in terms of the model just presented.

ECONOMIC IMBALANCE AS A CAUSE OF MARGINALIZATION

The accelerated industrialization of Latin American cities after the Second World War represented a major perturbation in the ecosystems of those cities. Economic imbalance between city and countryside accentuated the relative deprivation of the latter as the economic resources of each nation were increasingly channeled into urban industrial development. The cities became islands of wealth, modernization, administrative power, and social mobility in the midst of a backward, stagnating, traditional economy. This situation generated economic and demographic tensions, particularly among the more deprived sectors of the peasantry. Many people in the rural sectors found it easier to migrate than to survive in their villages.

The causes of the economic imbalance have been discussed by a number of social scientists (Sunkel 1971; Quijano 1970; among others). In many Latin American nations, the process of industrialization was not so much generated from within as introduced from abroad. After 1945, these nations began to attract an increasing amount of foreign investments in the consumer industries. Investors identified the major cities as their primary markets. An important part of the industrialization process was based on imported technology, usually far in advance of the technological level which prevailed in the local system. The ensuing economic dependence between the local system and the foreign financial centers was not merely a dependence on capital, but also on technology and other aspects of the imported culture.

The term "underdevelopment" has been proposed to describe a situation whereby a more industrialized economy extracts raw materials from a more backward economy and uses the latter as a market for its manufactured products. When this situation goes unchecked, modernization becomes increasingly concentrated in urban centers at the expense of rural development. This commonly results in a relative devaluation of traditional occupations as compared to industrial labor, and of the village with respect to the city, thereby setting the stage for the development of marginality.

MARGINALITY

According to Quijano (1970:53–65), marginality is a condition that excludes a labor force from participating in industrial production. It is a general effect of technological revolutions that reduce the need for human labor, particularly unskilled labor. Subsequent industrialization is accompanied by a saturation of the labor market and the more or less permanent rejection of a sector which was formerly employed in traditional occupations (journeymen, small artisans, *peons*), or in the small trades or small-scale, low-productivity industries.

As Adams (n.d.) points out, marginalization is inseparable from technological development, but it does not always result from an exploitative relationship between systems with different levels of industrial development. The industrialized nations have marginalized certain sectors of their own populations as well as those of dependent countries through the process of industrialization. While the industrialized nations have perfected new social techniques for dealing with their marginal populations, that is, social welfare (in the capitalist systems) and massive underemployment (in the socialist systems), most Third World nations have not succeeded in implementing either of these two options to any extent approaching all-inclusive coverage of their populations. Hence, the Latin American marginals are not merely excluded from most means of access to decision-making matters which concern their economic and social welfare; they also suffer from grinding deprivation to an extent which is no longer found in the industrialized countries.

If it is true that underemployment is caused by the effect of massive, imbalanced industrialization on traditional economies, there is no reason to expect that it can be cured by increasing the rate of industrialization, as some advocates of the "economic development" school optimistically predict. One reason for the invalidity of such predictions is that economic development, no matter how rapid, tends to lag behind local population growth.

In Mexico, despite sustained rates of annual economic growth which are among the world's highest, official statistics show that the contrast between the modern industrial economy and the traditional sector has not been bridged in recent years. For example, a recent economic survey prepared for the President of Mexico (Alejo 1973) notes that the annual rate of population growth in Mexico had jumped from 1.8 percent in 1930 to 3.4 percent in 1970. The growth rate of the economy was 6.4 percent in 1970, but the distribution of growth favored the modern sector of "industry, high-productivity services, and high-yield farming" at the expense of the traditional sector. Between 1940 and 1970, the urban population jumped from 20 percent to 40 percent of the total population of Mexico: "This implied a challenge . . . to create an increased number and better types of jobs. . . . There is some evidence that the Mexican economy has not yet been able to meet this demand for jobs, and that this is a major cause of the sharp concentration of incomes in Mexico" (Alejo 1973:1–2). In 1960, a full 40 percent of the total labor force was employed in so-called "low-productivity" jobs, that is, low-wage, traditional, or unskilled labor. Ten years later the proportion remained unchanged. Alejo estimated on this basis that underemployment in 1970 reached a level of 35–40 percent of the total labor force (1973:7–9).

MIGRATION

Imbalance in an ecosystem is a dynamic rather than a static feature. If the rural population in Mexico has remained relatively stable, it is because the excess population has been siphoned off to the cities at an increasing rate. The rural ecological niche has been saturated for several decades. No new resources have been created in the countryside. At the same time, industrialization has produced phenomenal economic growth and modernization in the large cities. The response of the rural population was to be expected; many of them abandoned the villages and flocked to the cities.

Most social scientists working on the subject have described the migration process in terms of a "push-pull" hypothesis, that is, listing factors of rejection in the communities of origin in relation to factors of attraction in the city. It is not particularly difficult to identify factors of either kind: excessive subdivision of land holdings, impoverished soils, lack of farming technology, lack of credits, lack of services, natural disasters, and political violence on the rural side, and the lure of better economic rewards, better services, better educational opportunities, and eventual participation in the modernization of the country on the urban side. Other relevant variables include age and sex of the migrants, distance to the city, available roads, public transportation, and, especially, the presence of relatives in the city (Butterworth 1971:90).

From an ecological point of view, the "push" and "pull" factors are two sides of the same coin. They are the results of the economic imbalance between city and countryside. The actual consequences of this imbalance may vary among different rural communities and may lead to variations in the migration pattern. However, the end result is substantially the same: the majority of migrants succeed in finding a new ecological niche in the city.

There has been some argument among students of Latin American migrants about the significance of migration in terms of the rural ecological niche: "Some believe that the migrants are badly fitted for urban life . . . while others claim that the migrants are among the fittest elements within a rural community who decide to leave in search of better opportunities" (Kemper 1970:617). Of course, these two hypotheses are not incompatible. In general, it is found that the majority of the peasant migrants are unable to gain access to the urban industrial economy after the available positions become saturated by earlier migrants or by the children of industrial workers.

After a review of the literature and on the basis of an extensive field study (Lomnitz 1974), I became convinced that migration involves no technical skills as such, but rather social resources. The earliest migrants from a community are usually aggressive, single, young men. At a later stage, migration is conditioned by the presence of relatives or friends in the city. These relatives or friends provide shelter and assistance to the new migrant family during their initial period of urban adjustment. Studying the history of migration in a rural community thus reveals a network of social relationships that may persist in the city as a form of mutual assistance.

RECIPROCITY NETWORKS

In Cerrada del Cóndor, a shantytown located in the southern part of Mexico City, certain social groups can be defined by three criteria: their physical proximity, social closeness, and highly generalized patterns of reciprocal exchange (see Sahlins 1965a). The latter criterion is invariably present in these groups and appears to provide an economic justification for their existence throughout the shantytown. I describe these groups as *networks,* that is, as social fields based on relations between individuals and defined by some specific underlying criterion (see Barnes 1964:98–99). The most important in this case is the presence of a continuous flow of exchange of goods and services among the network members. The additional criteria of physical and social proximity represent important accessory conditions for maintaining the flow of reciprocal exchange.

In studying Cerrada del Cóndor, I identified a total of 45 such networks, representing about two hundred households. The social composition of these networks was as follows: 30 were composed entirely of consanguineal and affinal kin; 8 contained at least one nuclear family that was unrelated by kinship to the rest; and 7 were composed entirely of families unrelated to each other by kinship. In all cases, membership in a network tended to involve the nuclear family as a whole, rather than specific individuals. Usually, a network comprised three or four nuclear families; however, 11 networks contained at least five nuclear families. Optimal size is limited by the requirements of spatial proximity, and by the economic potentialities for exchange among its members.[3]

Reciprocity patterns are anchored in a series of spatial clusters. Within each network, the women maintain daily exchanges of favors, including borrowing food and money, assistance in child-rearing, and mutual gossip. The men assist each other in finding jobs, share labor and expenses in emergencies and for the celebration of ritual occasions, and spend much of their free time together. The children play together, under the vigilance of any woman belonging to the network; they may also perform errands suited to their age. Reciprocity is also maintained between close kin who do not live in immediate physical proximity. However, the intensity of such extra-network exchanges is necessarily much lower than within the network.

A network is not a group constituted invariably over time. Its membership fluctuates as a result of the structural instability that characterizes marginality; many families are frequently on the move in search of inexpensive housing and job opportunities. As a network grows larger, it may create offshoots elsewhere within or beyond the shantytown. It may also subdivide or disperse under these conditions. The evolution of networks is a dynamic process which involves growth, division, regrouping, and dissociation in time. Networks based on kinship tend to be relatively stable and may also grow to a larger size than those based on neighborhood alone. The latter did not exceed a size of three families in my study. The average network in the shantytown included four to five nuclear families.

TYPES OF NETWORKS

Some of the basic variations in shantytown networks can be classified as follows:

A. *Kinship-based:* 1. Extended-family, with expense-sharing
                       2. Extended-family, without expense-sharing
                       3. Compound
                       4. Mixed
B. *Other:*   5. Non-kinship based

The *extended network* with expense-sharing is an extended family household in which living expenses and cooking responsibilities are shared. An extended network *without* expense sharing is similar to the former in that all members live in the same household, but each nuclear family manages its own economy, including meals. The *compound network* is a kinship group composed of nuclear families living in adjoining residential units. Each family conducts its own domestic affairs, although there is usually an outdoor area held in common which is used for washing and other activities. The *mixed network* is similar to the preceding, except that one or more of the nuclear families are not related by kinship. Finally, the *non-kinship network* is a group of mutually unrelated families who live in adjoining residential units.

Each type of network is situated in an exchange continuum which goes from greater to lesser intensity of flow in reciprocity, and from an unconditional sharing to the balanced exchange of goods, services, and other resources. The continuum is economically significant, but it also denotes "intervals of sociability" (Sahlins 1965a:139). For example, the extended network with expense sharing demands extreme social and physical closeness in a form consistent with the generalized pooling of most or all resources. At the opposite extreme is the non-kinship network, where the flow of reciprocity is less intense in accordance with the lower level of *confianza* among its members. This scaled pattern is similar to that observed, say, among Ellice Islanders (Brady 1972a:296), where reciprocal exchange is largely conditioned by "genealogical" and residential proximity and by the presence or absence of strong affective ties. Within the shantytown networks, however, "genealogical" proximity tends to override all other factors as an inducement of reciprocal exchange, as the following case histories illustrate.

Case 1. An expense-sharing extended network: The Gonzalez S. family lives in a rented lot, where five nuclear families have set up a common household. A sixth nuclear family of the same stock maintains separate domestic functions, although it shares the lot and the latrine with the others. This extended family spans four generations.

The Gonzalez S. family originally came from the State of Michoacan. Don Francisco (the first migrant in this family to reach the Federal District) was a trucker's helper in the fruit trade who "jumped ship" at age 16. Eleven years later, don Francisco brought his parents and three younger brothers to a neighborhood on the southern outskirts of Mexico City. After two intermediate moves, they moved to Cerrada del Cóndor in 1958. The family rents a lot on a small, natural esplanade near the bottom of the ravine; the rent, paid jointly to one of the two slumlords, is 200 pesos per month ($16 U.S.). The lot has natural boundaries and requires no fencing. New dwelling space was added as the family group increased.

In 1972 the head of the group was señora María, the widowed mother of don Francisco, aged 68. Her sons married in Mexico City. Don Francisco and another one of Maria's children, Albertina, are now dead, but their descendants are members of the extended household. The matriarch herself (señora María) shares a room with a daughter and her illegitimate child; this particular grandchild is being raised by señora María as if she were her own daughter. Another room houses the single surviving son of señora María, his wife Rosa, and their six unmarried children. Rosa's family lives in Cerrada del Cóndor and they maintain an active reciprocal exchange which includes Rosa herself. Don Francisco's three orphaned children occupy three rooms, as two of them (both males) have nuclear families of their own; the third room contains a young couple without children and two unmarried brothers. Finally, Albertina's widower and his three children share a room of their own. Altogether, 25 people live in the compound; 19 of them share all expenses and prepare all food in common. The others belong to the nuclear family of Concepción (one of don Francisco's sons), whose wife Soledad is closer to her own brother and sister-in-law who live nearby. Soledad cooks on an oil stove of her own, but gets along with the other women. She does her own marketing, often accompanied by other women of the extended family group. However, she never asks them to buy any food for her. She buys her tortillas from doña Rosa, señora María's chief assistant in preparing the communal meals.

All working members of the network contribute to the expenses of the household. There are no fixed contributions except by the non-participant family, which contributes 20 pesos ($1.60 U.S.) per month toward the rent and electric bill. The common kitchen has a wood stove and the gathering of firewood is one of the standard, twice-a-week, joint activities. There is also joint gathering of paper, cement, glass, and tin cans for sale. There is complete cooperation in such matters as fixing the roof, building a new addition to the dwellings, watching the children, and so on. The rooms are used chiefly for sleeping; most activities take place in the outside patio. Adults belonging to the expense-sharing network may borrow any clothes or personal articles from one another; their children take anything they need. All rooms may be entered by any member without asking. One of don Francisco's sons has purchased a television set and his room has become the site of family gatherings for watching it.

Doña Rosa's daughter is married and dwells in the shantytown, but whenever her husband is out working she visits with the network. She brings her child and both share the communal meals. She usually brings some food or money as a contribution. There are no regular hours for meals; anybody may casually dip his or her hands in the communal pot at any time of the day. There are no eating utensils. Soup is drunk from the plate and a rolled tortilla is used for a spoon. Whenever one of the nuclear families buys extra food from its own money, the food may be shared or reserved at will; if it is offered to the communal kitchen, the family may keep the best part for itself.

The children's bath is a joint activity; two or three women carry the necessary water and firewood, with the assistance of the children. Laundry is done in much the same manner. Any mother belonging to the expense-sharing network may scold any child in the network. Care of the sick is done jointly, and ritual expenses such as funerals are borne together.

The income and occupations of the network during the year 1971 were: Doña María, from washing stairs at the Mixcoac Market three

times a week, 15 to 20 pesos a day ($1.20 to $1.60 U.S.), plus tortillas
and stale bread. The latter is used for raising pigs in the patio. She
also makes 10 to 15 kilograms of tortillas daily for sale; the pigs get
any leftovers. She and the other women sell tortillas in the shantytown. When they have no pigs, they sell the stale bread and tortillas
to neighbors who raise animals. Rosa's husband earns up to 280
pesos a week ($22.40 U.S.) as a peon in construction or trucking.
Two grandsons of doña María each earn 30 to 40 pesos a day ($2.40
to $3.20 U.S.) as a trucker's helper and a locksmith's helper. Alber-
tina's widower takes care of cows in a nearby farm (his income is unknown). Doña Rosa sells tortillas. One child sells newspapers in the
mornings and goes to school afternoons, earning 10 pesos a day ($.80
U.S.). One of the granddaughters takes in washing two or three
times a week for 35 pesos a day ($2.80 U.S.), while another is a
housemaid in a nearby middle-class neighborhood but sleeps at home
and earns 25 pesos a day ($2.00 U.S.). There is also communal rais-
ing of pigs or sheep (at one time the group had 30 sheep). Finally,
there is communal gathering and selling of rags, cans, and assorted
waste materials for reprocessing. Altogether, this is a relatively autonomous, self-sufficient network. There is very little contact with
outsiders but great personal friendship and intense mutual assistance
among the network members themselves. The group managed to
survive both physically and socially, year after year, even though no
member of the network has ever had a steady job.

   Case 2. Evolution of a Compound Network: The Contreras family
comes from a commune in the State of Guanajuato. The parents-in-
law of the earliest established migrant, Juan, lived in a shantytown
near Cerrada del Cóndor, so he joined their household for a time with
his wife and children. There he learned the trade of tombstone polisher (there is a major cemetery in the area). He subsequently found
a room for rent in Cerrada del Cóndor. A few years later, his parents
joined him while he trained his father as a tombstone polisher. An
unmarried brother came with them and has learned the same trade.

   Two of Juan's married brothers and one married sister remained
behind in Guanajuato; but eventually both brothers and their families
moved to Cerrada del Cóndor. They lived with their parents at first
while becoming tombstone polishers. Juan and their father took them

to the shop, taught them, and shared money with them until they could fend for themselves. The two brothers' wives were sisters, and their kin soon began to arrive in the shantytown. First there was an unmarried sister, then an unmarried niece. The two unmarried relatives found work as live-in maids, but they stayed with their shantytown relatives on their days off or whenever they were out of work. The married niece, Josefa, found a room of her own and was joined by her unmarried brother from Guanajuato; he slept on the floor and worked with Josefa's husband. A few years later, the two sisters (Valentina and Gabriela) were periodically visited by their only brother during the slack field season. This brother had no land of his own but worked with his in-laws and rented a couple of oxen. When staying with his sisters in the city, he polished tombstones with his brothers-in-law.

Each nuclear family in this network occupies a separate room with separate household arrangements. They lived in close proximity within a U-shaped compound, with the rooms on one side, across from the kitchen.[4] When an adjoining room became vacant, the husbands of Gabriela and Valentina arranged for a good friend and working companion to move next to them. The network thereby became "mixed" through the incorporation of a non-kin family. This family became "related" to Valentina's family through *compadrazgo*. The unmarried sister who worked as a maid had a daughter (who was sent to be raised by her mother in the country), then a son (who was left in the care of Valentina and Gabriela). Two years later this sister, named Meche, began living with the father of her male child in a neighborhood a few blocks away from the shantytown, subsequently taking her small daughter back to live with her. She visited her sisters every day and was, for all practical purposes, a member of the network. Then the unmarried niece, Marcela, began to stay with Meche on her days off. There she met and married a neighbor. This newly married couple stayed with the parents of the husband, thereby creating another network just beyond the limits of the shantytown.

Meanwhile, the country brother began making his seasonal stays in the city longer and longer. He would have moved to the city permanently but for the opposition of his mother and his wife. At present, he sleeps at Meche's while a sister and her husband take care of his family and his oxen back in the country. This is a fluid situation that entails a great deal of personal interaction.

For a time, Gabriela's husband stopped drinking and began to rise economically; the household acquired a number of goods such as a television, a dining-room set, and a radio–record player console. Because of her new economic status, Gabriela lost interest in her former exchange activities within the network; she began turning down requests for assistance in family emergencies. Inevitably the personal relations cooled toward Gabriela, and she and her husband finally moved away to an urban-type room just beyond the shantytown.

Two years later, due to natural deterioration, two of the rooms in the compound fell in and altered the composition of the network. Josefa (the married niece) moved to another shantytown where an uncle had succeeded in purchasing a small lot for both families. The non-related neighbors also moved away to join the network of their in-laws in Cerrada del Cóndor.

Sometime thereafter, Gabriela's husband again fell under the influence of his father, brothers, and brothers-in-law: he resumed his old drinking habits and mistreated Gabriela, who shamefacedly returned to her former network. With her children she moved into a vacant room in the compound; she fell ill and was cared for by her sisters. Gabriela later gave birth and the network members paid for the clinic, thereby demonstrating high solidarity to an errant member. Gabriela and her children were fully supported until her husband returned to a more acceptable form of behavior.

The fluidity of this network and its many changes in recruitment and composition thus derive in part from fluctuations in the availability of space for rent, alcoholism, illness, pregnancy, and the physical deterioration of the dwellings. Many other examples could be given. Toward the end of the period of observation, Valentina's husband and his brother Juan had purchased a small lot. Meche helped with money and was invited to join the new network. Gabriela was said to be willing to move into the room to be vacated by Juan, thus joining the original Contreras network. This development suggests that the Valentina-Meche-Juan network may become more stable, as they will now be sharing property.

All the networks entwined with cases 1 and 2 are defined by the

flow or reciprocal exchanges among their members. Other relationships are possible, of course, but they never attain the intensity or
amount of solidarity of network reciprocity. For example, Valentina
had a special friendship with an older lady in the compound. This
lady had no children; her husband, a drugstore attendant, had a
steady job and was, consequently, better off. According to Valentina,
"It's a very good lady; she once gave me 20 pesos [$1.60 U.S.] so I
could take a sick child to see the doctor. But I am ashamed to ask her
for any favors." In this case the requisites of personal interest and
neighborhood were present, but the higher economic status of the
childless couple prevented them from joining the network on the
basis of reciprocity. Eventually they moved away and their room was
occupied by the returning Gabriela.

The more visible forms of reciprocity among kinship members of
the network include the joint care of children by any available adult;
this relationship includes the prerogative of scolding and sending the
child on small errands. When a child is not related through kinship,
it is generally scolded only by its mother, not by other women in the
network. There is also much borrowing of food, money, kitchen utensils, and clothing among all members of the network. If someone gets
sick he or she is cared for by the others, and the children of a sick
mother are automatically provided for.

The flow of reciprocity is also conditioned by residential proximity,
as previously mentioned. Meche, for example, used to travel about
eight blocks to visit her sisters every day, or her sisters regularly went
to see her or dispatched children as messengers on all kinds of occasions. Meche also left her child with her sisters while she was out
working. When Meche's husband was out of work, the sisters loaned
him money during a two-week period. A few months later, Meche's
husband noticed that his sister-in-law (Valentina) had torn shoes; he
subsequently gave Meche some money to buy new ones for her.
When Gabriela fell ill, Meche visited her every day and took care of
the children, even though the network women were willing to do so.
This was an intense flow of reciprocity for an outsider, but it hardly
compared with the reciprocity level inside the network, or with the
amount of reciprocity that developed when Meche actually joined the
network.

Meche's interest in her sisters' network began to wane as her family grew and she was no longer able to get about as easily as before. A specific incident contributed to this cooling of relations. Miguel (the seasonal visitor from Guanajuato) had been a regular participant in the Contreras drinking circle until one day he had a drunken fight with his in-laws (the husbands of Gabriela and Valentina) and was badly beaten up. He moved out of Valentina's room, and Meche's husband (who does not work or drink with the Contreras men) took him in. This represented a strain in the relations between Meche and both Contreras networks.

Compadrazgo and affinal relations are also widely used to strengthen kin-network relations or to establish potential ties with other networks (see Lomnitz 1973:75–78): Josefa had reciprocal ties with her husband's kin in a neighboring shantytown; when her home fell in she was able to move into her husband's kin network. Similarly, an unrelated member of the network, Teófila, used to visit her sister-in-law in Cerrada del Cóndor (who lived a couple of blocks away). As a non-kin member, her *compadrazgo* relationship with Valentina nevertheless gave her a fictive kinship status. There were also *compadrazgo* ties between the husbands of both Teófila and Valentina, between Josefa and Valentina, and between Gabriela and Valentina. Furthermore, all networks were work-mates (tombstone polishers), as well as neighbors and drinking companions. All these relationships can be important sources of support on occasions when things go wrong.

In the non-kinship networks, reciprocal exchange is more formally balanced and the intra-network situation is more sensitive to small changes in status or in the quality of the reciprocity; such networks are inherently less stable than those based on kinship. Yet, the basic principle of network organization remains the same: reciprocal exchange is the primary mechanism for survival.

NETWORKS AND NICHES

The preceding case histories exemplify the fact that rural migrants, at least in Mexico City, have been able to generate a new socioeconomic environment—an ecological niche—that provides the essentials of physical and cultural survival within the city. This niche is typically marginal to the urban industrial economy. Shantytowns are enclaves built on undervalued or marginal land (the ravine of Cerrada del Cóndor has been systematically bypassed by developers), and the economic basis of the residents rests on types of occupations which are undervalued or unwanted, largely because they afford no steady employment and no security. The niche of urban marginality may thus be described as interstitial to the urban-industrial ecology proper. It is symbolized by the gathering and reprocessing of waste materials as a way of life—by the proliferation of menial occupations such as watching over parked automobiles or shining shoes, which are customarily rewarded only with tips. The niche, itself, does not provide an adequate basis for individual survival, however. Any illness or period of joblessness could prove fatal if the marginal possessed no social resources of his own. Hence the network organizations found in the shantytowns must be regarded as integral parts of the marginal ecology; they are primary mechanisms for survival, representing a kind of spontaneous social security system for the participants.

When a human group is confronted with a situation of extreme scarcity, the normal patterns of social solidarity may deteriorate (see Laughlin and Brady, article 1; Turnbull, article 2). Thus, when individual survival can be secured only at the cost of disregarding elementary social relations, sociability (if not society itself) may disappear. Laughlin (article 3) has observed among the So that extreme deprivation causes a decrement in reciprocal exchange between kinsmen and other So, as well as an enhanced reliance upon rudimentary, external-market exchange.

At the other extreme, social solidarity tends to lose much of its immediate utility when the mean level of resources becomes much higher than subsistence level. Such conditions may even handicap the economic rise of ambitious individuals. In industrial contexts, market exchange and its profit values then become a dominant concern (Polanyi 1968:68–76). Competition is valued above reliance on others, and the "rules of the game" replace the older rules of propriety. Success is sought in preference to harmony within a social role.[5]

The middle ground between these two extremes comprises the vast majority of social groups which are neither starving nor economically affluent. Such groups may sustain a subsistence base that is precarious, scarce, unpredictable, or inadequate. This amounts to a structural insecurity of resources that may derive from different environmental, ecological, or socioeconomic causes. In such cases social solidarity might be mobilized as a resource for survival by the cultivation of interpersonal relations through reciprocity and exchange, and that is precisely what happens in the shantytowns described above.

THE CONCEPT OF CONFIANZA

Social closeness, physical proximity, and equality of economic wants are the basic ingredients of reciprocal exchange in Cerrada del Cóndor. These three conditions are reflected and expressed through *confianza* (Lomnitz 1971; 1974). This widespread native category is commonly employed to evaluate the status of actual or potential reciprocal exchange between two partners. Ego feels *confianza* in alter to the extent that he perceives alter as willing and able to enter (or continue) a sustained relationship of reciprocal exchange. *Confianza* is not a static category like genealogical distance: it evolves in time according to the variable intensity of the flow of goods and services between the partners.

Additional insight into the nature of *confianza* may be gained by comparing it to what Simmel (in Wolff 1964) calls "confidence." According to him, confidence is "one of the major synthetic forces in society," and its main aspects are: (1) cognitive, as a state intermediate between knowledge and ignorance of a person or persons; (2) dynamic, because it evolves through a reciprocal development of interpersonal relations; (3) personal, since the intimate knowledge of character becomes relevant where objective grounds for predicting future behavior are lacking. While Simmel seems to recognize implicitly a connection between confidence and reciprocal exchange among partners, this connection becomes essential in the concept of *confianza*. One might say that *confianza* is the kind of confidence that comes into play when one plans to ask for a favor in the hope of not meeting with a rebuff, and with the expectation of returning a similar favor upon request at an unspecified time in the future. It is a type of confidence that is directly related to generalized reciprocity as a form of exchange.

Confianza may be based on different factors, depending on the social setting. For example, the residential proximity which seems to be essential for *confianza* in the shantytown may be replaced by the use of the telephone among the middle class. In either case, however, the individual transactions in a reciprocity relation are delicate, since the expectation of a return remains unspecified and is in fact unmentionable. No kind of open accounting may be kept in such a relation; yet a balanced and sustained series of transactions is essential to its usefulness. *Confianza* is like a letter of credit, to be drawn in time of need: the stronger the *confianza,* the greater is the amount (literally and figuratively) which may be withdrawn.

At a more elementary level of social interaction, one might argue that some form of *confianza* intervenes whenever two persons relate, no matter how casually. Thus, for peaceful relations to obtain, encounters between strangers must include some sort of implied reciprocal agreement to abstain from unprovoked attack. Goffman (1966:197) has analyzed the symbols used among members of modern complex societies to induce this elementary relationship: body movements, facial expressions, styles of clothing and haircuts represent different signals directed toward (or against) different sets of people.

It is equally important to recognize in the case of urban marginality that the group is interstitial to a market economy, and that it derives its livelihood from market exchange. Even such hidden forms of mendacity as automobile-watching in Mexico City keep up the pretense that some sort of service is rendered. Reciprocity in the social network is important as a system of economic security, which it achieves by spreading the risk of loss of livelihood over a number of individuals. In urban industrial societies this security is likely to be provided either by the state or by the employer in the form of insurance policies. But marginal populations are not covered by such systems. Hence survival must be achieved through the more spontaneous mechanisms of social solidarity. Individuals who are either unwilling or unable to join one of the shantytown networks simply do not survive in that environment.

CONFIANZA IN THE NETWORK

All exchange is dyadic, yet the reciprocity network represents a clustering of dyadic relations to the point where each member trades goods and services with all other members. The presence of a sufficiently high level of *confianza* among the members is a requirement for the existence of reciprocity networks, as the following example suggests.

A survey of 142 women in Cerrada del Cóndor yielded an ideal scale of favors in terms of social distance, as summarized in table 6.1. This table does not necessarily reflect *actual* behavior: hypothetical questions tend to elicit responses which agree with the ideal model. Still, the table reveals a definite gradation of types of exchange over a continuum of social distance. The ideal model sets relatives above neighbors, and neighbors above *compadres,* as far as most forms of exchange are concerned; the ideal partner for reciprocity is obviously a relative who is also a neighbor. *Compadres* are rated most approachable in emergency matters; this is an agreement with the ideology of *compadrazgo.*

TABLE 6.1   OF WHOM WOULD YOU ASK A FAVOR?

Social Distance	Kind of favor				
	Emergencies	Money loans	Any kind	None	Total
Relatives (other than nuclear fam. members	6	58	50	16	130
Neighbors	7	48	10	45	110
Compadres	12	35	6	63	116
Friends	7	30	3	72	112
Acquaintances	6	4	0	92	102
Total	38	175	69	288	

SOURCE: Author's fieldnotes, 1971.

What *confianza* really measures is individual departures from the expected pattern of exchange; that is, the difference between actual and ideal social distance. It is evaluated by each partner subjectively and fluctuates with the changing intensity and quality of the exchange event. Even among close relatives there is a continuous adjustment of reciprocal relations; differences in socioeconomic status cool the relationship even between brothers, as does geographical distance (which may be quantitatively evaluated in minutes of walking, or in bus fares).

The dimension of personal liking or esteem among network members is somewhat more difficult to evaluate. It is a fact, however, that *paisanos* (migrants from similar geographical origins) find it easier to get together than people of widely dissimilar regions. Thus, there is even a degree of *confianza* implied in the sharing of a given regional subculture.

Another important stimulant of *confianza* is the joint consumption of alcohol by men. The institution of *cuatismo* "male friendship" implies a high degree of *confianza* through sharing intimate or confidential information under the effect of alcohol. This circle of *cuates* is generally recruited from among the male members of the network.

In other cultural contexts the factors of personal liking may be based on interactions of a different sort. Among the middle class of Chile, for example, one finds an ideology of friendship which presupposes a certain amount of intimate knowledge between friends. This ideology is nurtured from childhood on: "A good friend is generous in the broadest possible sense, he shares both the good and the bad, his experiences and feelings in life, and he is always ready to do a favor for a friend" (Lomnitz 1971:100). In general, one may say that within any given social context, two individuals will tend to feel *confianza* toward each other to the extent that they share similar expectations of behavior in the reciprocal exchange of goods, services, and information.

SOME FINAL THOUGHTS

The idealization of reciprocal and redistributive exchanges by Polanyi (1968) and his followers provoked a widespread reaction among adherents to the so-called formalist school of economic anthropology. The latter believed that every kind of economic exchange involves some kind of maximization of gain and that reciprocal exchange theory is merely a product of the romantic, anti-market mentality of some anthropologists (see Firth 1970; Burling 1962; Nash 1966; Cook 1968).

However, the widespread occurrence of systems of reciprocal exchange among large sections of the urban population in underdeveloped countries cannot be dismissed. In Cerrada del Cóndor, reciprocal exchange is an integral part of the marginal economy that operates on the borderline between the demands of the marketplace and those of personal and social solidarity. Maximization of gain may be present in either case. Although the gain obtained from reciprocity is not clearly defined in each transaction, it is nevertheless present as a long-term benefit to all partners.

Maximization of gain in a market economy presupposes the existence of plausible alternatives of behavior: to buy or not to buy, to choose a job among various offers, and so on. Marginals possess no such freedom of choice, since they have very little to sell and, therefore, not much with which to buy. Reciprocity frequently appears in situations that lack many alternatives, and this is a source of its strength and persistence. Concepts such as "generosity" applied to reciprocal exchange should be understood not so much as a moral quality but rather as an effect of economic necessity: "People are made generous through want, not through plenty" (Evans-Pritchard 1940:90–91).

Equality of wants, which I have proposed as a requisite for membership in shantytown reciprocity networks, has also been found by other authors as a more or less implicit condition of reciprocity. Thus Sahlins (1968:166) points out that "Economic inequality would reduce the content of sociability in balanced transactions." Blau (1967) has attempted to explain the mechanism of unbalanced transactions in terms of power transferred from one partner to another, as in the case of the poor relation, for example, who must bear the intromission of rich relatives in his private life as compensation for the imbalance that obtains in his reciprocal relationship with them. "The danger of being subjected to the power of another is an incentive to fulfill the obligations [of the exchange], by reciprocating for any favors or services received" (Blau 1967:28–29). It is easy to understand how, under the tense conditions of marginal life, only a symmetrical reciprocal relation can remain stable for any length of time.

CONCLUSIONS

Marginality in Latin America is not a short-lived phenomenon; it endures. A shantytown is not a transit camp of rural migrants bound for modernization through incorporation into the urban proletariat or the middle class. In fact, the urban workers conspire with the urban middle class to keep the marginals out of the urban industrial system. There is a complicity of underdevelopment in the fact that all social classes in the "modern" sector of the economy have a vested interest in excluding the marginals.

According to Alejo (1973), Mexico will have, at best, the same proportion of unemployment and underemployment in 1980 as it has today. This means a considerable projected net increase in the marginal population. New industrial jobs are increasingly costly to create, as the economy requires an ever smaller, more specialized labor force. The priority for new job openings belongs to the descendants of those workers who are already incorporated into the industrial production system. This is not to exclude as a possibility the eventual stabilization of the marginalization process; but under the present circumstances it seems unrealistic to expect the marginals to be absorbed (no matter how gradually) into the urban industrial economy.

The reciprocity networks described in this article suggest an opportunity of using the social resources of the marginal population, and perhaps of channeling these resources into new forms of production for the benefit of all concerned. Existing mechanisms of cooperation are being utilized for individual survival that, if reoriented, could yield social energy toward the progress of the ecosystem as a whole. To begin with, the problems of the marginal populations themselves could be approached in terms of utilization of the network structure. It is obvious that the gigantic housing problems of marginality cannot possibly be solved unless the marginals have access to housing credit; at present, they are excluded from such credit because of their marginality.

Corporate residential patterns are not foreign to the Mexican tradition. They have existed since the days of Teotihuacan and Tenochtitlan (Bernal 1973). If reciprocity networks were legally empowered to acquire urban property, it would soon be realized that their land use is very efficient. A lot of 100 to 150 square meters can house four and more families, that is, up to thirty persons per lot. The geometry of dwellings around an open yard or patio represents an optimum arrangement for the combination of suburban housing with gardening and animal husbandry. The production of hogs, chickens, and turkeys by marginals represents today a major (though quite unknown) contribution to Mexico's foodstuff production.

Survival through solidarity in the Mexican shantytown may thus be viewed as a successful adaptive response of a population to conditions of extreme deprivation. This response is evolutionary in the sense that pre-existing or latent cultural mechanisms are brought into play to confront new economic challenges. Shantytowns in Mexico, and probably in other Latin American nations as well, may thus be regarded as the results of a successful process of natural and social selection against great odds. The specific forms of survival which have evolved among marginal populations deserve further study, since they may well represent a reserve of social energy and creativity well beyond the immediate tasks of survival.

NOTES

1. I have explored the question of how to account for the survival of Latin American marginal populations in other publications (see Lomnitz 1973, 1974).

2. In addition to the more central concepts of human ecology, some attempt will be made to incorporate a number of other empirically or theoretically weak concepts applied by other investigators to urban marginality: (a) *Rural-Urban migration:* this is a relevant component of the marginalization process; however, not all marginals are of rural origin, and the urban descendants of rural migrants do not necessarily remain marginal, nor do all migrants become marginals; some enter the proletarian or middle classes. (b) *Reserve labor force:* a likely category, but there is no proof that marginals can significantly permeate the industrial labor market. In general, the barriers established against the marginals by the urban industrial system (including the organized labor force) have been increasingly efficient. (c) *Surplus population of dependent capitalist economies:* while providing a coherent explanation of the marginalization process, this concept (Quijano 1970:27–41) does not fully account for the economic relationship between marginality and the urban system. For example, marginality supplies the urban middle class with an inexhaustible source of cheap menial labor. (d) *Residents of tenements and shantytowns:* an operational definition on the basis of residence is inadequate, because many industrial workers also live in shantytowns or in downtown slums. However, the study of shantytowns did give rise to the concept of marginality, first as an ecological phenomenon, and later as a structural economic process.

3. Identification of a network in the field is achieved through participant observation; it is an analytic rather than a native category.

4. There was one latrine for this compound. The room had no windows, the door was the primary source of light and air; but since some of the neighbors in the compound did not belong to the network, it was necessary to use curtains in the doorways for privacy. The kin-related members of the network walked in and out of each other's rooms without knocking.

5. An actual situation of conflict between these two ideologies has been described in some detail for the Chilean middle class (Lomnitz 1971:100).

7

Cultural and Biological Adaptations to Deprivation: The Northern Ojibwa Case

Charles A. Bishop

As we have seen in previous articles, the expansion of Western industrial systems into other niches and habitats can have differential effects on societies displaced or subordinated by such growth. Charles Bishop gives us yet another example of this kind of environmental restructuring. Like the So of Uganda, the Ojibwa are seen as adapting simultaneously to both progressive and recursive environment change. The Ojibwa data show in diachronic perspective the nature of a societal transformation that establishes adaptive diaphasis in response to recurrent patterns of ecological stress. The decimation of one strategic resource base—big game—led to a shift in dependence to another base. In the case of the So, the shift was to pastoralism. In the case of the Ojibwa, it was to trapping. Both sets of changes increased the power of industrial agents to exploit local resources. The Ojibwa case also demonstrates that a system of increased exploitation, dependence, and subordination can be engineered as environmental change by industrialism even when the dominant group is only peripherally located in the area so affected. The mode of integration established between the expanding industrial complex of the Western world and the Ojibwa differs from the previous two cases in terms of both geographical location and intensity of direct domination. The problems posed for population survival and sociocultural persistence are no less severe than in the other cases, however, and the outcome provides still another example of relatively successful adaptation to progressive and recursive environmental restructuring.

Adaptability is probably the most distinctive characteristic of life. In maintaining the independence and individuality of natural units, none of the great forces of inanimate matter are as successful as that alertness and adaptability to change which we designate as life—and the loss of which is death (Selye 1973:699).

This article will examine the effects of ecological stress upon the Northern Ojibwa during the nineteenth century.[1] Most of this stress derived from: (1) a faunal catastrophe (between A. D. 1810 and 1829) reinforced by alterations in contact relationships with Euro-Canadians after 1821, that is, a disaster; and, although mediated in part by cyclical fluctuations in resources, (2) a long period of deprivation involving reduced resource availability. The Indians were thus forced to adapt to both progressive changes, constant and nonrepetitive, and recursive or cyclical changes in their environment (Laughlin and Brady, article 1) during this period.

To explicate more fully the nature of the disaster and subsequent deprivation, it is appropriate to begin with an outline of Northern

Ojibwa sociocultural arrangements as they appear to have existed immediately following European contacts, and then to give an account of the progressive changes that culminated in the stressful conditions. Following a discussion of the nature of deprivation, the specific conditions of the Northern Ojibwa are related to general theoretical issues of survival, deprivation, and adaptation.

THE EARLY CONTACT OJIBWA AND THE FUR TRADE

When first visited by French explorers and missionaries during the early seventeenth century, the people who came to be known as Ojibwa occupied the region near the north shore of Lake Huron and at the east end of Lake Superior (Bishop and Smith 1975). They lived a semi-sedentary existence, occupying a number of strategically located village sites during the warmer months of the year. There may have been about twenty such village camps altogether at the time of contact, ranging from 100 to 400 occupants each and representing a total population of perhaps 4,500 persons (Bishop 1976). The economic and ecological niche of these semi-sedentary villages was filled with a rich array of resources, especially fish, but including deer, moose, beaver, and a variety of plant foods. The Ojibwa of this era were not likely to have been in any danger of starvation, since food surpluses offset periods of potential scarcity. Indeed, the proto-historic Ojibwa appear to fit well Sahlins' model of "the original affluent society" (Sahlins 1972:1–39). Each village community bore an animal name which, it is argued, symbolized a clan-totem group that was further characterized by patrilineality and patrilocality (Hickerson 1962; Bishop 1974, 1976). In winter, it is suggested, these clan villages segmented along lineage lines, the segments forming hunting groups which exploited game in the hinterland. Although politically, and for the main economically, autonomous, the clans were linked together by bilateral cross-cousin marriage and the Feast of the Dead ceremony held by each group approximately every seven years (McPherron 1967:292; Hickerson 1960). In pre-contact times, the Feast appears to have been an instrument to perpetuate alliances and redistribute surplus food and other goods.

Following contact and the introduction of the French trade, the intensity of social life increased as the Ojibwa and neighboring tribes gathered near Sault Ste. Marie to exchange fur pelts for European items. These were first obtained from other Indians (Ottawa and Nipissing) who acted as middlemen, and later directly from French *coureurs de bois*. After 1650, the Feast of the Dead ceremony grew in scope to include great quantities of surplus goods which were exchanged or destroyed at multitribal gatherings. Feasting, dancing, and gift-giving came to overshadow the more solemn purpose of the Feast, while the clan chiefs (captains) hosting a feast manipulated social relations to accumulate surplus goods for both consumption and exchange (McPherron 1967:292–93). According to McPherron, the florescent Feast functioned "to reduce the quantity of goods through simple destruction and through redistribution of the proceeds of the fur trade, serving as a mechanism to forestall the social disruption that was occurring as a result of the enormous change in economic relations" (1967:293).

In order to extend their middleman role and also to avoid the wrath of the Iroquois, a number of Ojibwa groups began to shift westward along both the north and south shores of Lake Superior during the late seventeenth century. My study is concerned primarily with the Ojibwa who began expanding in a northwesterly direction.

Until the 1670s when the newly founded Hudson's Bay Company began establishing trading centers along coastal Hudson Bay and James Bay, the Ojibwa acted as middlemen to the Cree and Assiniboin to the northwest. Although after this date they were forced to trap furs themselves to obtain European wares, they continued to return to Sault Ste. Marie and later Michilimackinac to fish and engage in intertribal trade fairs. By the 1730s, however, some Ojibwa began residing permanently in the boreal forests northwest of Lake Superior as the Cree and Assiniboin retreated westward in the van of the expanding fur trade. The abundance of resources in the northern interior, the advantage of being closer to the source of French and English trade rivalry, along with the depletion of game and furs farther east had lured Ojibwa trader-settlers in a northwesterly direction by the early eighteenth century. The Ojibwa groups (and perhaps other groups such as Ottawa and Algonquins) who came to occupy the southern two-thirds of northern Ontario and eastern Manitoba were few in number but large in size, often including as many as 80 people. It would seem that either whole clans or lineages of parent clans formed basic social groups. Over each band, or "tribe" as they were called by the traders, was a leader or "captain" who dealt directly with the traders on behalf of his "young men." Survival and trapping by large bands under competitive conditions required considerable mobility. Subsistence patterns subsequently began to focus on abundant large game animals, such as moose and caribou, while fishing declined in importance and was left to be done by women and children. While interclan sharing of foods and even trade goods continued at ceremonials and feasts, the fur animals trapped appear to have been coveted as band (or lineage) property.

After a brief interlude during the 1760s when the Hudson's Bay Company controlled the trade stemming from French problems in Quebec, a new wave of traders from Montreal entered the Northern Ojibwa area and were soon capturing the bulk of the trade. No longer did the Ojibwa have to make long treks to distant trading posts for their supplies. In order to compete effectively with the Montreal merchants, the Hudson's Bay Company was forced to erect numerous inland posts during the late decades of the century in the area occupied by the emergent Northern Ojibwa. At this time, rivalry between the Hudson's Bay Company and the Montreal merchants who united to form the Northwest Company grew intense as the two concerns vied for the pelts obtained by Indians. Indeed, great quantities of European goods were distributed to Indians at a low cost to gain their allegiance, but even then some groups might fail to pay their debts if bargains looked better at a competing post. Traders of both companies were often forced to give Indians what they requested, lest they lose the trade of whole bands. Nevertheless, despite the ease with which Indians could obtain goods, it is evident that the Ojibwa were growing increasingly dependent upon European substitutes.

With the settling of the interior by traders during the last decades of the century, mass Indian migrations ceased as Indians adapted to more localized trade conditions. The large bands or clans of earlier times segmented into smaller more viable groups of from 20 to 35 persons, an apparent adaptation to the new trade and ecological conditions. This process of segmentation was also related to population growth during the last half of the eighteenth century, despite occasional epidemics and intergroup conflicts that derived from resource and status competition.

THE DISASTER: FAUNAL DEPLETIONS AND TRADE MONOPOLY

The focus on furs and venison by a growing population that consumed the flesh and also supplied traders with considerable quantities could not continue for long. The valuable beaver supply as well as larger animals were slaughtered in such numbers that they began to grow scarce by 1810. Dwindling fur returns directly affected the trading companies. Adapted to expanding trade conditions, the Northwest Company, when faced with diminishing returns and resulting economic losses, was forced to amalgamate with the Hudson's Bay Company by 1821. Changes in trade policies and subsistence activities brought about by the untempered exploitation of food and fur resources during the era of trade company rivalry also altered the primary adaptive strategies of the Northern Ojibwa. As the fur animals, particularly beaver, declined through overhunting, the Ojibwa found it increasingly difficult to meet their trade needs. This was further enhanced by a parallel decline in cervines, moose and caribou, the main subsistence source for Indians. Thus, more time had to be devoted to hunting large game animals and correspondingly less effort was spent trapping at the very time when furs were becoming scarce. As stated by the Lac Seul trader, John Davis, in 1824: "[F]ew large animals could be killed though many of the Indians employed their whole time in going after them[.] Consequently the trade suffered particularly in Martins, want of the first necessary of life is the source of most of the miseries of the poor Indian as well as of great injury to the trade . . ." (HBC Arch B107/e/1). Since the hides of the large animals were manufactured into clothing and snowshoe lacing, among other products, the scarcity meant that Indians had to rely upon substitutes, particularly European cloth and blankets acquired in trade. But these were among the more expensive items and hence were becoming quite difficult to obtain at the very time when they were most needed. In some cases, Indians were forced to cut up their furs to make clothing.

Cases of starvation, even cannibalism, occasioned by the dearth of large animals became relatively frequent by the 1820s. While Indians could and did eat the flesh of the fur-bearing animals, including the pelts themselves in times of extreme shortage, this resource alone could not sustain them. Thus, to prevent starvation, the traders encouraged Indians to snare hare and set nets for fish. Yet, because snaring and fishing were considered womens' work and beneath the dignity of male hunters, some Indians had to be pushed to the limit before they would engage in such activities. For example, after seven Crane Indians starved to death trying to live off caribou in 1826: "[T]hey are obliged now to have recourse to rabbits and fish—the very few of them could snare one of the former animals two years ago—necessity . . . taught them to *choke* rabbits . . .—and had they been wise last year and gone to the rabbit ground so many of them would not have starved to death" (HBC Arch B155/a/38).

Nevertheless, the switch in subsistence patterns became mandatory if the Indians were to survive, since the few remaining moose and caribou were soon exterminated. Hares came to provide both sustenance and clothing, their pelts being woven into skin robes and blankets even though it was a humiliating experience for a hunter to have to resort to such apparel. Thomas Vincent remarked in 1825 that: "[T]heir former pride and ambition to excel each other is vanished. A young man may now be seen wearing an old tattered Rabbit Skin garment that a few years ago he would have considered a degrading covering for a helpless old Woman" (HBC Arch B3/e/10).

By the late 1820s, hare and fish had become the chief source of livelihood during most of the year and remained so for the next seven decades. In 1830, Charles McKenzie summed up the situation:

> ['T]is not many years past since they have taken entirely to their present way of living. Any young man would think himself disgraced even to be seen setting a Net to catch fish or a Snare for a Rabbit & when recourse was had to such means in the times of scarcity, it was left entirely to the women's province. Yet both young & old men lean their assistance now, without considering

it a disgrace, so strong is the call of nature over prejudice. (HBC
Arch B107/a/8)

Changes in subsistence patterns and trading post dependency relationships were intimately connected. The termination of competition
between the Northwest Company and Hudson's Bay Company in
1821 placed the latter concern in a more favorable position in regard
to tightening up its trade policies and entrenching itself in the life of
the Indians. Although the Northern Ojibwa had been partially dependent upon European materials prior to 1821, they had been able to
take advantage of the trade rivalry and had had comparatively little
difficulty obtaining their trade supplies. After this date, the Hudson's
Bay Company had greater latitude to experiment with and manipu-
late its relationship with the Indians. The effects of this monopoly
were evident in such remarks as Charles McKenzie's comment
regarding the conditions of trade with the Lac Seul Indian, Grand
Coquin, in 1822: "I was well aware of his old Shams which have lost
their wonted efficacy . . . nothing but a good hunt would answer
now . . ." (HBC Arch B107/a/2).

Among the policies implemented after 1821 were: (1) the withdrawal of a number of posts which no longer merited expenditure
and which had been operated at a loss during the period of trade rivalry; (2) a general increase in the price of trade goods; (3) restrictions for conservation purposes placed on the taking of beaver and
muskrats; (4) a concerted effort to establish family hunting territories; (5) the termination of deferential treatment of band chiefs;
and (6) developing what was termed the "ready barter" system of
trade. The purpose of these changes was to improve trade (from the
company's perspective) and to make the Indians more dependent on
the trading post. Both aims were achieved, although the ability of Indians to cope with these political and economic changes also affected
policy-making.

The withdrawal of all but a handful of posts during the 1820s
meant that many debt records were transferred and consolidated.
This reduced costs and lessened the chance that Indians would rove
from post to post. The debts of individual trappers had been kept
since about 1810 and it was evident from the records that many large

unpaid balances remained as a legacy of prior trade competition. Although Indians could choose where they wished to trade initially, once the choice was made, their furs were either not accepted elsewhere, or their debts were transferred to the new place. Accurate records of individual balances could be maintained by such tactics. On the basis of these data, new credit could be withheld and pressure to produce could be applied to "lazy" trappers. Similarly, increasing the value of trade goods was an attempt to recoup losses.

The restrictions placed on taking beaver and muskrats were meant to assure their recovery after virtual annihilation during previous decades. Summer pelts, which were formerly taken, were rendered valueless and were no longer accepted by the traders. For such conservation measures to work, the Indians had to recognize some sort of territorial rights over resources. Otherwise, there was no way to prevent trappers from moving about and taking fur-bearers wherever they were found. That conservation policies and family hunting territories were coordinated is indicated by Governor George Simpson:

> On the subject of nursing the country . . . We are endeavoring to confine the natives throughout the country now by families to separate and distinct hunting grounds[.] [T]his system seems to take among them by degrees, and in a few years I hope it will become general, but it is a very difficult matter to change the habits of Indians, altho they may see the ultimate benefit thereof to themselves and families. (HBC Arch D4/92)

There are several reasons why family territories did not develop immediately. For one thing, so long as some Indians persisted in taking furs wherever they could find them (to others this meant trespassing), it was difficult to enforce conservation practices. For another, it was exceedingly difficult to convince starving Indians not to kill beaver. Finally, Indians who had formerly practiced communal hunting were evidently reluctant to partition their band territories (Bishop 1970).

The deferential treatment of band leaders—the "captains"—by providing them with a special coat, medals, and a keg of rum was discontinued because it was considered detrimental to the trade. Instead, it was argued, regardless of their status Indians should be recognized according to their abilities as trappers.

Finally, the "ready barter" system (which was put into effect only sporadically after 1824) required that Indians exchange furs directly for their trade needs, rather than obtaining such goods in advance in early autumn as had previously been the custom. Although materials could be obtained more cheaply on the direct barter system, it meant that Indians had to begin the fall trapping season without the necessary supplies they would normally obtain on the debt system. These changes eliminated the risk element of the debt system from the Company's point of view, but placed severe hardships on Indians, especially since both food and furs had become scarce.

DEPRIVATION AND SURVIVAL: CHANGING ADAPTIVE STRATEGIES

The Northern Ojibwa were forced to make a number of immediate adaptive adjustments to the faunal depletion and new trade conditions in order to survive, despite being nominally unprepared for these events. The long period which followed involved severe hardship and deprivation for these people. But unlike conditions preceding the initial disaster, for which they were unprepared, the Indians came to expect repetitive and cyclical occurrences of resource deprivation. Given that most Northern Ojibwa survived the disaster, it becomes pertinent to investigate the adaptive strategies that evolved to accommodate the later, cyclical and hence predictable conditions of environmental stress.

All the evidence indicates that, after 1821, the Northern Ojibwa could not have survived without relying on the trading post. This dependency was related to environmental shifts, alterations in trade policies implemented by the Company, and to the replacement of native wares by European substitutes during prior decades. McKenzie, manager of the Lac Seul post, summed up this relationship in 1851:

> The Indians also must be provided with their most necessaries
> . . . the natives stand in the same yearly necessity, having
> nothing within themselves to cover their nakedness—save a few
> miserable Rabbit Skins when kind providence sends that most
> necessary Supply—both for their Sustenance and Covering—yet
> so very simple a thing as a *Rabbit Snare*—must come out of the

Trading Shop—They not even wherewithall to Sew their
Shoes—without recourse to the Shop. (HBC Arch B107/a/30)

The Northern Ojibwa became extensively dependent upon such
items as guns, ammunition, hatchets, knives, kettles, twine, nets,
leather, and European cloth. Indeed, traders endeavored to foster this
dependent relationship since it gave them more power to implement
new policies. Dependent Indians were subject to the sanctions of the
trading company as well as to sanctions within their own system—a
circumstance ripe for what Spicer (1961:520–21) calls "directed culture change."

The Ojibwa had to adapt not only to trading post dependency, but
to periodic changes in trading policies. As mentioned, one such policy
was the ready barter system, which often created difficulties for Indians who had to face the winter without any supplies. However,
because of complaints from Indians *and* traders, the ready barter system was either abandoned after a few years or was modified by Company officials to allow Indians several items on credit which were
deemed essential in the autumn. Charles McKenzie, an outspoken
critic of these policies, commented on such compromises in 1852:

> 'Tis certain if we wish the Indians to work, that we must supply
> their necessaries—now in the olden times when the country
> was rich "Necessaries" were understood to go no farther than
> putting *Tools* into their hands. But now comes the word Neces-
> sities which has a Greater latitude—I should like to ask you Gen-
> tlemen—when you tell us to give the Indians no more than their
> *Real necessaries* I should like to know what you mean by real
> necessaries—That after putting Tools into their hands does not
> Clothing come under the head of necessaries—or is clothing as
> necessary to a naked Indian as tools? Is not a Gun absolutely
> necessary for an Indian—or what is an Indian without a
> gun—he can kill Squirrels only—with his Bow & Arrows. One
> thing clear the Lac Seul Indians did not get their Real Necessi-
> ties this season. . . . You'll say d—n them let them cover them-
> selves with Rabbit Skins—Aye let them—as they must—and
> God help them should Rabbits fail them—both for covering and
> food and I often Shudder at the thought . . . and that would be
> ruinous to you also—being as you are Gentlemen Responsible
> for their lives. (HBC Arch B107/z/2)

In addition to these newly introduced trading policies and subsequent dependencies, the Indians also had to adapt to the exigencies of the wider environment. If hare proved to be numerous, the Indians could spend most of their time trapping. If they were scarce, however, as was frequently the case, trapping was abandoned in favor of more direct food quests. In 1850, for example, the scarcity of hare prevented Indians from trapping even though fur animals were relatively abundant. The Indians suffered so much from starvation that winter, according to George McPherson of Osnaburgh House, that "not an Indian is Making any hunt in furs. . . . The Indians . . . say, they did nothing else but Angle Jackfish from day to day to Save their lives" (HBC Arch B155/a/61).

Subsistence on small game also substantially reduced the mobility which had become a significant part of the Ojibwa life style during the lush days of the early fur trade. As McKenzie suggested in 1827:

> Fish and Rabbits became the Chief & only food of the natives which binds them to certain spots where these are to be found in greater abundance . . . [they] have destroyed all the Furred Animals within a wide range of these places. Were there large animals to enable the Indians to live & rove in the forests as formerly no doubt they [would] collect a number of small furs such as Martins, Cats, & Otters in the season when these are of most value but the miserable state of the Country not admits of this . . . they cannot live where these animals abound. . . . (HBC Arch B107/e/3)

In sum, trapping had become a basic subsistence activity. It was only through the trade in furs that the Northern Ojibwa could obtain materials necessary for survival. Actually, survival was balanced precariously between the food quest and trapping. Although both were essential, the immediacy of starvation often necessitated the search for food over furs. The food quest, which frequently interfered with trapping activities, then, influenced the type and quantity of furs traded, which, in turn, defined the limits of an Indian's purchasing power. In terms of maximization theory, the limited variety and quantity of resources (both food and furs) required a flexible mode of production and a range of strategy alternatives.

Environmental changes combined with policies designed to obligate and maintain a permanent Indian population nucleated about the post also had a decided influence on the restructuring of Ojibwa social organization. Ecological and trade conditions tended to mold the nature of social groups while setting limits on their size.

One effect was a deemphasis on unilineality as a result of the atrophy of descent group functions. During the late eighteenth century, hunting groups were, for the most part, named patrilineages (lineage segments or remnants of aboriginal clans) that shared food resources and trade goods, mortuary rites (the Feast of the Dead ceremony), social control, as well as defense and predation functions. The clans of the mid-nineteenth century operated only to regulate marriage through the residual practice of totem group exogamy. The last Feast of the Dead ceremony uniting lineage mates that I was able to discover in the historical records occurred at Lac Seul in 1845, and it was anomalous under the altered conditions: "Assiniboine died at a Small Lake—in the forest—but his Tribe—Eagle Tribe came in a Body and took the Corps to Lac La Glaize and Buried it among his fathers—The only instance of the Kind I have known for many years" (McKenzie, HBC Arch B107/a/24).

Similarly, the altered environment, the termination of deferential treatment of leaders, and the stress placed on individual efforts and rights in trapping had all but destroyed the former pattern of succession by primogeniture. McKenzie, in 1831, mentioned an Indian who had "some ideas of taking his late father's Title & honours to which he is entitled by birth—being the Eldest son of the late old Nabagache—a chieftain of former days" (HBC Arch B107/a/10). Such attainment at this date, however, meant little more than ego gratification. The tendency for the eldest son to inherit his father's title and reside virilocally was all that remained of a once universal pattern that had ensured the corporateness of the clan.

Adaptation to variable birth and death rates in a context where food and fur resources were also scarce and scattered required that lineage mates disperse themselves spatially, thereby inhibiting former clan functions. Adaptation to a degenerated environment where resources were both limited in variety and low in productivity had, during prior decades, generated a flexible social structure with flexible patterns of post-nuptial residence.

The fission of extended kin groups of 30 or so persons into winter units only slightly, if at all, larger than the primary family was related to the atrophy of lineage group functions. In the late eighteenth century, members of clan-named groups of similar size had been able to reside together regardless of the season. The new subsistence difficulties, however, led to the formation of isolated patricentric families for seven or eight months of the year, except during optimal winters. Resource abundance generally prevented such atomization. Such was the case in 1853 for members of the Pelican clan. As McKenzie noted: "Greean and his tribe of Pelicans 10 men in number came in from the Cat Lake quarter—with their wives and children . . . These brought the best haul of Furs that came in for many Years . . . I gave him . . . a present which he is well deserving—by keeping his band together" (HBC Arch B107/a/31). When possible, then, Indians seem to have preferred to live in larger social enclaves. The above case was, however, the exception rather than the rule; fission and dispersal were more common than fusion.

The abundance and type of food hunted set definite upper limits on group size. Hare and fish (which periodically fluctuated in quantity and which were low in fat content) could not support groups larger than families except for very brief periods during the winter season. The actual quantity of meat from such small animals when compared with large game is quite striking. For instance, Edward S. Rogers (1966:100) estimated that the 88 moose taken by the Round (Weagamow) Lake Indians in 1958–59 produced approximately 35,200 pounds of meat. By comparison, 7,500 hare produced only 11,200 pounds. Thus, the pursuit of small scattered game necessitated small scattered hunting units. However, the pursuit of such resources, as noted, reduced mobility patterns and bound families to areas where hare and fish could be found.

Two ecological factors appear to be primary in setting limits on the size of hunting groups: (1) the type and abundance of food; and, (2) the overall population density of a region. Where food was scarce and the population relatively dense, the territory available to each group for exploitation would be comparatively smaller than in areas less densely populated. Thus, a smaller territory could probably be most efficiently exploited by single family units. There is support for this in the historical literature. Winter groups nearer Rainy Lake were equivalent to nuclear families, whereas those farther north where the population density was half as great were sometimes twice as large. It is not surprising, then, that the more densely populated areas were the first to develop family hunting territories (Bishop 1970). They were also the first to experience the decimation of beaver and large game animals. Because of these conditions, they came to exhibit more extreme forms of social atomism. It is thus not surprising that the classic example of Ojibwa atomism has been Ruth Landes' Emo Ojibwa of the Rainy Lake region.

Group size is only indirect evidence of social atomism. In order to acquire direct information, the manner in which productive activities are conducted and the type of reciprocity systems maintained need examining. Modes of production and reciprocity provide a measure of the degree of individualism or collectivism present under fluctuating resource availability. For the Northern Ojibwa of the mid-nineteenth century, production involved the acquisition of both food and furs but neither trapping nor the snaring of hare and other small game required group participation. Both activities could be performed most efficiently by single persons or hunting partners within territorially bounded regions. Production, then, was largely individualistic. This was in marked contrast to the situation half a century earlier when large mobile bands collectively hunted big game animals as well as fur bearers. Indeed, Edward Rogers has indicated (personal communication) that the number of large game animals taken per capita increases with the number of men cooperating in the hunt. That is, where 4 or 5 men hunt together, the average number of moose taken per hunter is greater than when only 2 men hunt together. Maximum efficiency is attained when about 6 or 7 men are involved. Beyond this number the per capita kill declines. Relating these data to conditions in the late eighteenth century when big game hunting prevailed, it is of interest to note that groups averaged about 25 persons or slightly more with about 7 hunters per group.

During the mid-nineteenth century, the exchange of resources outside the family unit was not entirely lacking. However, reciprocity patterns varied both with the type of resource involved and with the degree to which scarcity, and hence deprivation, was present. In regard to the former, furs were definitely the personal property of the trapper who exchanged them directly for trade goods. Such relations with the trading post involved what Sahlins (1965a:148–49) has termed "negative reciprocity," meaning an attempt to get something for nothing—or at least for as little as possible. The journals clearly indicate that relations between Indians and traders frequently involved haggling over price or even begging. This was true even when furs were given in the guise of gifts. For instance, one Indian known as Kingfisher gave a "gift" of ten prime beaver pelts to Charles Mc-Kenzie after which the Indian made a speech to have an outpost established at Red Lake. McKenzie then gave the Kingfisher what he thought was a generous gift. However, the Indian thought differently: "[H]e knew well the value of the present he made & the furs he traded—& was not a little surpised that 'so great a man as me' (these were his words) did not know the Etiquette of these things better" (HBC Arch B107/a/9).

Once trade goods were received by individual trappers, it would appear that they were shared to some extent with other members of the co-residential group. Survival probably would have required this. Unfortunately, there are few data on the extent of sharing. It would seem, however, that trade goods remained within the group whose trappers procured them.

Food was the one commodity which was voluntarily shared with no explicitly defined return expected, that is, as a form of generalized exchange (Sahlins 1965a:147). Survival demanded that this be so. Failure to share food was considered a most heinous crime. Yet, when food shortages became critical, there were occasions when self-interest threatened even the family structure. In times of extreme duress, family members would frequently abandon one another, or resort to the ultimate subsistence recourse—cannibalism. For example, in 1831, McKenzie reported that an Indian known as "Stump has Eaten his winter hunt & what is more awful & revolting to humanity, that this Indian has Killed his poor old Mother! & devoured her!!!" (HBC Arch B107/a/10).

Again in 1846, when a measles epidemic struck Lac Seul, many Indians abandoned their relatives to survive as best they could. Mc-Kenzie gives some vivid descriptions: "Aye the Indians are going off as many as can—leaving many at the point of death—Sons leaving

their Fathers and Mothers—brothers leaving brothers—careless
whether they ever see them again . . ." (HBC Arch B107/a/25). Such
examples bring to mind the case of the IK (Turnbull 1972), who
evidently exhibited similar behavioral patterns under comparable conditions of deprivation.

Although starvation often forced Indians to adopt extreme measures to ensure personal survival, deprivation could at times be temporarily overcome by taking refuge at the trading post. As McKenzie
reported in 1831: "Young Tripie came to join his father . . . He
parted . . . some time ago—being too many to live at one place—we
have no less than 12 of the Tripies to feed now to whom I serve out
daily Rations of fish & potatoes" (HBC Arch B107/a/9). By spring the
post had been depleted of food, and young Tripie, although still starving, presented McKenzie with the flesh of a beaver. McKenzie added
that "[H]e did not forget that he owed his life to this house the greatest part of the winter." The journals indicate that food was often voluntarily shared with traders as well as kinsmen, if available, although
traders had generally adopted a policy of paying for it. In turn, Indians expected to be fed in times of scarcity provided that they had
the strength to reach the post to get food donations.

In the past, anthropologists have discussed social atomism in terms
of individualistic patterns of proprietorship and self-sufficiency. However, when viewed in terms of patterns of production and reciprocity,
it may in the future be possible to measure the degree to which
atomism is present, and thereby acquire more precise conceptual re-
finement. The extent of atomism at a given time will fluctuate in accordance with the conditions for existence. As Laughlin (1974b:
382–83) has argued, reciprocity (one measure of atomism) exhibits
"a periodic centrifugal/centripetal fluctuation of the inner bounds of
negative reciprocity." He calls this the "accordion effect" of negative
reciprocity "which forms a constantly fluctuating and systematic adaptation of a society to the environmental conditions." In sum, atomism may not exist in perpetuity: "Rather, socioeconomic relations
change in a systematic and predictable fashion in order that the society can adapt to shifting ecological and external social conditions"
(Laughlin 1974b:392). Adaptation, then, involves both internal and

external alterations: internal when pertaining to shifts in the nature of social relations, and external when concerned with variations in exploitive activities.

One biological consequence of the shift from large game hunting to the intensification of efforts on small non-migratory fauna was an evident population growth during the nineteenth century. In the face of recurring episodes of extreme deprivation, this, at first, would seem to be contradictory. Nevertheless, demographic materials from all trading post records throughout the Ojibwa area attest to it. For example, the Lac Seul Indian population of 1838, according to Mc-Kenzie had been "greatly on the increase since 1821" (HBC Arch B107/a/16). Between 1829 and 1838, it had increased from 219 to 339 persons. Similarly, the population dependent upon the Osnaburgh House post grew from about 200 in 1825 to 474 persons in 1881 (Bishop 1974:157).

It is an accepted principle that "equilibrium systems regulate population density below the carrying capacity of the environment" (Binford 1968:328). Equilibrium, it should be stressed, does not refer to a constancy in the numbers of persons, but rather to a balanced relationship between the population and its basic resources. Population growth can be caused by a number of factors. In the case of the Northern Ojibwa, demographic changes seem to have been primarily due to an increase in labor input and to social reorganization for subsistence ends (cf. Dumond 1972b:325–326; Lee 1972:338).

With respect to the labor input, there can be no question that more effort had to be put into survival activities as large game diminished in numbers and eventually disappeared. Traders like McKenzie were aware of the marked contrast with earlier conditions: "The Indian life is become a most miserable life . . . the procuring of the means of existence keeps the very best Indian in constant employment every day of the year & not to live as Indians were want [sic] to live 20 years ago but merely to exist" (McKenzie 1831; HBC Arch B107/e/4). Every capable Indian regardless of age and sex was now employed in the food quest rather than merely the adult hunters and the women who set nets and snares as was the case prior to the disaster. The labor input was thus considerably higher in relation to the productive results. Nevertheless, except during winters of extreme scarcity, efforts generally proved sufficient to maintain the now scattered population despite a rather dull and arduous life style.

The social reorganization for subsistence requirements involving small game and fur bearers required separation of family units for much of the year. The disappearance of big animals resulted in the fission of former hunting groups into family units which dispersed to areas of food and furs. Trapping and hare snaring, as previously stated, demanded less mobility and hence less territory than big game hunting. Where livelihood on moose and caribou required that hunting groups move frequently and over extensive regions, the exploitation of small fauna meant that a greater number of smaller units could survive provided that they were scattered over the country. Thus, for example, a territory of 3,000 square miles might support a group of 30 persons, 10 of whom are, as big game hunters, the food getters. In contrast, that same 3,000 square miles would be capable of supporting, say, three extended family units of 15 persons each (about 45 people altogether) if subsistence is on small nonmigratory fauna such as hare and fish.

The fact that families scattered during the harsh winter months to exploit given regions does not mean, however, that they necessarily returned to exactly the same location from year to year. Where they might settle was largely a function of resource abundance and location. Usually several related families, upon leaving the trading post for the winter, would travel to a relatively permanent base camp located near strategic resources on a water route. Rogers and Black (1976) have recently termed this the "home base" model which they relate to survival strategies among the Weagmow Ojibwa. It was from these base camps that individual families radiated out to exploit their territories. The degree of permanency of residence at a base camp during any given winter was a function of resource availability. In extremely good years (which were comparatively rare) several households might winter together at a camp except for brief periods when individual families scattered to satellite settlements for purposes of trapping and foraging. In contrast, during lean winters, the family groups were forced to remain apart, each striving to stave off starvation. The survival alternatives were thus more limited than in good years. A similar dichotomy existed between general summer abundance and winter scarcity. As Rogers and Black put it, the subsistence strategy "must allow for stretching tight during hard periods—so that even with sophisticated evaluation of a depth of environmental knowledge, the last contingency plan may be the only option if one is to survive—it also allows for contraction during easier times."

The restructuring of social relations to accommodate environmental shifts involved a balance among the satisfaction of material requirements, affective social relationships, and the expenditure of efforts. This balance was achieved by altering modes of production and reciprocity to minimize relative deprivation (cf. Dumond 1972a: 288–89). It also involved considerable individual social mobility from group to group, a practice related to the maintenance of effective and efficient group size under conditions of fluctuating and periodic resource scarcity. At another level, the new adaptation entailed a cognitive reorientation, one tailored to survival needs involving the new and relatively permanent situation of deprivation where resources both in the natural environment and obtainable from the store were in finite quantities. Putting it another way, Northern Ojibwa social structure was more expendable than human lives. When viewed from this perspective, the Northern Ojibwa of mid-nineteenth century were not poorly adapted. Indeed, they demonstrated an ability to maximize survival potential by sociocultural readjustment in a poor environment. Thus, despite occurrences of starvation, exposure, disease, and cannibalism, all of which operated to retard the rate of growth, the fact of cultural viability is confirmed by an evident population growth.

SUMMARY AND CONCLUSIONS

After the fur trade first reached the Ojibwa during the early seventeenth century, it led rapidly to alterations in socioeconomic arrangements. In certain respects, the situation parallels that of Northwest Coast tribes where an influx of quantities of trade goods led to changes in the structure and function of the potlatch. For them and for the Ojibwa, ceremonials grew in scope and became a primary means of status aggrandizement for chiefs and their bands through the redistribution of large quantities of furs and European goods. So important had these trade materials become, both for social and economic reasons, that the Ojibwa expanded into new ecological niches to acquire them. This expansion resulted in rivalries and physical conflicts with other tribes and sometimes between different Ojibwa bands.

In their new northern habitat, Indians engaged in an almost unrestricted slaughter of animals to supply competing traders. The competitive nature of the fur trade itself fostered dishonesty (at least from the traders' point of view). Indeed, it may be postulated that the art of playing off competing traders against each other to acquire extra debts was itself a channel to status enhancement. At the same time, these very trade goods had by the late eighteenth century totally replaced many items of aboriginal manufacture. Yet it was not the trade goods alone that led to the dependence of Indians, since, prior to 1821, greater quantities were received than for several decades thereafter. It was only after big animals and beaver became depleted and trade rivalry ended that a state of total dependence was reached. As beaver declined, Indians found it increasingly difficult to procure sufficient quantities to obtain trade supplies. Simultaneously, however, as big game grew scarce, the survival value of fur bearers increased. Further, the decline of large game also meant that more time had to be devoted to hunting them until, finally, the law of diminishing returns in regard to the amount of effort spent in searching for them exceeded the limits of survival. At this juncture, survival requirements forced the Ojibwa to adapt their subsistence technique to taking hare and fish. However, neither these resources nor the requirements of trapping allowed for the maintenance of large cohesive hunting groups characteristic of former years. Hence, the relationship with an altered environment and external conditions of trade tended to mold the nature of social groups while setting limits on their size and the extent of territory which they could effectively exploit. It also destroyed the functional basis of their unilineal organization.

The Ojibwa case, then, is additional support for Laughlin's hypothesis that any society with a normative unilineal-residence rule faced with a deteriorating economic situation where goods become limited in type and quantity "will develop a tendency to become increasingly more randomized in relation to directionality of descent" (1974a:212). That is, the ecological pressures for flexibility produced groupings whose structure became increasingly bilateral. It is important to note, however, that the principle of complementary filiation (Fortes 1969:98, 253–54) was retained through the cognitive and behavioral distinctions between non-kin (including cross-cousins) and kin or cognatic relatives.

In short, Ojibwa social structure underwent adaptive shifts in response to fluctuations in the nature and availability of resources. Both the modes of production involving trapping and foraging along with exchange networks shifted accordingly. Production, because of the nature of the resources exploited, became highly individualistic, while exchanges within the Ojibwa system became largely limited to foods shared among close kin or relatives. In these respects Ojibwa society can be called atomistic. Basic exchanges from the perspective of survival also involved those between families and the trading post. Rephrasing this in terms of maximization theory, as Martin has recently done in her discussion of exchange-dependent foragers: "The act of exchange . . . became a resource in itself, to be effectively exploited for the acquisition of subsistence goods" (Martin 1974:26).

In the cognitive realm, there was a short period during the disaster when the Ojibwa failed to adequately integrate their perceptual structuring of reality with the operational realities of the environment. Some died as a result. But the majority were able to synchronize their "operational" and "cognized" environments and to establish diaphatic equilibration (see article 1). They were able to suppress overt expressions, especially aggressive ones, while at the same time allowing for much permissiveness. With the disappearance of any higher political authority and where survival required both cooperation and individualism, such cognitive reorientations were highly adaptive (see also Brady, article 9). A contingency mechanism employed in the absence of physical force was witchcraft, which, judging by the historical evidence, became an important means of social control during the nineteenth century. There can be no doubt that deprivation and stress, at times, were extreme. Yet the Ojibwa, faced with the need to adapt to a situation where the immediate reward was only survival, showed flexibility in altering subsistence style, organizational networks, and cultural motifs so as not merely to exist, but through efficient ecological adaptation, to devise new adaptive strategies that would allow the population to grow.

In sum, the Ojibwa had readjusted their adaptive strategies to conform with survival requirements. Although at first several changes required the advice of traders since they went against traditional norms, the ultimate decision-making lay with the Ojibwa. In most cases, they chose survival under deprived conditions over extinction.

NOTES

1. Most of the data pertaining to the nineteenth-century Northern Ojibwa were obtained from the Archives of the Hudson's Bay Company. In that regard, I thank the Governor and Committee of the Hudson's Bay Company for permission to view and cite from their archival materials. The research for this paper was sponsored by grants from the National Museum of Man and from the State University of New York Research Foundation.

Survival or Extinction: Reflections on the Problem of Famine in Tsimshian and Kaguru Mythology

John J. Cove

Myth is the mode, par excellence, for the storage and transmission of vicarious experience in a society's culture pool (see Laughlin and Cove 1977). In the following article, John Cove argues that Tsimshian and Kaguru myths constitute a valid source of information on solutions to environmental problems such as famine, not only for the anthropologist but for the people who tell and hear them. Diaphasis in social action in a situation of recurrent environmental stress requires cognition of the recurrence, its potential effects, and the range of appropriate alternatives for behavior. Optimal adaptation entails such conceptualization in order to remove much of the superoptimal noxity that derives from intense environmental disruptions. Myth serves as an important part of the feed-forward process in adaptation by encoding, storing, and transmitting knowledge of potentially dangerous environmental events to subsequent generations. Without it, infrequent but recurrent deprivation in a particular environment would appear as a discontinuous set of disasters, each calling for novel resolutions to escalated levels of environmental noxity. It is thereby difficult to overestimate the importance of the transgenerational continuity encapsulated by mythology. The information so encoded may be highly symbolic and even focused primarily on the "inappropriate" actions of the past under specified conditions. But all such information adds to the cognitive wherewithal that subsequent generations may bring to bear in sorting out the realities of their own environmental difficulties. In fact, mythology is such an integral and strategic element in adaptive infrastructures that, should it be replaced by religious material alien to the operational environment with which the traditional material is isomorphic, the cornerstone of adaptive diaphasis may be removed for that population.

Without some functional substitute through innovation or acculturation, such changes can be intensely maladaptive.

> And the whole congregation of the people of Israel mur-
> mured against Moses and Aaron in the wilderness, and
> said unto them, "Would that we had died by the hand of
> the Lord in the Land of Egypt, when we sat by the fleshpots
> and ate bread to the full; for you have brought us out into
> this wilderness to kill the whole assembly with hunger"
> (Exodus 16:2–3).

This article examines some important relationships between famine mythology and population survival in Tsimshian and Kaguru culture. It is argued that myths constitute a valid source of information on solutions to environmental problems such as famine, not only for the anthropologist, but for the people who tell and hear them.

My initial interest in the relation between myth and famine came about through an examination of the literature on resource variation on the Northwest Coast. It was once assumed that this culture area thrived on a surplus of resources which permitted population densi-ties and complexity of social organization unknown to other hunters and gatherers (Codere 1950:4–5, 63–64; Ford 1941:8). More re-cently, ecologically oriented anthropologists have concluded that "the population lived sufficiently close to the margins of subsistence so that variations in productivity which fell below normal could threaten parts of the population with famine and death from starvation" (Pid-docke 1965:248).

One of the difficulties with such arguments is the shortage of pre-contact data on Northwest Coast subsistence. Both Piddocke (1965:248) and Suttles (1968a:59) use the existence of famine themes in myth as support for their contention that starvation was a problem for human populations in this area. However, neither goes beyond the mention of famine in myth to determine if it provides any evidence regarding the kinds of indigenous solutions employed.

Ecological theorists have posited two competing explanations for how the population survived periods of scarcity. Both assume the functional importance of redistribution, although one stresses the redistribution of resources and the other of labor.[1]

The coastal tribes depend largely on marine resources, many of which are migratory. Salmon, for example, are available for only a few months each year, and even then the runs tend to be concentrated and sporadic. The quantities present in any given year are contingent in part on the number spawned three to five years earlier that managed to reach maturity. Variations in rainfall, temperature, and the frequency of natural disasters such as forest fires can lead to major differences in the size of annual runs. Such annual fluctuations tend to have relatively localized effects, typically confined to a single species of salmon and a few spawning rivers. Since no precontact population depended exclusively on one resource for subsistence, it is unlikely that famine occurred more than once in a generation (Suttles 1966:60).

Piddocke (1965), Suttles (1960, 1968a, 1968b) and Vayda (1961) have argued that groups experiencing food shortages could exchange wealth for food with groups who had a surplus. For that solution to be viable over the long run, some mechanism was required to ensure that each group had surplus wealth and that some groups had surplus food. Potlatching ensured that accumulated wealth was redistributed and that over-production was motivated by institutionalizing competition for prestige.

The second theory is that some production units at a point in time could have too many people for existing resources, while others have too few in terms of needed labor (Adams 1973:87–106; Ruddell 1973). This situation could occur as a result of either resource variations or demographic imbalances. In either case, redistributing people to more abundant resource areas might provide an effective solution.[2]

MYTHOLOGY AS A DATA SOURCE

The notion of using myth as a data source about traditional culture is not a new one. Malinowski (1962) was one of the first to point out the importance of myth for understanding social life. Boas (1916, 1935) and Erlich (1937) used myth to reconstruct culture. The validity of mythological descriptions has been queried, however, by later anthropologists. Köngäs Maranda (1973:9) and Simmons (1961:137–39) state that the intended audience has no need or interest in being presented with the details of their everyday life; hence mythological descriptions will inevitably be incomplete. Lessa (1966:86) feels that myths may contain many elements that are alien or imaginary, which leads to distortions of reality. Lévi-Strauss (1967:29–30) has raised the problem of mythic thought itself, which can transform the reality upon which it reflects.

If myth is to be used as a source of information on native solutions to famine, these difficulties must somehow be overcome.[3] In terms of the incompleteness of mythological description, it would only become critical if the anthropologist's interests were different from the native's. Since intensive threats to survival are not an everyday experience in most cultures, it is likely that myth would more fully elaborate on such a problem. Similarly, it is unlikely that any group would borrow the theme of famine from another, unless the experience was common.

The remaining difficulty is dealing with what may be called "plays of the imagination," or transformations of mythic thought. Lévi-Strauss (1967:30) states that divergences from reality portrayed in myth exist precisely to show that such divergences are socially "untenable." In other words, myths explore the potentialities of social life and present alternatives which are believed to be inherent in those situations. Some possible resolutions may be disruptive to the social order, and hence must be rejected. Since famine is a condition which itself is "untenable," I assume that the alternatives presented are potentially practical solutions rather than flights of fantasy. Using Boas (1916:393), I also assume that the course of action in myth is sanctioned in the same way as in everyday life. Hence, what the natives view as viable and appropriate answers to the problem of famine can be determined by the consequences of action.[4]

A number of Tsimshian myths dealing with famine are presented and analyzed in the following section, revealing a range of solutions that the Tsimshian traditionally envisaged and considered valid.

These myths and their properties are then compared to the theories of redistribution previously outlined. The results confirm the notion that mythology itself may have significant pro-survival value (see Laughlin and Brady, article 1).

TSIMSHIAN REFLECTIONS ON FAMINE

The available corpus of Tsimshian myths gives us nine which are concerned to some extent with the problem of famine. I shall recount them in some detail first and then summarize their importance for the present thesis:

1. *The Spider and the Widow's Daughter* (Boas 1916:158–60)
   Famine was common in winter because the people lacked nets. When famine occurred, the rich would abandon the poor and leave the village. It once happened that a widow and her daughter living in the mother's brother's village were left behind. They in turn left the village and the widow attempted to catch salmon to keep her daughter alive. She was unsuccessful. While the widow was away fishing, a stranger came and slept with the daughter. The next day he showed them how to make nets, and they caught many salmon. After many huts were full of food he left for his own village, taking the daughter with him.
   The rich returned to their village and buried their poor relatives. Later the widow returned, but did not tell anyone what had happened. The next winter she gave salmon to the village, and soon became famous. Other villages came to her to buy salmon, and as a result the widow became wealthy.
   At the stranger's village the widow's daughter discovered that her husband was a spider. She was warned not to eat their food if she wanted to remain human. The spiders showed her how to make different kinds of nets, and in the following summer she returned to her mother. This was how the people learned to make nets.

2. *Local Winter in G.it-O!A.DĀ* (Boas 1916:250–51)
   Because of a blizzard, people were unable to get food. Soon only a prince and his wife and child were left alive. When their food was gone, the child died due to its mother's lack of milk. A bluejay gave the woman some elderberries which she shared

with her husband. They traveled to a place of summer; all the
while the prince was suckled by his wife. At this new place, he
made a fish trap, and his wife caught trout. She continued to
suckle him until his strength returned. They made larger traps
to catch salmon. Finally they went downstream to a different
location and settled.

3. *The Young Chief Who Married His Cousin* (Boas 1916:
238–43)

A young girl married a supernatural being and they had a
son. The supernatural being allowed the girl to spend a year
with her father's people. The grandfather gave a great feast in
honor of his grandson. As the child grew up he became a great
hunter and also gave greater feasts. When his grandmother
died, he with his grandfather and mother left the village.

The supernatural being brought them food, and soon they
had houses full. At the same time many people in the village
died because they had no food. The old chief returned and offered them food from his camp. They accepted and presented
him with gifts. The old chief then gave a great feast for all the
peoples and gave his name to his grandson. A little later the old
chief died and his grandson gave a great feast to all the tribes.
He became rich because of his father's help, and was famous
among all the peoples.

4. *The Four Chiefs and Chief Grizzly Bear* (Boas 1916:292–95)

There were four brothers who were chiefs. A starving man
came to their village during a winter famine. The three eldest
brothers refused the stranger food, but the fourth had pity and
gave him the last of his food. The next day the stranger presented him with many gifts. Due to them the youngest chief became a successful hunter and supported the village. The
villagers presented the youngest chief with many gifts. By his
generosity and feasting, he became a famous chief.

5. *Little Eagle* (Boas 1902:169–87)

A prince fed salmon caught by his father's people to the eagles. When winter came, food was scarce and the chief ordered
everyone to move. The prince, his grandmother, and a slave
were left behind. The eagles brought them food in repayment
for the prince's generosity.

His father and the other villagers were starving. The chief

sent men to find his son. The prince fed them but asked them not to tell his father that he was alive. The chief found out, however, and they all returned to the village. At first the son would not let them land, but then became ashamed and fed them. The prince married and became a great chief. When his parents died, he gave great potlatches.

6. *The Grizzly Bear* (Boas 1902:201–10)

A chief had four sons. One winter the people had no food. Three of the sons were killed by a grizzly bear while out hunting. The fourth went to look for them and was mistaken by the bear for her husband. They married, and the youngest brother remained with the bear for many years.

The prince became homesick for his people, and the bear agreed to accompany him to his village. At first the people were afraid. She helped them get food, and was scolded by one young man for feeding them with excrement. In anger she killed the man and left the village. Her husband followed, and after warning him to go back, killed him.

7. *Asi-hwîl* (Boas 1902:225–29)

The people of two villages were starving. Sisters, living in different villages, decided to go visit the other and met on the way. Each had a little food which they shared. That night a man appeared and slept with one of the sisters. He got food for them.

The sister gave birth to a son. When the sisters' brother came looking for them the man hid. After they left he returned to the camp and said it was time to separate. The sisters with the boy returned to their village, and a great potlatch was given for the boy.

8. *The Story of Asdi-wal* (Boas 1912:71–147)

In winter a famine occurred. A mother and daughter living in different villages lost their husbands, and went in search for each other. They met between the two towns and shared a rotten berry. That night a man came to their camp and slept with the daughter, and left in the morning.

The stranger gave the daughter help in finding food and returned to their camp. They married and soon after had a son. The father then disappeared. All the people heard of their great fortune in finding food. They bought meat from them, and soon the grandmother, daughter, and son were wealthy. When the grandmother died, the daughter gave a great potlatch to all the people. The boy was given a name, and they returned to her village.

9. *The Story of Gunaxnesēmg⁰a'd* (Boas 1912:147–91)

A young woman was taken by bears to live in their village. She married one of them, but was homesick for her people and so escaped. She was taken to safety by a man after she promised to marry him. They had a son, though the woman was still homesick. The man agreed to let her and their son leave, and gave her hunting equipment for their son.

She returned to find her parents dead from grief. Her brothers refused to let her live with them, with the exception of the youngest. She and her child lived with him, although in the corner of the house with the poor people. One winter a famine occurred and the people died of starvation. The son called his friends in the village together and they went hunting for food. The mother gave him the equipment presented by his father. He was successful, and brought back food to the village and gave it to the people. Then his mother sold meat to those who were starving. She gave a potlatch and the boy received his name. The prince wished to marry the daughter of an uncle but he refused; so the prince and his cousin escaped from the village to marry and did not return.

One striking feature of these myths is that the cause of famine is never social.[5] In all but two of them, winter is presented as a contributing factor, and in one the absence of technology is mentioned. This fits the seasonal character of Tsimshian exploitation, in which spring and summer are the major periods. Winter is defined as the time for village aggregation and ceremonial activity. In those months, food catches may be depleted; and if weather conditions are unfavorable, it may be impossible to hunt or fish.

A second feature is the use of characters, which seems to direct the myths to the attention of specific types of individuals. Four of the myths appear to speak to chiefs, six to wives, six to sons, two to husbands, and two to women's brothers. To the larger audience, these characters represent marriage, descent, residence, and authority as principles by which both solutions and concomitant problems emerge. With respect to those in authority, the message is generosity.

Since Tsimshian chiefs control the means of production, and hence access to resources for members of their respective houses, their position in times of famine would be critical to group survival. Given the problems of famine, and tempered by certain social realities, one tendency would be for individual survival to take precedence over collective responsibility (see Laughlin and Brady, article 1). In myths 1, 5, and 9 individualism is shown to be unsuccessful in the long run. The abandonment of dependents is presented as ultimately detrimental by inverting the relationship and making the chiefs' survival contingent on the generosity of those who had initially been left behind or unaccepted. These myths deny the apparent asymmetry of authority relations and acknowledge the reciprocal character of dependency. In myth 5 generosity is extended to strangers, who lie outside a chief's sphere of authority. In every case, those who are generous are rewarded through increased wealth and prestige. Generosity is shown to be equal in importance to control over resources as a base for power.[6]

If the means for survival cannot be found within a group, its members must go outside. Affinal relations provide a basis for the second alternative. Since the Tsimshian are exogamous and matrilineal, emphasis is placed on support received from husbands of a clan's women. Only in myths 2 and 6 is support provided directly by the woman, and that is restricted to their husbands. Myth 5 is the only instance of a son helping his father's clan. In myths 1, 3, 7, 8, and 9 the support given by men to their wives' clans is restricted in type and works through an intermediary. It is not food which is given but the means of production. This is not given directly to the clan but to either the wives or the sons. Members of the same clan, marriage partners, and strangers can be given food; but members of a clan cannot receive it from non-members.

This oblique recognition of survival through affinal relations indicates that the Tsimshian recognize inherent strains that could be intensified through dependency of this kind. In myths 7 and 8 the potential conflict between affinal and descent ties are brought out. After their husbands die, women of the same clan, in one case sisters and in the other a mother and daughter, attempt to find support through a reestablishment of relations. Their failure to provide food for each other, subsequent salvation through remarriage, and final separation from their husbands in favor of their brothers expresses this tension.

In myths 1, 6, 7, 8, and 9 an additional dimension of that tension is expressed. In addition to matrilineal descent, the Tsimshian have avunculocal residence and patrilateral cross-cousin marriage.[7] This means that the wife resides in her husband's clan's territory. In myths 1, 7, 8, and 9 the wife feels homesickness and returns to her people unaccompanied by the husband. In myth 6 it is the husband who is residing inappropriately and it is he who wants to return, again inappropriately, to his father's village.[8] The woman's action of accompanying the prince back to his territory ultimately leads to hostilities and the death of the husband.

The tension shown in myths 5 and 6 between father and son can also be understood as a consequence of residence rule and descent rule. The son, too, lives in the wrong place until marriage, and thereby has potentially conflicting sources of identity. The gifts from father to son at their time of separation in myths 7, 8, and 9 recognize this bond. To remain with one's father's clan is to take his authority and at the same time deny one's descent and obligations to one's mother's clan. In myths 1 and 9, the mother's brother is warned that his survival may depend on his sister and her offspring, and that marriage and change in residence do not nullify clan obligations.

If these mythological explorations are compared with the competing theories of redistribution, some interesting similarities occur. Although changes in membership are not explicitly mentioned, the notion of redistributing people is supported. For the Tsimshian, the production unit is the house, which is not a kinship unit although it includes members of the same clan. Each house is under the leadership of a chief; hence changes in allegiance need not involve a change in clan. In the myths it was argued that ability to provide food and generosity determined the prestige of a chief. In a number of the myths, gifts were given to generous providers, which can be viewed as an alliance, particularly since those gifts were used by the chiefs in potlatch.

In the case of the alternate theory, the evidence is more direct. The purchase of food by others is mentioned a number of times, and affinal ties provide one means of acquiring food during periods of scarcity. The only qualification is that there is no mention of purchasing food from affines, though that may be a function of wanting to recognize dependency only indirectly. Potlatch is also discussed as a means of converting wealth to prestige.

The analysis and comparison above show that both kinds of solutions may have been employed in pre-contact times. The redistribution of people would seem to be an appropriate internal solution to famine, and the exchange of wealth for food an appropriate external solution. More importantly, the myths recount dangers with either alternative. Famine is not only a threat to the survival of a population; it is also a threat to the existing social order. It demands new courses of action, all of which are potentially disruptive. The appropriate solution is one which permits a population to survive and at the same time does not destroy the social framework. In the following section, the analysis of a Kaguru famine myth attempts to determine if the same kind of rational, mythic solution exists in a different culture.

A KAGURU REFLECTION ON FAMINE

The Kaguru are sedentary agriculturalists living in lowland, mountain, and plateau areas of eastern Tanzania (Beidelman 1967:38–41). As with the Tsimshian, Kaguru experience famine infrequently because of variation in rainfall (see Laughlin, article 3) which can produce droughts or flooding (Beidelman 1963:57; 1967:39). A Kaguru myth entitled "Hyena and Rabbit" explores the condition of famine (Beidelman 1961a:61–74):

> There was a famine in the land. Rabbit and his uncle Hyena come together to discuss how they will survive. Rabbit suggests selling their mothers, but Hyena rejects the idea in favor of killing them and selling their meat.
> Rabbit reluctantly agrees, and Hyena kills his mother. Rabbit postpones doing so, and finally is able to substitute the meat of a bushbuck. Hyena still needs food, and begs Rabbit for more. Rabbit refuses, and his uncle dies of starvation. Rabbit takes his mother out of hiding and they live peacefully.

The myth begins with the problem of who shall survive. The relationship between Hyena and Rabbit is one of authority, which fits the traditional power structure of Kaguru in which authority is passed down matrilineally from uncle to sister's son (Beidelman 1963:59). The Hyena is also a symbol of witchcraft (Beidelman 1963:64). In combination these properties represent authority as immoral and hint that the uncle may have been responsible for the famine, since drought is within a witch's power (Beidelman 1963:63).

The solutions given by the two characters also comment on the immorality of authority. Rabbit wants to sell their mothers so that Rabbit and Hyena can buy food. Although he is the subordinate, Rabbit's idea is moral, since all the members of the clan can survive. His alternative permits the mothers to be bought back when conditions improve, which would reconstitute the clan in original form (Beidelman 1961a:61).

Hyena's solution is immoral, in that survival would be based on the death of others and the permanent dissolution of the clan, which is matrilineally based. By treating his mother as food, Hyena is stating that she is an animal and implicitly resorting to cannibalism—additional characteristics of a witch (Beidelman 1967:67).

Hyena's rejection of his nephew's suggestion is an assertion of his authority and concern with his own survival. Rabbit appropriately obeys his uncle by not selling his mother and providing him with an equivalent in bushbuck meat. The substitution is also appropriate, since the Kaguru regard wild animals as female and witches treat animals as human (Beidelman 1961b:256; 1963:67). Through that substitution, Rabbit is able to fulfill his responsibilities to his uncle and to his lineage.

The remainder of the myth is an inversion of that authority relation and a rejection of Hyena's solution. By killing his mother and wanting Rabbit to kill his sister, Hyena denies the basis on which his authority in the clan rests. When Hyena asks for more food after being given the bushbuck meat, he addresses Rabbit as "sir" and "uncle," which is a reversal of their earlier positions. Rabbit does not provide him with food, since Hyena has removed himself from the lineage. Hyena's solution is shown to be ineffective in that he dies of starvation after receiving the bushbuck substitute.

In general, this myth reveals themes similar to those of the Tsimshian. Emphasis is placed on authority relations and the need for collective orientations. A temporary redistribution of people is presented as an alternative. Similarly, the Kaguru myth is equally concerned with the problem of maintaining social order and the return to a normal state when conditions improve.

The commonality of issues addressed by myths from two different cultures with different ecological bases argues that myth may be a powerful survival technique in itself. We may now examine the survival value of myth in more general terms.

MYTH AND SURVIVAL

As Laughlin and d'Aquili (1975) have argued, one of the functions of myth is the storage and transmission of information. This function is critical to human survival insofar as man can learn vicariously from past experience, avoiding many of the risks encountered by the original participants. For conditions such as famine, which may be very infrequent, there is a possibility that successful solutions might be lost and therefore have to be rediscovered.

Myth, however, is more than a charter for action. It not only presents solutions that others have discovered but explores alternatives. This exploration, too, is critical in that solutions to problems such as famine may have unrecognized consequences for the social order. Myth thereby presents to people a series of cultural experiments, some of which may be unsuccessful. By doing so, it makes explicit the dangers of inappropriate means of coping with newly faced exigencies. When both successful and unsuccessful courses of action are made available, the temptation to try unstated avenues is avoided.

Myth is the ideal storage facility for such information. Its sacred character ensures that it will be preserved and transmitted. In addition, the use of themes such as authority relations, marriage, and descent are of sufficient general interest that they have timeless relevance which transcends varying conditions of social life. Through the use of symbolic language, a multiplicity of messages can be stored within a single myth. Depending on the particular context, different relations and themes may be emphasized or received by the intended audience. That audience is a culture's future members, and the messages come from the past. What is learned at a point in time is projected into the future through myth and is there to be drawn upon when needed.

The structure and function of myth therefore can have high pro-survival value. Myth constitutes, in part, a set of proven recipes whose validity is demonstrated through contrasts and consequences. It is a storehouse of vicarious experience, both positive and negative, a legacy from the past which can help those in the present have a future.

NOTES

1. Adams (1973:90) feels that famine in myth may be more an idiom for legitimizing authority than a threat to survival.

2. The questions of scarcity and redistribution of labor have tended to be dealt with as if the resources alone were the determining factor. It is more conceivable that it is the available resources which set the minimum limits and technology/labor the maximum. Given highly concentrated and temporally separated runs of different species of salmon, potlatch may not be important motivationally. It is more likely that a group will catch the maximum at time 1 in anticapation of poor runs at times 2 or 3. The decision to underproduce may be relevant only for the last runs of the fishing season. Even here, preference for variety in diet and knowledge that other groups have done less well may lead to maximizing catch. Similarly, the technology may set limits on the maximum labor requirements of any production unit rather than available resources. Given the lack of pre-contact data, a computer simulation may be the most feasible way of determining these limits.

3. For a more extensive discussion of reconstruction see Cove (1975b).

4. This criterion has been successfully employed by Ackerman (1975) in his re-analysis of The Story of Asdi-wal, which can usefully be compared to Lévi-Strauss's treatment (1967).

5. In Exodus, and in the Kaguru myth analyzed in this paper, social responsibility for famine is attributed to those in authority.

6. For a detailed analysis of a single Tsimshian myth dealing with strains in authority relations see Cove (1975b).

7. This position is at odds with most discussions of Tsimshian social organization and was first suggested by Ackerman (1975). His arguments for these rules are sufficiently cogent to make them the likely ones in pre-contact times.

8. The grizzly in this myth can be understood as a clan emblem (Boas 1916:505).

Stability and Change:
Wherewithal for Survival
on a Coral Island

Ivan A. Brady

The importance of studying the interrelationships between environmental stress, adaptive infrastructures, and cross-cultural influences has surfaced in various ways as a common theme in previous articles. The following contribution by Ivan Brady brings this theme into central focus. Emphasizing the place of change processes in an "environment-choice" nexus, Brady analyzes some of the major cultural transformations that have altered the range of social action alternatives available to a small island population in responding to both physical and sociocultural changes in their environment. He argues that the transmission of information as culture-pool content across the cultural boundaries of Funafuti Island—accomplished largely by missionaries and a colonial government—has neither been presented nor responded to in any manner we might call purely random or fortuitous. Even with considerable dominance from outside sources, the ecological circumstances of the islanders appear to have selected for certain kinds of cultural acceptance and rejection patterns, and some of these transformations have carried a heavier functional load for adaptive consequences than others. It is common knowledge that a population's life style and life chances can be severely compromised by such imported influences, and some of the impact of missionaries and the colonial government on Funafuti's adaptive profile has in fact been negative. However, as this case illustrates, cross-cultural exchange may also result in an increase in adaptive diversity for either one or both of the populations involved, depending largely on the modes of acceptance and rejection engineered in the long run and on the kinds of environments in which the transformations occur.

Social science is replete with descriptions of sociocultural change.[1] Many studies focus on rural societies that have been influenced extensively by industrial nations (see Cochrane 1971; Brady and Isaac 1975). Histories are presented with varying attention to culture-trait combinations and developmental sequences as particular groups attempt to adjust their life circumstances to changing environments. However, the generative or enabling processes underlying such transformations, that is, "the mechanisms by which entities are transformed from one state to another" (Barnett 1965:223), are seldom specified or evaluated systematically (see Barnett 1965:221; Barth 1966:2ff.). Consequently, the analysis of process in studies of rapid change in human societies is not nearly so advanced as in, for example, the definition, measurement, and documentation of cultural evolution generally (see Naroll and Divale 1976:98).

This article examines a limited set of these problems. It is an analysis of the interplay of certain adaptive selection processes and social action patterns on Funafuti Atoll, a small coral island society in the British colony of Tuvalu (formerly the Ellice Islands), in western Polynesia.[2] The physical environment of this island is marked occasionally by such recursive phenomena as droughts, tropical cyclones, and tidal waves. The people of the island have also been confronted by diverse cross-cultural exposure for more than a century, representing environmental input that is largely progressive (see article 1). In an attempt to relate local effects to internal processes and external causes, and thereby to incorporate both microscopic and macroscopic dimensions in the analysis, the concept of an "environment-choice" nexus (see Britan and Denich 1976) is developed and applied to cultural and behavioral transformations across local group boundaries. This is the nexus of social action in which changes in culture content, social behaviors, and institutional alignments of personnel and resources emerge and are played out in relation to changing environmental stimuli.

The nature of "adaptive diversity" as an index of social forms, cultural complexity, and behavioral alternatives is also explored and related to the condition of ecological resiliency demonstrated by the islanders in their capacity to survive a recent tropical cyclone. In attempting to explain this apparent resiliency, it is suggested that, despite some negative consequences, Funafuti's adaptive diversity has been increased by local connections to Britain's industrial resources, and specifically by the mode through which these relationships have been incorporated into the islanders' culture pool (see Dunn 1970; Goodenough 1971). Some of the major psychological and sociocultural processes underlying these patterns are identified as part of the analysis.

ADAPTIVE DIVERSITY AND CROSS-CULTURAL CHANGE

Resource decimation and depopulation caused by droughts, tidal waves, and tropical cyclones are infrequent but recurrent facts of life for most of the coral island populations in the Pacific. Small land areas and limited natural resources frequently exacerbate the problem of survival in complex ways (see Wiens 1962). Successful adaptation requires specific and concerted responses to these conditions. It follows that an adaptive premium may be placed on sociocultural interdependencies and the internal organization of personnel and material resources in specific ways on coral islands, all other things being equal. But observers are by no means agreed on the particulars of these adaptive patterns, for the responses engineered by similar populations to comparable environmental stimuli are often divergent, at least on the surface (see Fosberg 1965; Brady 1976e; cf. Sahlins 1957, 1958).

While pertinent to the present article, an extended review of the literature on sociocultural and biological adaptation to island environments is precluded here by space limitations. It may be sufficient to point out that: (1) there is no simple relationship between the availability of food and human population densities on coral islands (Hainline 1965); (2) social stratification appears to be positively (if not causally) correlated with increased population *size* on islands and elsewhere (Orans 1966; Cancian 1976), although under certain circumstances in small island populations it appears to be inversely related to increased population *densities* (Hainline 1965); and (3) if coral island populations select for egalitarianism in social and economic relations as one possible response to environmental constraints, as Sahlins (1957, 1958) has argued,[3] that condition probably has never been realized at the total expense of more hierarchical forms of exchange in Micronesia and Polynesia.

Nevertheless, the widespread lateral organization of coral island societies on more or less egalitarian grounds has a compelling logic and perhaps a compelling adaptive selection process behind it. A premium placed on direct rather than hierarchical reciprocity (such as chiefly redistribution) ideally facilitates a relatively free flow of goods and services between any two groups or points on the island, with surplus resources gravitating to individuals and groups who are most in need of them *when* they are in need of them, hoarding strategies to the contrary notwithstanding (see article 1). Furthermore, the membership of every adult in each major type of socioeconomic group on the island ideally provides individual access to each type of resource exploited in the system, and it may do so in a manner that minimizes the need for intervening acts of exchange across group boundaries or through hierarchical flow in the event of shortages (see Sahlins 1957, 1958; cf. Sahlins 1972; Laughlin and Brady, article 1). The reciprocal flow of goods, foodstuffs, and services on the strength of widely calculated kinship, alliance, and community obligations is added survival insurance in that it potentially levels out production deficiencies in any of the groups so connected (see also Goodenough 1955). Similar benefits derive from extending the socioeconomic network over more than one island, each island then coming to the aid of others in need on the basis of shared kinship, political, and material bonds (see Schneider 1957; Alkire 1965; Lessa 1968; Mason 1968). Sahlins suggests that "the more diversified these organizations become, the better adapted is the group" (1958:236–37).

One potential line of diversification not considered by Sahlins, but that can be consistent with the adaptive principles above, is the extension of rural island subsistence and survival networks to include the industrial world and its resources. Where this occurs, it has usually been accomplished by colonial or missionary intervention, or both, rather than as a specific adaptive response to indigenous conditions. Either way, there is great potential for increasing local diversity in sociocultural interdependencies, personnel alignments, and resource options. A positive outcome on all fronts is by no means assured, however, as any quick glance at the ethnography of Third World peoples today will attest. Local access to strategic resources in the wider arena may be severely constrained by the power demands and political inclinations of the dominant group, and such byproducts of colonialism as selection for sedentary life in administrative centers may inadvertently undermine traditional alliances and trade networks that include other groups in the area (see Alkire 1965; Waddell 1975:268–69), among other possibilities.

Moreover, one of the first casualties in such liaisons is intergroup egalitarianism, at least on the cross-cultural level. Cross-cultural expansion inevitably leads to some inequality in the new arena. Where this is realized in an extreme form of imported dominance, the displacement of internal adaptive strategies may result in rapid homogenization in favor of the dominant group rather than in increased cross-cultural diversity in the culture pool of the subordinates. The adaptive success of the subordinate population thus depends on several critical factors. In addition to the inherent adaptive potential and diversity of the new traits themselves (see Brady and Isaac 1975; Waddell 1975; Naroll and Divale 1976), one of the most important factors to be considered is the manner in which imported features are synthesized in the local culture pool.

PROCESS, DIALECTIC, AND CROSS-CULTURAL SYNTHESIS

Regardless of the way one views culture or culture change, the problem of how cultural elements and behavior are synthesized invariably surfaces in extended analysis (see Brady and Isaac 1975). The processes that generate or enable such syntheses are elusive; they are neither simple in makeup nor plainly visible in action. In their purest form, processes are recurrent and distinguishable from the various effects they produce; they are also amenable to analytic descriptions independent of any conscious values held by the populations in which they operate (Barnett 1965:221ff.). The values themselves are cultural constructs and, as such, ultimately represent an arbitrary assignment of meaning to things, perceptions, and events that theoretically have nothing intrinsically to do with the symbolic load assigned to them (see Schneider 1968; Wagner 1975); they help to define "appropriate" behavior for individuals and otherwise facilitate the development of normative structures in the population's culture pool and cognized environment. They are critical components of adaptive infrastructures in the sense that the behaviors and social alignments coordinated by the population's culture pool must correspond approximately to the demands posed for the population by its operational environment; adaptation is otherwise impeded (see article 1).

A dialectic relationship is engaged in this manner between external stimuli that enter the reaction system of individuals, on the one hand, and the patterns of social action produced as responses, on the other. The psychological processes of cognitive structuring and symbolic interpretation of environmental stimuli represent intervening variables in the dialectic, insofar as they produce conscious charters for social action in the organism. Sociocultural processes activate these charters in the form of behavioral outputs; they are anchored in (but not limited to) language and exchange as modes of cultural expression and forms of social behavior, and they represent the primary means through which the system of symbols and meanings conceptually controlled by individuals is translated into wider networks of communication, institutionalized behavior, and social alignments. This is not to say that all conceptual material is ultimately given sociocultural expression, or that it necessarily is given sociocultural expression in precisely the same form in which it is conceptualized (see Piaget and Inhelder 1969). Furthermore, the same processes may underlie both stability and change in a population's adaptive profile over time, so that changes in behavioral patterns do not necessarily emanate from the alteration of cultural value systems or of the processes themselves, but from the alteration of action possibilities within an existing value system (Britan and Denich 1976:69). Traditional responses to recursive environmental change normally take the latter form.

Cast in this framework, the identification of processes that generate or facilitate the development of particular social forms, cultural complexes, and human behavior under changing environmental circumstances represents a sufficient level of explanation for those phenomena, at least on one level of ontological reality (see Barnett 1965; Barth 1966).[4] Such an approach demands an advance of theory over surface-level "facts" (see Lévi-Strauss 1967) and does not seek explanations of sociocultural change simply by juxtaposing sequences of historical patterns in particular populations. It also requires that the dialectic relationships that obtain between processes and their historical products be delineated, ideally connecting cause and effect in a context suitably specific for the identification of both (see Bee 1974:3ff.).

At the risk of oversimplifying the complexities of this problem, it seems clear that changes achieved through cross-cultural contact depend in part on the predominant mode through which new traits are introduced by the external group, and in part on the predominant mode of acceptance or rejection engineered by the internal group (see Barnett 1953). The results of each process can be influenced by the other, especially if the mode of introduction is militaristic and oppressive (see Dirks, article 5). Moreover, the linking networks in human societies are such that the effects of processual action in any sphere of behavior can produce a variety of complex feedback reactions in others connected to it (see Rappaport 1968). Acceptance and rejection patterns under cross-cultural circumstances are thereby pertinent not only to surface-level changes in behavior, but may also have sweeping ecological repercussions in the wider adaptive profile of the target group.

Ignoring for the moment the problem of rejecting certain imported influences, which is also a potentially important source of change (see Worsley 1957), two general possibilities emerge in terms of cross-cultural acceptance. The first is acceptance through direct substitution of the new traits for old ones. Beliefs, behaviors, artifacts, and sociocultural alignments acquired or produced in this manner are normally internalized in the public culture of the recipients and marked as "own" culture in the short run, although not necessarily in precisely the same context in which they are proposed. Some innovation and syncretism is inevitable in cross-cultural exchanges; one-to-one substitution is highly unlikely in terms of the meaning constructions placed upon imported traits, if not in terms of the forms and functions of the traits themselves (see Barnett 1953). The second possibility is acceptance through cross-cultural compartmentalization of some or all of the new order by differentiating it as "other" culture at the outset and maintaining the distinction in ideology and behavior as possible in the long run (see Barnett 1971; Brady 1975b; Singer 1975). This may result in a classic "bicultural" situation in which individuals participate in the imported cultural and social domains according to their skills, inclinations, opportunities, and abilities without necessarily sacrificing much of the integrity of their traditional culture pool (see McFee 1968).

In reality, some measure of both modes of acceptance is likely to be achieved. The psychological processes underlying the synthesis of diverse material of whatever type probably start with some form of compartmentalization as conceptual staging for comparative purposes. Similarly, conceptual compartmentalization may give way to direct substitution of newer forms for older ones in behavior in the short run, and what is overtly compartmentalized in sociocultural forms may give way to a new synthesis of old and new in the long run, amounting to substitution by displacement and innovation over time. But, where one type of acceptance prevails over the other in the extreme as sociocultural expressions, radically different results may obtain in the society's culture pool and adaptive profile. Cross-cultural compartmentalization is a transformation of expansion that theoretically produces greater diversity in the number and kinds of social alignments and action alternatives possible; direct substitution is a transformation of replacement that eliminates rather than adds to diversity in the same context, all other things (such as the inherent or acquired diversity of the imported traits) being equal. Each type of transformation may thereby carry a different functional load for ecological consequences in both the short and the long run. Furthermore, the changes induced by each process are not likely to be governed by purely random or fortuitous criteria. There are always certain features in the target groups that predispose them to accept or reject alien influences (Barnett 1953:313ff.).

Cross-cultural interference through migration and diffusion thus can reduce, regularize, or totally restructure the social action alternatives available to individuals and whole populations by substituting new elements for old ones in their traditional culture pools, by adding new elements at little immediate expense to the existence of older ones in a transformation of expansion, or by some synergetic and innovative measure of both processes. The mechanisms that select for acceptance and rejection of new culture content and social action patterns are most immediately cognitive and perceptual, and the stimuli are environmental in the widest sense of the term. The resultant changes are operationalized through sociocultural processes whose effects are expressed overtly through learned and shared behavior and perhaps covertly in terms of the psychobiological and physiological welfare of the population (see Gross and Underwood 1975; Cawte, article 4). Individuals enter environments structured by these and other variables as decision-makers and actors in a wider ecosystem. Their collective ability to matriculate in the existing environment and to respond successfully to subsequent fluctuations in it from a variety of physical and sociocultural stimuli can be taken as a crude index of the population's adaptive diversity, sophistication, and potential. The entire field can be conceptualized as an "environment-choice" nexus (Britan and Denich 1976).

AN ENVIRONMENT-CHOICE NEXUS

Social action alternatives emerge and are played out in a complexly structured field of social identities and relationships, institutional alignments of personnel and resources, technological capacities, and wider environmental constraints. These actions, in turn, help to define and perhaps reorganize the specific culture content and possible behavioral consequences that enter into future calculations for social action by the same individuals and all others in the population with whom the experiences are shared. Similarly, new options for social action may be engineered as innovations from existing or imported culture content. The analytic problem is to determine what kinds of environmental stimuli in particular sociocultural and ecological contexts are likely to select for change in the first place, and perhaps select for a preponderance of one form of change over others, and then to identify the key processes or combinations of processes that produce such patterns over time in that society's environment-choice nexus. Furthermore, as Britan and Denich (1976:57) argue, "To understand the sources of behavioral patterns, it is necessary to integrate the analysis of individual choice with an appraisal of the total environment that defines the nature of action possibilities" (cf. Leach 1960; Barth 1966).

Integrating the analysis of individual choice with an appraisal of the environment in which choices are made can be accomplished on various levels of specificity and analytic satisfaction. One alternative is to map the specific actions chosen by individuals in a mazeway of social action alternatives, and then to represent these data explicitly through flow charts (or comparable descriptions) of decision nodes that pertain to changing the actor's status from an antecedent to a consequent condition (see Howard 1963, 1970; Barth 1966; Keesing 1967, 1970). The rigor and detail potentially encompassed by these sorts of analyses are desirable components of an environment-choice scheme *if* the wider environmental conditions from which action possibilities derive are also specified and incorporated into the model (see Britan and Denich 1976:57).

Another alternative that sacrifices some elegance and detail control is to generalize beyond the flow of social actions taken by specific individuals or classes of individuals by concentrating instead on the collective patterns their choices represent. The wider environmental conditions from which action possibilities emanate must also be specified in this instance, of course, with full acknowledgement that the cognitive processing of information done by individuals as they monitor environmental stimuli for purposes of social action is a key element in understanding the broader forces of change at work in that system. The present study is cast in this framework, primarily because the data collected on Funafuti lend themselves to more efficient analysis in this form.

The analysis of an environment-choice nexus thus may proceed in broad terms by focusing on: (1) the ways in which external conditions are translated into human behavior; (2) how both local and supralocal conditions may impinge simultaneously upon the reaction system of a given population; (3) alterations in behavior produced by the collective interactions of individuals and groups in monitoring changing environmental stimuli; (4) the specific nature of those environmental stimuli; and (5) identification of the major processes that link these elements together and assist in their transformation through various stages of development. A temporal perspective must be added if these analytic dimensions are to be contextualized properly. The following historical overview of Funafuti's environment-choice nexus is calculated with these dimensions in mind.

FUNAFUTI: PATTERNS OF CHANGE AND STABILITY

Physical Environment: Funafuti is one of nine coral atolls and table reef islands in the Tuvalu chain. The total land surface of the group is about ten square miles, not all of which is suitable for the production of subsistence resources (see Brady 1970, 1974). Funafuti itself measures about one square mile in surface territory (map 9.1). The climate is maritime-tropical and is generally hospitable by coral island standards, that is, insofar as debilitating endemic diseases are few in number and the frequency of tropical cyclones and tidal waves is modest in comparison to some other atoll groups in the Pacific (e.g., in Micronesia). Rainfall averages about 120 inches per year for the group as a whole and is slightly higher than that on Funafuti. Extended droughts are uncommon, but not unknown (Roberts 1958:410–11). They are minimized today by the widespread use of rain barrels and cement cisterns as catchment devices. Funafuti is also one of two islands in the chain with a lagoon that can be navigated by large ships.[5] Its anchorage is highly favored by mariners who visit the area.

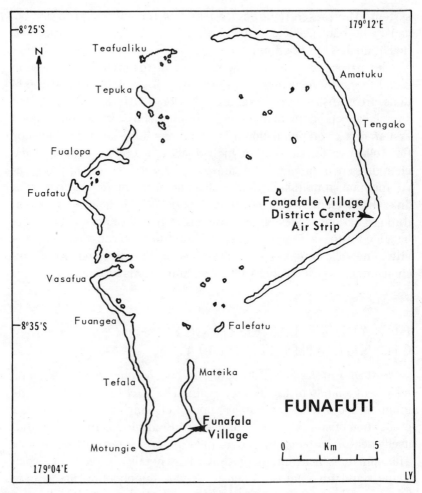

MAP 9.1 FUNAFUTI ISLAND

Population: The population in 1968 consisted of 830 persons, 30 percent or more of whom were non-indigenous to the island (Zwart and Groenewegen 1970:66).[6] Population densities are sufficient to support widespread notions of relative land hunger and stimulate competition for land resources in the community (see Brady 1970, 1974).[7] There are two villages of unequal size on the island. Fongafale represents the main settlement (map 9.1). Funafuti is the only island in the group with a functional airstrip at the present time. Air Pacific makes weekly flights to the island on its way through to Nauru and Fiji. As a port of entry into the former Gilbert and Ellice Islands Colony (GEIC) (map 9.2) and now the seat of the Tuvalu government, Funafuti has frequent contact with outside populations. The New Zealand Meteorological Service maintains a weather station on the island and provides a radio communications link from the Tuvalu area to other places such as Fiji and Tarawa (previously the seat of the GEIC government). This external contact and the availability of air transport and modern shipping facilities encourages local population mobility. Most movements away from the island are for employment elsewhere, especially at Tarawa and the phosphate mining complexes on Ocean Island and Nauru.

Social Organization and Land Tenure: Kin group membership represents the primary means of access to land on Funafuti. Customary tenure rules automatically provide children with a share in the land estates of their parents by birthright. Kinship identities are calculated largely on the manner in which land and "blood" are shared with particular persons. Both land and "blood" symbolize communion with the ancestral past. Descent ideology is cognatic with a patrilateral bias applied to matters of inheritance, residence, succession to traditional political positions, and domestic authority. Kinship is calculated bilaterally, forming a network of overlapping kindreds that covers each village and extends to other islands.

The actual groups holding rights to coconut land and taro gardens are chartered primarily by common descent in a maximal ramage category, as intersected by parental residence and previous tenure patterns in the ramage, and they tend to cluster around a senior sibling set in each case. Group affiliation is optional (ambilateral) to the extent that people can change their primary membership to other related groups (on a priority scale of relative social and genealogical distance), provided that the members of the other groups are willing to accept additional coparceners on their estates. The primary functions of each group include the maintenance, allocation, and transmission rights in the estate its members hold in joint tenure. The loss of members through death or permanent migration, the incorporation of new members through birth, marriage, or adoption, and the rate of absolute property divisions in each generation have a direct effect on land group composition. Depending upon the number of living members and the history of land distribution in each generation, members of the same ancestral estate category may have formed several separate land groups. Each of these units is likely to be a lineal or extended family unit that ranges in size from 2 to 60 members, with the average active membership on Funafuti now being about 7 members. A landholding group thus may be only one of a set of like units that are related to one another in various ways; but each group by definition today has jurally exclusive control over its own land (Brady 1974:138ff.).

Land group activities are operationalized primarily in terms of household organization. A land group may comprise several households linked together in one or more household clusters, or it may be represented by only one household unit. The eldest male of this group normally serves as the manager of the group's strategic resources such as money, land, canoes, and other tools of production. The managers of related land groups are usually real or classificatory siblings who have formed their own groups as a result of previous estate divisions.

The wide integration of people through ties of kinship, descent, marriage, and adoption forms an important network for hospitality and reciprocity in the community (see Brady 1972a). Kinship, in fact, is the symbolic and normative charter through which most local political demands are advanced, economic goals are maximized, and adaptive social alignments are arranged (see Brady 1974, 1976a; Keesing 1975). The overall patterns of integration are such that group membership principles and social action patterns provide individual access to some resources of each type exploited in the system.

Technology and Economy: The people of Funafuti are primarily horticulturalists and fishermen.[8] A limited inventory of tools is needed for traditional subsistence, and most of them can be produced from raw materials available locally (e.g., wood for canoes, fishing poles). Metal axes, adzes, hammers, and imported nylon fishing line are also important additions to household inventories, and they can be purchased at the local cooperative store or acquired through exchange in the village.

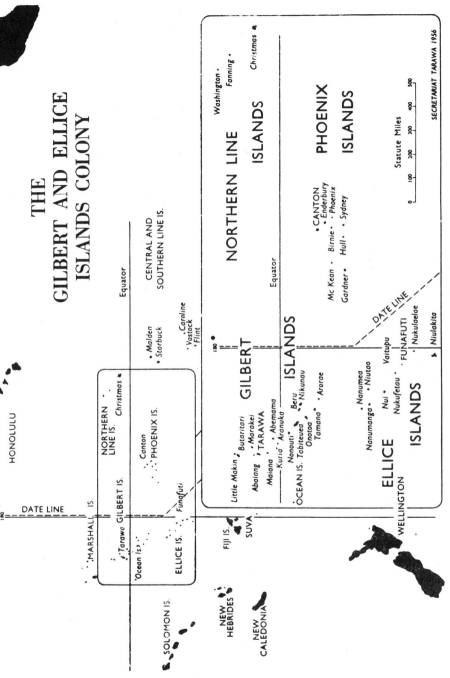

MAP 9.2 THE GILBERT AND ELLICE ISLANDS COLONY

As a center of government activity, Funafuti has various opportunities for local employment that do not occur on the other islands. The major employers are the colony government, the weather station, the Ellice Church, Air Pacific, and the local cooperative society. Together they represent an important source of cash income for the islanders. Copra, the only local resource produced for export on a regular basis, is sold to the local cooperative society. Cash obtained from employment, from copra sales, or from relatives through kinship reciprocity is normally converted to supplementary subsistence items, thereby relieving some of the pressure on traditional land and marine resources.[9] Some income is also spent for travel and for clothing, kerosene, flashlights, watches, sewing machines, bicycles, metal kitchen utensils, tobacco, radios, phonographs, outboard motors, and motorcycles, most of which can be obtained at the cooperative store.[10]

The reliance on commercial items and the range of market principles in the domestic economy, however, are not as extensive as they might appear to be at first glance. Subsistence is still geared primarily to harvesting coconuts, taro, *Cyrtosperma,* and marine resources. Households remain the primary producers and consumers in subsistence cycles, and these cycles are often carried out with few intervening acts of exchange. An average household seldom depends on imported foodstuffs for more than about 20 percent of its annual diet, although households with a high proportion of employed people in them tend to exceed this figure. Copra production is an important source of income for most households, but it has never been close to maximum output for the population. It fluctuates in part with variable demands for cash, and these demands do not ordinarily peak for large segments of the population at the same time. Moreover, kinship and community bonds regularly promote the diversion of some household produce for the benefit of the commonweal on a noncommercial basis. Households underwrite village construction and ceremonial projects by contributing labor and food. Institutionalized obligations to share strategic resources with kinsmen and friends—on a scale of relative need and social distance priorities—help to level inequities in the distribution of both indigenous and imported produce. Commerce is structurally and normatively inappropriate in this context according to local rules, with a few minor exceptions (Brady

1972a). The result is that kinship reciprocity rather than market exchange prevails as the dominant mode of allocating goods and services in the domestic sphere of the economy. This duality is maintained explicitly through cross-cultural compartmentalization as a mode of acceptance and participation in the market system imported by the colonial government (Brady 1975b). A similar type of compartmentalization applies to local land tenure patterns.

In accordance with the Ellice Islands Lands Code implemented after World War II, land can neither be given nor sold to persons other than the islanders themselves. Selling land in any case is strongly disapproved of on the premise that it tends to aggravate land hunger. It is also held to be inappropriate because of the commerce involved. Commerce is an impersonal mode of transaction and is generally viewed as an inappropriate mode of transacting land between fellow islanders. This attitude also extends to leasehold transactions between islanders for the most part, the exceptions being leasehold among islanders who must acquire tenant and use rights to village land where they have none of their own. Traditional land relations symbolize communion with the ancestral past, nurturance, growth, and social solidarity. The impersonality of commerce conflicts directly with these meanings. Land is valued both as a source of subsistence and as an integral part of the social system itself, rather than exclusively as real estate (Brady 1974, 1976b; see also Lieber 1970; Silverman 1970, 1971). But leasing land to agents from the wider market sphere of the economy, such as the colonial government or Air Pacific, is often sought after with enthusiasm because of the cash it brings to the lessors. The cross-cultural identity of the participants makes these transactions normatively acceptable, and the differences between these transactions and more traditional ones are maintained through cross-cultural compartmentalization as a mode of accepting and adapting to external influences (Brady 1975b).

Political Organization: Formerly embracing a network of petty chiefdoms, Funafuti presently represents one political unit in Tuvalu's colonial hierarchy. No divisions smaller than individual islands are recognized by the colonial government, although some were possible in the traditional system. Funafuti is governed by an Island Council whose members are islanders elected in an annual plebiscite.

The council is supported by a Lands Court and an Island Court whose members are recruited through a combination of appointments by the colonial government and by the council. The Ellice Church has its headquarters near the main village and is closely integrated into the daily lives of the islanders. But it is not empowered to make legally binding decisions in local affairs. The power of traditional chiefs has been reduced by the influence of both the colonial government and the church to little more than token authority and prestige, although some contemporary chiefs enfranchise themselves as members of the local council or court system.

Aboriginal Environment and Settlement: The remote location and a paucity of natural resources suitable for commercial exploitation have helped to keep the islands of Tuvalu isolated from all but the heartiest entrepreneurs until recently. The pounding surf and treacherous reefs that characterize most of the islands have also interrupted more than one potential liaison with people from elsewhere in the past, and such problems continue to pose barriers to effective communication to some degree in modern times. Nonetheless, the relative isolation and insularity of the islands did not pose insurmountable difficulties for the early colonists: the Polynesians, the missionaries, and the British government.

Legendary and linguistic evidence indicates that the earliest Tuvalu settlers probably came from Samoa, perhaps by drifting before the southeast trades four or five hundred years ago. This population was augmented later by arrivals from the Tokelaus, the Gilberts, Tonga, Futana, Rotuma, the northern Cooks, and beyond (see Gibson 1892; Smith 1897; Kennedy 1931; Roberts 1958; Brady 1970, 1972b, 1975b). The presumed founder of Funafutui, a Samoan chief named Telematua, arrived about four hundred years ago in the company of his two wives. Population pressure on the island's meager resources,[11] serious political squabbles, and battles with marauding Tongans ultimately encouraged the development of a new village (Funafala—see map 9.1) and stimulated the movement of some people off the island for points north (Roberts 1958:409ff.). After hardship caused by droughts, some fighting over territory, the arrival of numerous immigrants from other islands, and some absolute divisions of ancestral estates that were previously monopolized by a few ranking chiefs, government by a council of chiefs emerged as the dominant political entity in each village. Fashioned on a model imported from Samoa, these councils were supported by an adjunct council of minor chiefs and elders (Roberts 1958:415; Brady 1970, 1975b).

High rank within particular land groups generated some prestige and influence in council affairs, but individual powers of persuasion and management in socioeconomic affairs were frequently more important. High rank on the council of chiefs was likely to be achieved or enhanced through generosity in the disbursement of goods and services across local production group boundaries. Chiefly powers were also augmented by bravery in warfare, skilled oratory, historical knowledge of the island groups, and a reputation for sound judgment. This relationship between ascription and achievement in chiefly power left room for persons of lower rank to jockey for more influential positions in the local hierarchy.

Individual households or extended family household clusters lived for the most part on their own ancestral lands and, as previously mentioned, formed the basic units of production and consumption in each community. Taro, *Cyrtosperma,* coconuts, and fish represented the bulk of each household's diet. Sea turtles were valued especially as a source of red meat and they were viewed as chiefly property. These animals symbolized ancestral ties to both the land and the sea and were not to be consumed by commoners or lesser chiefs without permission of the ranking chief nearest whose property they were caught.[12] Some aboriginal chiefs had more control over production in and beyond their ancestral land groups than others. But specialized production of land and sea resources was normally restricted to activities intended to underwrite special tasks (such as house construction) in particular land groups, to support community events, or to provide subsistence for ranking chiefs and their families.[13] Some of each household's produce was earmarked for chiefly consumption or subsequent redistribution to the islanders for these reasons.[14] Chiefs were free from manual labor unless they chose not to be. In any case, the demands of chiefly redistribution as a means of enfranchising both the chiefs and the specialized production interests of their constituents probably accounted for less material flow in the local economy than was possible and probably realized in more direct and egalitarian forms of reciprocity (Brady 1970, 1972a).

The fortunes of jockeying for position in and between the local village hierarchies in peace and war occasionally united all the islanders under a single paramount chief, as in the period of first settlement. Some chiefs (including Funafuti's legendary founder) tried to dominate other islands in the group through a combination of magic and physical force. But such relationships were difficult to maintain and were never established on an enduring basis by any individuals or groups in the aboriginal period. The island itself represented the widest functional expression of ranked political integration; the power of individual chiefs was more or less confined to their own villages, ancestral land groups, or village councils. More egalitarian interisland contacts were established through marital, adoption, and friendship alliances. These and other ties based on kinship and descent were reaffirmed in times of plenty by interisland competition in athletics, feasting, and dancing, and by mutual aid in periods of differential deprivation (Brady 1970, 1975b, 1976e).

Generally speaking, early life styles on Funafuti were grounded in kin-based economics, politics, and religion. Communalism pervaded each kin group as a primary strategy of adaptation, and government by council provided centralization for the community as a whole. Obligations to share resources among persons related by common ancestry or common territory, or both, formed the basis for many interpersonal relationships. Marital, adoption, and friendship alliances helped to extend the range of primary hospitality and aid as survival insurance. Peaceful strangers were either adopted formally into a local kin group, thereby providing access to land and community resources, or they were given produce and generalized hospitality in the form of service for the duration of their visit. Either way, what was given to them helped to establish a local identity that allowed them to participate in the life-sustaining activities of the community. Some of the earliest and most influential agents of change in the area—missionaries of the London Missionary Society (LMS) and administrators from the British colonial government—arrived under conditions approximating these (Brady 1975b: 119ff.).

European Contact, Diffusion, and Change: Whalers, explorers, traders, beachcombers, and blackbirders affected the Tuvalu population most directly in the nineteenth century by deporting and displacing people, and by importing material goods, diseases, and ideas about the nature of the rest of the world. Mendaña had been in the area much earlier. He charted an island in 1568 that was probably the island of Nui in the northern part of Tuvalu (Maude 1959). European discovery of the rest of the group proceeded sporadically from the time of Spaniard Mourelle's visit to Nanumea and Nanumanga in 1781 until Captain de Peyster's call at Funafuti in 1819. The American Wilkes, the Frenchman Duperre, and the Russian Chiamtschenko sailed through the area in later years (Roberts 1958:394ff.).

Between 1859 and 1870 Peruvian and Australian blackbirders took their toll of the Tuvalu population, most notably at Nukulaelae and Funafuti. Historical accounts suggest that about 200 persons from Nukulaelae and about 180 from Funafuti were taken by slavers in 1863 (Newton 1967:201). Traders were or had been in residence at Funafuti and other islands in the group by the time of the Reverend Murray's visits in 1865 and 1870 (Murray 1876:375–93; Maude 1950:65). Morrell (1960:276) indicates that the German company of Godeffroy and Son dominated the local copra trade in 1872, sending small schooners to the area to collect copra for shipment to Samoa. By the turn of the century, the once numerous resident traders were conspicuous by their absence throughout the islands. Itinerant merchants of the Samoa Shipping and Trading Company, and later Burns Philp and the Chinese firm of On Chong, monopolized local trade until World War II interrupted their activities. Germany secured rights to trade and otherwise conduct business and political affairs in the area in a treaty negotiated with Funafuti in 1878 (Morrell 1960:276). But Britain managed to render this agreement ineffective within a decade or so, and, on mandate of the islanders and the Crown, declared a protectorate government in the group in 1892. The islands were annexed officially to Britain as part of the newly formed Gilbert and Ellice Islands Colony in 1915. Funafuti was later designated as the seat of the Ellice Islands district (Brady 1975b:124ff.).

Samoan-based representatives of the LMS, some of whom were Samoan pastors, operated continuously in the group from 1865 until recently. The Ellice Church has since incorporated as an autonomous unit. Allied troops used the islands as a staging area for assaults on the Japanese entrenched at Tarawa and in other parts of the Pacific during World War II, and a major base for these operations was established at Funafuti. Actual warfare on Funafuti was limited to a few bombing raids made by the Japanese and was even less apparent on most of the other islands. But the presence of Allied forces represented some of the most intense exposure many of the islanders had experienced with the outside world up to that time, at least in terms of the numbers of people present and the diversity of material goods imported. Ships, firearms, heavy equipment, and marines were there in abundance, and some of the western passages into the lagoon may still be mined (Ward 1967:46). It is the missionaries and the colonial government, however, who have brought about the most conspicuous and enduring changes in Tuvalu society and culture.

The missionaries managed to sweep away or drive underground nearly all traces of the aboriginal religion, overt infanticide, abortion, polygyny, and warfare. Men with more than one wife were asked to choose their favorite and send the others back to their natal groups. Ancestral shrines containing the skulls of high-ranking predecessors were torn down. The remains of lesser-ranked ancestors were removed from houses and buried, along with nearly all ritual and actual articles of warfare. Conversion depended largely on the capitulation of local chiefs, and, although some chiefs were more reluctant than others to convert (see Murray 1876:403–10; Gill 1885:19–23; Whitmee 1871:10–26), resistance to the acceptance of Christianity throughout the islands was short-lived.

The inroads gained by the Samoan pastors in particular, altered the traditional power structure. The Samoans demanded and eventually were given the respect, authority, and badges of rank previously accorded to high chiefs (see Brady 1970, 1975b). Rank order came to depend more on the degree of assimilation and relative position in the church hierarchy than on traditional birth order and special skills in other contexts. Priority for village council membership was allocated accordingly to chiefs and elders who had been converted, thereby ensuring their domination by the pastors and the influence of the pastors in council decisions. Obedience to the pastors was sanctioned by threats of damnation and Divine wrath, and, in a more pragmatic sense, by community ostracism and a capricious system of fines levied in cash and local produce (see Brady 1970, 1975b; Macdonald 1971a, 1971b, 1972). Churches were built throughout Tuvalu by the 1880s. The demand for capital to buy imported materials for church construction stimulated local trade among the islanders, the missionaries, and the traders who were either in residence at the time or who included these islands on their itineraries. Literacy was introduced by way of the Samoan bible, and Samoan was instituted as the official language of the church (Brady 1975b:119ff.).[15]

In general, the Samoan pastors made every effort to replace traditional behaviors and beliefs from the *poo uliuli* "heathen darkness" (prior to 1865) with the enlightenment of *fakasamoa* "the Samoan way," and they were usually successful in getting their way.[16] Most of the missionary complex has been assimilated with a minimum of overt compartmentalization and a maximum of public substitution for traditional patterns (Brady 1975b:140). The few conflicting public and private interests that remain in local acceptance of the church orthodoxies have been maintained with reasonable harmony through compartmentalization (Brady 1975b:123).[17]

Many of the changes initiated by the missionaries have been supported in principle or codified in fact by the colonial government. But the colonial government has also had a direction of its own in influencing social and cultural change on Funafuti and elsewhere in the chain, especially in political and economic matters. The roots of a theocracy had been planted and developed with considerable success prior to the arrival of the colonial government. Agents for the latter competed with the missions in these areas from the outset, and subsequently began to diffuse some of the local power that had been usurped from the chiefs and concentrated in the hands of the village pastors. This was accomplished most directly through transformation of the existing island councils into a new form more consistent with British interests and policies. Eligibility for service on the new island councils was measured increasingly in terms of civil service requirements that included familiarity with bookkeeping and at least minimal literacy in English. No attempt was made to ensure direct representation of the various land groups on these councils, and the members selected by the islanders were not always chiefs. Islanders who were not always chiefs were also trained as magistrates to serve on the newly devised local courts. The combination of colonial and missionary intervention in local political affairs overall has eroded or eliminated all the bases upon which chiefs traditionally drew their authority and prestige. The new type of local "government man" is a link in a civil service hierarchy that transcends the petty chiefdoms of the past and unifies the islands of Tuvalu as a rural satellite of a modern nation state (see Brady 1975b).

Some other important changes on Funafuti and in the Tuvalu area as a whole that can be attributed primarily to the colonial government and its policies include revisions of customary land tenure practices and subsequent redirections in household production and distribution orientations. Centralization under the colonial government around the turn of this century required that villages be neatly aligned in rows and columns, and that the people on each island be clustered into a single village for the most part.[18] Many people who had been living on their ancestral land estates up to this time could no longer do so, and their relocation to one of the existing villages (usually the largest one on the island) posed new problems for group affiliation and tenure rights concerning the land they were asked to live on thereafter (Brady 1975b:127).

Similar legislation has contributed inadvertently to plot fragmentation rates and relative land hunger by encouraging absolute divisions of property where simple segmentation might have sufficed in the past, that is, when a land group grows too large to maintain itself efficiently as a cooperative and corporate unit (Brady 1974:141ff.). This increased nucleation of land groups is also functionally related to a diminishing sociability range in property and kin group networks on traditional principles, and thereby to a potential reduction in the flow of strategic resources among distant kin in times of crises (Brady 1975b:134). Household production and distribution strategies take these patterns into account, as well as the patterns presented by augmented material inventories, income, and diets through increased participation in the world market economy (Brady 1972a, 1975b).

Both the missionaries and the colonial government have contributed to Tuvalu population growth in the past century. The colonial government has done so most directly through its health and welfare services instituted since World War II. The role of the missionaries in this regard can be traced most directly to their elimination of such practices as infanticide, abortion, and, to some degree, warfare, prior to the arrival of the colonial government (Brady 1972b, 1975b). Population growth, in conjunction with some important but unanticipated reactions to colonial land legislation, has promoted increases in relative land hunger throughout the islands (Brady 1974). The population is no longer growing as rapidly as it once was, however, largely because of the colonial government's successful implementation of a birth control project in the past few years (Brady 1975b:136). Migration out of Tuvalu for employment has also relieved some of the population pressure on local resources, both by creating a large "floating" population and by providing income that can be tapped by relatives at home as additional wherewithal for subsistence.

In sum, the cross-cultural influences presented to the islanders on Funafuti and elsewhere in Tuvalu by missionaries and the colonial government have been extensive but not equal on all counts. For reasons pertaining to historical affinities between Samoa and Tuvalu, to differential culture content and appeal of the missions and the colonial government to the islanders, and to the modes of introduction and implementation strategies of the agents generally, the mission complex has been more thoroughly assimilated into Funafuti's culture pool. Most of the culture content that can be identified as imported by the missions has been closely integrated and subsequently labeled as "own" culture by the islanders with a minimum of overt compartmentalization and a maximum of public substitutions for the *status quo ante*. In contrast, the colonial complex has been conceptualized and largely operationalized by the islanders as "other" culture from the outset. The attitudes and plans of colonial personnel have helped to maintain this distinction in several important domains of Funafuti's environment-choice nexus in the long run (see Brady 1972a, 1974, 1975b).

The most strategic parts of the islanders' traditional culture pool from the standpoint of subsistence and deprivation recovery needs, such as economic and land tenure patterns, are among the areas of greatest direct influence by the colonial government in the past. They are also the most highly compartmentalized today. Funafuti has managed to keep some of the old and blend it with much of the new culture in cultivating current survival options. There has been some direct substitution for former practices in these and related behavioral domains, as perhaps might be expected in the wake of extensive political changes. But, combined with a high frequency of adoption, fosterage, and other customary options for household and land group affiliation (see Brady 1976b, 1976e), kinship and communalism continue to form the basis for most interpersonal relationships on the island and thereby continue to function as important means for getting resources to people and people to resources. The development of common interest groups through church membership and employment opportunities has added to rather than completely displaced more traditional structures and options for community integration. Furthermore, interisland travel no longer carries the high risk it had when canoes were the only source of transport, and many people argue that interisland alliances are more easily developed and maintained today as a result of modern communication facilities. The combination of these patterns and processes of cross-cultural and interisland integration represents an increase in local adaptive diversity over aboriginal conditions, and this has come about in part as a selective adjustment to the multiple and progressive cross-cultural influences that have been at work on Funafuti in the past century. The range of social action alternatives in the islanders' environment-choice nexus has been transformed accordingly. One thing that has not changed appreciably, however, is the physical environment. A recent tropical cyclone challenged the adaptive stability of Funafuti's new sociocultural profile by nearly demolishing the island's subsistence resources altogether and causing considerable disruption in domestic affairs.

A DEPRIVATIVE EVENT:
TROPICAL CYCLONE BEBE

With little or no advance warning to the island residents, tropical cyclone Bebe struck Funafuti with full force on the evening of October 21, 1972, killing six people, wrecking four ships, destroying innumerable canoes, demolishing a large concrete church, leveling most of the weather station complex, uprooting thousands of coconut trees, spoiling taro and *Cyrtosperma* gardens, leaving more than 700 residents homeless, and causing extensive erosion, among other damages. The storm surge that followed included a tidal wave estimated to be 80 to 100 feet high at its peak. It put the eastern half of the island completely under water before subsiding (Maragos et al. 1973).

A scientific team sent to the island in December 1972 to study the storm's climatic character and physiographic effects reported that Bebe was "the only severe storm ever recorded for the month of October since the beginning of written weather observations in the southwestern Pacific," and "only the third severe storm to strike Funafuti Atoll during the past 140 years" (Maragos et al. 1973:1163). My previous research in the area agrees generally with these estimates.[19] The history of such problems is thus not extensive on Funafuti or elsewhere in the group so far as I am aware. But the particular kind of environmental fluctuation represented by the storm is known and coded extensively in culture pools in the Tuvalu chain and all over Polynesia and Micronesia (see Sahlins 1958; Firth 1959; Alkire 1965; Lessa 1968). These are recurrent (if infrequent) problems of adaptation that people who live on coral islands must confront and adjust to if they are to survive, as previously mentioned. The exact timing and great intensity of Bebe, however, were unexpected attributes according to several informants who were on the island at the time. The psychological and physiological stress experienced by some islanders may have been escalated as a consequence (see article 1).

Nevertheless, reactions to the storm were generally swift and effective and are indicative of Funafuti's present sociocultural circumstances.[20] Within three days of the incident, the people from Funafala were evacuated and brought to the main village for aid, and the airstrip was cleared sufficiently for New Zealand to land a plane carrying emergency supplies of food, tents, clothing, and communications equipment. An extensive relief operation was mounted at Tarawa by the colonial government, church groups, and private citizens. The arrival of experts with various reconstruction skills followed shortly thereafter, and a variety of kin-based and community-

level task groups were formed to help implement reparations. Some
looting of the cooperative store was reported in the immediate aftermath of the storm, mostly for foodstuffs (Hall 1972:2). But the traditional mandates for widespread sharing in times of need prevailed
throughout the community with few reported incidences of hoarding.
A communal task group of islanders and visitors quickly re-roofed the
main village meeting house as a temporary shelter.

Through its connection to Britain as a commonwealth country,
New Zealand agreed to take most of the responsibility for cleaning up
the island. Heavy equipment was subsequently flown in for that purpose. Some islanders with kinsmen and land on other islands were
transported there by the government. Most government employees
were taken to Tarawa. Immediate or long-term recovery aid has also
been provided by other commonwealth countires, by the United
States, and by island communities in the colony and elsewhere, including Samoa. Total reconstruction is nearly complete at the present
time, and most of the island's indigenous subsistence resources have
been regenerated.

In all, local resourcefulness and the pipeline to prompt government
aid appear to have averted what otherwise would have been a much
more intense period of deprivation in the aftermath of spoiled water,
scarce food, damaged raw materials for shelters, and disorganization
in domestic affairs. Of perhaps more importance is that the imported
wherewithal for survival available to the islanders during the storm
(including shelter for some people aboard ships then anchored in the
lagoon), the aid delivered in the immediate aftermath, and the combination of reconstruction efforts since then constitutes an environmental message of considerable impact beyond the storm itself. The
particular alignments of personnel and resources in place before and
after the storm fulfilled a critical survival function: they allowed the
islanders to endure a severe deprivative event without seriously undermining population survival or sociocultural persistence patterns.
The value of the existing traditional strategies for action and the
manner in which these principles have been integrated with the
cross-cultural network have been reinforced for the most part.[21] To
that extent, these patterns may represent a conservative force for
change in the future, if not a platform for involution by intensifying

the existing network of relationships. If so, a conservative force for sociocultural integration and social action possibilities will have been fashioned from a recent history of extensive progressive change under recursive environmental conditions, which is not an altogether unexpected result of dialectic and diaphatic processes at work in the same society over time (see article 1).

Endurance also implies a capacity to change, however, and the reorganization patterns developed by a population in attempting to recover from the effects of resource disruption by physical or social forces in the environment may present an especially favorable climate for innovation (see Barnett 1953; Chapman 1954; Wallace 1956). Similarly, dissatisfaction with certain sociocultural alignments or resource control patterns prior to a disaster or deprivative cycle may be resolved deliberately in the aftermath, perhaps by taking advantage of the discontinuity produced by the event itself (see Danielsson 1955; Lessa 1968). In Funafuti's case, it is perhaps significant that the vote to form a colony separate from the Gilbertese was affirmed in August 1974 while reconstruction in Bebe's wake was still under way. One of the initial interests in starting the separation move was to offset a long history of perceived and actual inequities in the distribution of colonial aid between the Gilberts and Tuvalu. The Gilbertese initiated the move in part because of job competition: the people of Tuvalu had more and better jobs per capita, especially at Tarawa. In terms of actual numbers of people and in nearly all other aspects of access to colonial resources, however, the Tuvalu islanders were always the minority population in the combined colony. Tuvalu support for separating from the Gilbertese was struck in part in the hope of increasing colonial service and aid and in part as an attempt to gain more control over internal affairs. Bebe may have acted as a catalyst for the realization of these plans.[22]

SUMMARY AND CONCLUSIONS

The processes underlying the development and integration of culture are varied and complex. Some are deeply embedded in the adaptive infrastructures of the population; others are more plainly psychological and sociocultural. Psychological processes operate through cognition and perception and are the basic mechanisms through which individuals receive, sort, transmute, and otherwise assemble symbolic information. Sociocultural processes translate the system of symbols and meanings conceptually controlled by individuals into wider networks of interpersonal relationships and institutional alignments. They are mechanisms for social action that relate individuals to populations and ultimately to the ecosystems inhabited by those populations. Both types of processes are thereby essential components of cultural change and adaptation. Adaptive patterns proceed as alternations between conscious and unconscious selection for cultural integration and behavior modification in response to changing environmental stimuli; they are action patterns that flow through networks of individual perceptions and information pools, and they also represent the mediating influence between a population's cognized and operational environments as these environments are articulated over time (see article 1).

Processes so constituted are amenable to description independent of any conscious values held by the populations in which they operate, although in reality processes and their products and the values assigned to them are closely bound. The values themselves are cultural constructs that ultimately depend on arbitrary assignments of meanings to things, perceptions, and events that have nothing intrinsically to do with the symbolic load assigned to them. They are part of the system of symbols and meanings that help to define "appropriate" behavior for individuals and otherwise structure their cognized environment as a charter for social actions. These actions must correspond approximately to the demands posed for the population by its operational environment if the population is to adapt successfully. A dialectic relationship is posed in this manner between environmental stimuli that enter the reaction systems of individual organisms, on the one hand, and the patterns of social action produced as responses, on the other. The processes of cognitive structuring and symbolic interpretation of environmental stimuli represent intervening variables in the dialectic. As these processes and their products are integrated in the functioning of human ecosystems, certain selective patterns of behavior and sociocultural alignments develop and begin to characterize as well as structure social action for the population. These patterns and their corollaries overtly represent the wherewithal for survival a population brings to bear on environmental contingencies, including those that destroy or disrupt access to strategic resources. The capacity to endure such contingencies can be interpreted as a crude index of adaptive sophistication.

On islands subject to resource disruptions by tropical cyclones, tidal waves, and droughts, such as on the coral island of the Pacific, an adaptive premium may be placed on social actions that support sociocultural interdependence, the internal organization of personnel, and material resource flow in specific ways. For example, an emphasis placed on direct rather than hierarchical reciprocity can facilitate an immediate and relatively unencumbered flow of goods and services between any two individuals, groups, or points on the island, with surplus resources ideally gravitating to people who are most in need of them *when* they are most in need of them, hoarding strategies to the contrary notwithstanding. Similarly, the membership of every adult in each major type of socioeconomic group on the island ideally provides individual access to each type of resource exploited in the system with few intervening acts of exchange. The reciprocal flow of goods, foodstuffs, and services on the strength of kinship and community obligations potentially levels out production deficiencies in any one of these groups. Additional benefits derive from extending the socioeconomic network over more than one island, where each comes to the aid of others in need as a form of survival insurance. Furthermore, it has been suggested that the more diversified these organizations become in social forms, cultural complexity, and behavioral alternatives in a time of need, the better adapted is the group, all other things being equal. The extension of rural island subsistence and survival networks to include hierarchical liaisons with the industrial world and its resources can be consistent with these adaptive principles as an alternative or complementary form of diversification.

The actual form of diversification achieved under cross-cultural influences depends in part on the predominant mode through which new traits are introduced, and in part on the predominant mode of acceptance or rejection that is engineered by the recipient group. Two general possibilities for acceptance include a transformation of replacement, where new patterns are substituted directly for older ones in the recipients' culture pool, or a transformation of expansion, where some of the new order is added to older patterns as a means for articulating social action in both. Of the two, the latter process theoretically produces greater diversity in terms of the number and kinds of sociocultural alignments and action alternatives possible. The process in this instance is cross-cultural compartmentalization. In reality, all cross-cultural interchange is likely to produce some measure of both modes of acceptance, where acceptance occurs. But each mode in the extreme can produce radically different results for overall change in a population's culture pool, and each, therefore, may carry a different functional load for ecological consequences. Compartmentalization in this context has the distinct advantage of allowing acceptance of new traits without necessarily sacrificing the traditional baseline of survival. Depending on the balance of acceptance and rejection of new traits and on the predominant mode of their introduction and integration, then, cross-cultural interference through migration and diffusion can reduce, regularize, or totally restructure the social action alternatives available to individuals in particular environments.

Funafuti has frequently been in the vanguard of changes begun in Tuvalu by agents of an imported church and state, in part because of the island's accessibility to large ships, and in part because of relations developed independent of the islanders in international politics early in the period of European contact. Beyond these and other purely situational factors, the islanders' environment-choice nexus has been structured by individual assessments, evaluations, and choices among alternatives for achieving both subsistence and general survival goals from environmental possibilities (see Britan and Denich 1976:69). The development of this nexus has been regulated by the psychological and sociocultural processes of cross-cultural acceptance and rejection of culture content, innovation, and strategic resource management in local affairs under variable resource conditions. The results have been such that the present system thrives more or less on traditional resource mining and management patterns while extending its material and social interdependencies into industrialism. The culmination of these general processes and specific historical patterns provided the wherewithal needed for surviving and recovering quickly from tropical cyclone Bebe.

The selective nature of many changes instituted on the island is further exemplified by the relative distribution of compartmentalization and direct substitution as modes of acceptance. The most strategic parts of the traditional culture pool from the standpoint of subsistence and deprivation recovery needs, such as economic and land tenure patterns, are among the areas of greatest potential displacement by colonial actions in the past. These domains are also the most highly compartmentalized today. Some direct substitution of new elements for older patterns has occurred, of course, especially in political organization, and not all of the changes have been positive. Some have added directly to local population growth and thereby adversely affected the islanders' socioeconomic patterns. The increased nucleation of land groups under colonial direction has also undermined some traditional obligations to share strategic resources with distant relatives in times of need. But the overall patterns of integration on the island provide every individual with access to some of each type of basic resource now exploited in the system, and this has been facilitated by the preservation of traditional patterns despite important changes in related areas. Cognatic descent, optional affiliation rules for moving membership from one land group to another, bilateral inheritance, alliances formed through marriage and adoption, and the continuing obligations of kinship reciprocity on a scale of relative social distance are some of the important features of island life in the past that are fundamentally the same today.

Similarly, the structural persistence of government by council from the aboriginal period to the present day—although radically altered in culture content—has eased the transition from petty chiefdom to satellite of a modern nation state. There has also been continuity insofar as the early history of political change on the island was marked by a diminishing concentration of power in the hands of a few chiefly families. Competition from rivals, demographic pressure on both land and marine resources, some absolute divisions in land estates, and a model of Samoan politics drawn from past experiences inspired the development of a council of chiefs. The missionaries picked up the trend, modifying it to suit their special interests, and the colonial government continued the transformation in content. Because of the effect this transformation produced in isolating exchange and social integration patterns that once were firmly linked to chiefly redistribution and authority over land and community activities, it might be argued that egalitarianism was being selected for simultaneously in domestic affairs. But, if so, it did not come about exclusively as a result of adaptation to aboriginal conditions. In fact, what was begun as a diffusion of power within certain limits in the aboriginal period has now become a highly stratified domain of political action in the cross-cultural arena, and one that is characterized more by direct substitution in culture content than by compartmentalization between the old and the new.

Furthermore, it is important to recognize that certain types of change may have greater and more direct impact than others on a population's life chances, and this impact is not necessarily coextensive with the degree to which imported culture traits are either visible on the surface in everyday affairs or "internalized" by the recipient group. Despite the more overt and intensive level of compartmentalization applied to the colonial complex on Funafuti, that is, its being less overtly integrated in much of the local culture pool than the mission complex, the colonial government appears to have been quite influential in redirecting the islanders survival chances. Many changes induced by the missionaries have been superficial or at best indirect in their effects on local subsistence, exchange, and population mobility patterns, for example, irrespective of the extensive influence of the church on other aspects of the islanders' culture. The reverse is true in nearly all respects for the colonial government (see Brady 1975b). It is the combination of these particular patterns and processes of change across traditional boundaries, however, that represents the primary increase in adaptive diversity for the islanders in the past century.

One thing is clear: the islanders are better prepared to survive disruptions in the physical environment than they ever were in aboriginal times. The cost of this security has not been especially high in the sense that some important features of the traditional system have been maintained while adding new alternatives from elsewhere. But there is no way of knowing just how long these mixed patterns will endure in their present form. A new synthesis will inevi-tably result in time. If events of the past century are any indication of future directions, it would appear that the new synthesis will be anchored more in favor of Western emulation than in success with preserving traditional culture. Dependence on the colonial complex has increased progressively for several decades; it was intensified most recently by tropical cyclone Bebe and was reaffirmed for the most part in the separation of Tuvalu from the Gilberts. These cir-cumstances augur for greater homogenization of the islanders' cul-ture pool in days to come, and therein lies a problem. In the lopsided dynamics of borrowing from industrial nations, the islanders may be hard-pressed to discover that "more is not *always* better." As Elman Service has noted in another context (1971, 1975), involution on ex-isting opportunities ultimately becomes non-progressive as an adap-tive strategy, thereby posing new problems for survival.

NOTES

1. This article is an expanded and revised version of a paper presented at the Sev-enty-third Annual Meeting of the American Anthropological Association in Mexico City, 1974. Some of the data were gathered while I was conducting doctoral disserta-tion research in Tuvalu in 1968 and 1969. Financial support was provided by a Na-tional Institute of Mental Health fellowship (MH 40529) and research grant (MH 11629), and by the Department of Anthropology, University of Oregon. Additional in-formation was gathered in 1971 through the assistance of a National Science Foun-dation Research Grant (GS 29695). I am grateful for the support of these institutions, and for the many suggestions offered by Charles D. Laughlin, Jr., and Doug Munro on a previous draft of this article.

2. The Gilbert and Ellice Islands Colony was officially divided into two new ones in 1976. The Ellice Islands are now known by the traditional name for the group, *Tuvalu* "group of eight," although there are nine islands in the chain (see Brady 1974).

3. Notwithstanding the various qualifications of Sahlins' (1958) thesis, for some of the implications here are problematic: see Goodenough (1959), Freeman (1961, 1962, 1964), Suggs (1961), Finney (1966), Ember (1966), Orans (1966), Goldman (1970), Sahlins (1972), and Cancian (1976).

4. That is, at least in terms of *how* these phenomena were transformed from one state to another, if not *why* they were (see Bee 1974:5).

5. Nukufetau is the other island with a large, navigable lagoon.

6. This figure was slightly lower in a survey I conducted in 1972. The results of the 1973 colony census are not yet available to me.

7. By "relative land hunger" I mean a perceived or actual scarcity of land. The per-ception of relative land hunger in Tuvalu is often more intense than can be justified on the basis of demonstrable shortages of land for subsistence (see Brady 1974). More-over, population densities alone are often inadequate indicators of actual land hunger. Other factors such as the land tenure system itself intervene (Brady 1975b:132).

8. These resources are normally clustered within the exploitative capabilities of individual households or household clusters, although high plot fragmentation on the island may interfere with the ease of access enjoyed by particular groups in harvesting their daily needs (see Brady 1974).

9. Local diets include several varieties of fish and crustaceans, as well as taro, *Cyrtosperma*, breadfruit, bananas, coconuts, pandanus, pork, chicken, sea mammals from time to time, an occasional dog, and other miscellaneous items. Imported foodstuffs include such items as rice, butter, sugar, flour, fish, canned vegetables, sea biscuits, and candy.

10. Funafuti's cooperative store accounted for more than 40 percent of the total retail sales in Tuvalu in 1972.

11. One probable response to this pressure was infanticide. Nukufetau, Niutao, and Nanumanga practiced the killing by smothering or drowning of all but one boy and girl from each mother for some indefinite period prior to the arrival of the missionaries. In special cases, a third child of either sex could be adopted in order to save it from elimination in this manner. Funafuti apparently did not discriminate by sex of the child. Only the first two children were allowed to live, regardless of their sex, unless special arrangements were made for adoption plus the payment of a fine to the community as a whole. The fine was usually a large bundle of produce (see Brady 1972b, 1974, 1975b, 1976b).

12. The heads of turtles were especially prized as chiefly food, or perhaps better said, as symbols of chiefly authority. The missionaries explicitly eliminated the practice of presenting turtle heads to chiefs.

13. This support has been redirected to the village pastors today (see Brady 1975b, 1976a).

14. Each village also had a battery of specialists who applied their skills to such diverse interests as canoe and house construction, navigation, magic, sorcery, divination, curing, midwifery, and tattooing. Most of the specialties directly involving religious ritual were banned or reordered into a new context by the missionaries (see Brady 1975b).

15. However, the Tuvalu (Ellice) language replaced Samoan as the official language of the local government in 1931 and was permitted in the church thereafter (see Macdonald 1971a:88).

16. Most of the Samoan pastors have been replaced in recent years by people from Tuvalu, in accordance with the recent independence of the Ellice Church from the LMS. But the role created by the Samoans is indelibly imprinted in the church hierarchy of today, and many of the changes engineered by them persist throughout the whole of Tuvalu society and culture (see Brady 1975b:123ff.).

17. Sorcery persists, for example, in some quarters in clandestine opposition to the church. Similarly, a belief in mana, ghosts, and some ancestral spirits prevails in contradistinction to the teachings of the church. But open opposition to the church is rare, and most of the church complex has been firmly integrated into both the public and private domains of the islanders (see Brady 1975b).

18. This was done around 1911. Nanumea and Funafuti are the only islands in the chain with more than one active village today (see Brady 1970, 1976a).

19. Wiens (1962:474) reports that the last tidal wave with widespread repercussions in Tuvalu occurred in 1891, although he does not cite details or the source of his information. Murray (1876:414–15) notes that Vaitupu Island had the walls of its chapel torn down and flooded by a large wave in 1869. My informants from this island have indicated that Murray's account was accurate and that another wave swept through their village during the westerly season in the 1920s. Several houses were torn down; the copra shed, the central meeting house, and the schoolhouse were damaged; nobody was seriously injured. Since then, reports have filtered into the district adminis-

tration of waves that put one or two islets awash on other islands in the group, evidently without doing much damage. In January 1967 the houses at Tangitangi Village on Nukufetau were swamped by a large wave that transported several huge coral boulders from the seaside to the lagoon. Damage to the houses was light and no injuries were reported. In 1962, a large wave washed through Funafala Village on Funafuti (some distance away from the main village and the district center—see map 9-1), apparently without causing much damage to people or property. Funafuti also had a gale force wind that swept the island for more than eighteen hours in January 1958. This storm was rated at the time as the worst in fifty years. It created considerable structural damage to houses, destroyed most of the island's banana plants, ruined taro and *Cyrtosperma* gardens from the coast up to about 200 yards inland, and wrecked several canoes. Tropical cyclone Bebe thus appears clearly to be the worst in Tuvalu in this century, if not for a much longer period of time.

20. Data on reactions to the storm have been collected from newspaper accounts, personal correspondence with island residents, and discussions with some of the people who visited the island immediately after the storm struck. The government did not think it would be prudent for me to investigate the aftermath in person in 1974, for "fear of raising the dust on issues that had only just begun to settle." The "issues" were unspecified.

21. Evidently, some of the island residents were dissatisfied with certain aid programs such as attempts to reconstruct houses from cement blocks. One entrepreneur reportedly attempted to sell sand to the government to mix with cement the latter had provided for house reconstruction—giving some indication of the relative social distance involved between this islander and the colonial agents, despite the government's contextualizing the matter as "aid" and "generosity." A few other accounts similar to this one have been reported to me, but none have been verified to date with the actual persons involved.

22. If so, the pattern is similar to the situation reported by Lessa (1968) for the island of Ulithi in Micronesia after a comparable storm. An intense tropical cyclone there had the effect of intensifying progressive changes that had already begun in relations with a colonial power (see also Firth 1959).

Epilogue:
Adaptation and
Anthropological Theory

Ivan A. Brady and
Charles D. Laughlin, Jr.

In adapting to particular habitats and environmental changes, human societies attempt to persist as sociocultural entities and to survive as biological populations. Biological survival is primary, of course, insofar as neither the population of a given society nor its sociocultural profile can continue actively in the absence of viable organisms. On the other hand, a human biological population can survive with a radically altered sociocultural profile, all other things being equal. It cannot survive without an *alterable* sociocultural profile, at least in the long run. It is within this framework of flexibility and change that the concept of adaptation comes most readily to the fore in anthropological analysis.

As we pointed out in article 1, adaptation refers to the processes "by which organisms, through responsive changes in their own states, structures, or compositions, maintain [homeorhesis] in and among themselves in the face of both short-term environment fluctuations and long-term changes in the composition or structure of their environments" (Rappaport 1971:60; see also Alland and McCay 1973). Adaptation emerges from this definition as a dynamic, systemic, life-serving—and in human populations—biocultural set of processes. The unit of adaptation is the individual organism as a member of a social group, and the processes are those of equilibrating biocultural structure to the environment. Adaptive processes impinge on the reaction systems of human organisms in several ways and on several levels of reality, not all of which are immediately or inevitably apparent to the organisms themselves or to the scientists who study them. The culturally entrained eye sees surface structure and highly symbolic behavior; the external observer is likely to see less in the cultural terms of the group being studied, and perhaps more in terms of the specific culture content of his own scientific and folk system. But mapping out surface structure and the actual patterns of behavior in a particular society does not necessarily engage the most critical levels on which adaptation takes place in that system's adaptive infrastructure, for it is the structure of the organisms themselves as well as that of their society that evolves, not behavior (see Count 1973). The goal in this final article is to review briefly some premises and to outline some of the methodological and theoretical difficulties that have kept anthropological theory focused on surface structural adaptations rather than on the more extensive complex of adaptive infrastructures in the past.

ADAPTIVE INFRASTRUCTURES: SOME ADDITIONAL CONSIDERATIONS

There has been a long and trying debate in anthropology over the appropriate level of analysis for studying the ontology of structure in human societies. Attempts to nail down the "correct" level of analysis are frequently confounded by differences between levels of reality and levels of analysis and also by the great diversity of special interests in the discipline. The result is generally confusion about the loci of structure in sociocultural and biocultural phenomena, and disagreement over the nature of causality in socially adaptive processes.

In philosophical terms, anthropologists intuitively tend to embrace one of two extremes. One is the *logical atomism* of Bertrand Russell (1956; see also Wittgenstein 1961). This position holds that reality, or statements about reality, may be reduced to ultimate constituents, and that the process of doing science is precisely the process of discovering the ultimate constituents in any particular universe of discourse. The other extreme is typified by Emile Durkheim (1938), and we can refer to it as *anti-reductionism*. This position holds that the proper level of analysis of any system is the one upon which the system appears to base its primary existence. Social systems, for example, should be studied in the analytically restricted domain of "social facts." Other levels of discourse, the argument goes, are unnecessarily reductionistic.

Extreme atomism and anti-reductionism obscure comprehension and analysis of the complex relations that obtain within and between progressively higher levels of systemic organization, such as we have faced in this volume in terms of the human biogram. Moreover, both extremes commit what Whitehead (1960:443) calls the *fallacy of the bifurcation of nature*—the creation of two worlds for conception, one of reality in general and the other of science. The reality of the situation in which we find ourselves is that all human social systems are multidimensional and exist on at least two levels of structure and performance: that of the cognized environment, on the one hand, and that of the wider operational environment, on the other. We have attempted to avoid the fallacy of the bifurcation of nature most directly in our discussions of cognized and operational environments by positing an empirical and transactional overlap between these two domains, and by recognizing that the empirical reality referred to by science and the folk systems it studies is the same reality in each instance, at least on the level of deep structure.

A comparable conceptual problem that has plagued metaphysicians and scientists throughout the history of Western thought is the simultaneous depiction of stasis and change in social systems. As Whitehead (1960:319) notes, "On the whole, the history of philosophy supports Bergson's charge that the human intellect 'spatializes the universe'; that is to say, that it tends to ignore the fluency, and to analyze the world in terms of static categories." Bergson's charge is quite apropos to the treatment of complex social systems by many modern anthropologists. The anthropological enterprise as normally constituted presents seemingly insurmountable obstacles to a dynamic and realistic depiction of human sociocultural systems. The field researcher is confronted with the ongoing life processes and products of a social system in motion; but the parochial skills, interests, and inclinations the observer brings to bear on this dynamism frequently result in the impression that the social structure, culture pool, or perhaps personality structure described is *the* state of affairs for all time.

Rather than tackle structural equilibration and environmental change in the same social system over time, anthropologists have all too frequently resorted to shallow surveys of surface structure in particular groups, which are then presented through such literary devices as writing in the "ethnographic present." By editing out cross-cultural interference and a temporal or evolutionary perspective, the reader is supposed to gain a "more controlled look" at a society as it might have been at some earlier time. Aside from the problem of pooling information from various time periods that appear to lie somewhere back in the "aboriginal" life circumstances of a particular group (see Murdock 1949), which further distorts the reality of the analytic model for lack of proper controls, the reader ends up with a synchronic "slice of life" as it was presumed to be in the past. However intriguing and useful such studies may be for certain limited purposes, there is no avoiding the fact that the "ethnographic present" is a hypothetical device that does not move the discipline on to more dynamic and realistic models of adaptation and change. If anthropology is ever to come of age as a viable science—in full control of a broadly integrated scientific paradigm against which one can measure the progress of the discipline—it must be prepared to delineate the multiple complexities of human social systems as they have existed through time and are presently constituted. But even this effort will end in stagnation without some conscientious effort to see beyond the surface structural variations and non-recurrent "histories" of particular populations. Studies of sociocultural change and adaptation must either be cast directly in an evolutionary framework or be carried out with sufficient rigor on lower levels of analysis that they lend themselves to broader interpretations. As Alland and McCay point out, "The study of evolution is most emphatically *not* the study of history writ large, but rather the search for those underlying factors that drive systems of human behavior" (1973:143).

We have attempted in this volume to identify some of the major processual and structural features of adaptive infrastructures in relation to surface structure and particular culture content in several societies, and we have done so with the premise in mind that analytic conclusions drawn on one level of analysis must be compatible with the body of facts and theory we control on other levels of analysis. It is true that our evolutionary interest has inclined more toward specific than general evolution (see Sahlins and Service 1960). But the building of a maximally satisfactory scientific paradigm requires investigation on *all* levels of reality and it demands consistency rather than contradictions in results when one changes the scope of analysis to a broader or narrower base in dealing with the same phenomena (see Rubinstein and Laughlin 1977). To quote Alland and McCay again, "the discovery of those mechanisms that underlie change requires careful attention to rather specific evolutionary episodes. The grand overview commits the sin of omission and risks superficiality" (1973:161), *unless* it is a body of facts and theory that is closely integrated with specific levels of analysis and reality in human existence patterns. There is a need in anthropology for theoretical consistency in both directions of analysis—from microtheory to macrotheory, and vice-versa. The biocultural and transformational model developed in this volume lends itself, we feel, to such analyses.

We have also treated cognitive systems, culture pools, and adaptive infrastructures from an "organismic" point of view—one that is in keeping with a Whiteheadian conception of systems in process:

> There are two species of process, macroscopic process, and microscopic process. The macroscopic process is the transition from attained actuality to actuality in the attainment; while the microscopic process is the conversion of conditions which are merely real into determinate actuality. The former process effects the transition from the 'actual' to the 'merely real'; and the latter process effects the growth from the real to the actual. Macroscopic process is efficient; microscopic process is teleological. The future is merely real, without being actual; whereas the past is a nexus of actualities. *The actualities are constituted by their real genetic phases. The present is the immediacy of teleological process whereby reality becomes actual* . . . each actual entity is itself only describable as an organic process. It repeats in microcosm what the universe is in macrocosm. It is a

process proceeding from phase to phase, each phase being the real basis from which its successor proceeds towards the completion of the thing in question. . . . An 'object' is a transcendent element characterizing that definiteness to which our 'experience' has to conform. In this sense, the future has *objective* reality in present, but no *formal* actuality. For it is inherent in the constitution of the immediate, present actuality that a future will supersede it. Also conditions to which that future must conform, including real relationships to the present, are really objective in the immediate actuality. . . . Thus each actual entity, although complete so far as concerns its microscopic process, is yet incomplete by reason of its objective inclusion of the macroscopic process. It really experiences a future which must be actual, although the completed actualities of that future are undetermined. In this sense, each actual occasion experiences its own objective immortality. (Whitehead 1960:326–28, emphasis added)

Whitehead's conceptualization of macroscopic and microscopic process is roughly equivalent to what Lévi-Strauss has called "structure" and "history," respectively (cf. Barnett 1965). The movement of microscopic processes into macroscopic processes occurs at a complex node comprised of the intersection of macroscopic process, history, and environment for a given population. The historical component is itself an infinite progression of such transformations. What makes a Whiteheadian analysis more palatable to us than a Lévi-Straussian one in this regard is that the latter explicitly rejects the historical and environmental components of the transformational node, thereby obfuscating any possibility of explaining the transformation from "historical" to "structural" as ongoing process and adaptation to changing environmental circumstances (see Lévi-Strauss 1967:1ff.). A Whiteheadian view requires analysis of all components of the node over time. Whether or not the node is anchored primarily in the emerging cognized environment of an individual or in the collective adaptive infrastructure of a social group, the study of adaptation in human populations is grounded in elucidating the node of transformation at which any conceptual or social system meets its future. Thus in Laughlin's analysis of systemic change among the So (see article 3), all three elements of a Whiteheadian transformational node are present and specified: progressive and recursive change in the environment, the particular microscopic processes evident in the history of So adaptation, and the macroscopic processes of diaphatic equilibration to recursivity in the environment.

PROSPECTUS

The importance of these issues for calculating future studies of adaptation in anthropology seems apparent. The structure of any organic system, including for our purposes cognitive and sociocultural systems, is multidimensional. Just as any complex organic system is, by definition, comprised of subsystems embedded in subsystems, so too are its subsystems comprised of temporal phases embedded in temporal phases. Thus, in order for the ethnographer to complete a minimally satisfactory description of adaptation in a social system, he must outline explicitly both the subsystem and the phase of reference. The minimal duration of structural phase so incorporated should be determined by the duration of environmental flux stipulated by his research problem. The maximal duration of phase for an individual conceptual system is the duration circumscribed by that individual's conception and death—one life cycle. On the other hand, the maximal duration of phase for any particular social system may range from many generations to virtual infinity. Lacking the methodological and theoretical means for encompassing maximal phase in all instances, it is still possible to operationalize anthropological studies of adaptation to encompass *maximal practical phases,* that is, all complete phases of cognitive and social structures that are efficiently operative in the adaptation complex being examined and are available for practical measurement and recording. The key to success in such studies lies not only in disencumbering history from structure and form from function, but also in applying a systematically calculated temporal perspective. As Count has said, "Only by following an individual or group through a whole period until all the processes commence to repeat (i.e., over an entire cycle) can we record its biogram" (1973:7). Furthermore, we have suggested that this be done through the study of tandem exploitation cycles that bridge the transactional relationships between a population's cognized and operational environments, through the discovery and analysis of structure and cybernetic processing in adaptive infrastructures, and through the comparative study of these structures as they have existed through time and are presently constituted.

Accepting these arguments, the major task for analysis becomes one of isolating and describing the activity systems of adaptive infrastructures as well as the infrastructures themselves. The position taken in this volume is that such activity systems are likely to be made more manifest under conditions of extreme deprivation and stress. It seems that nowhere are the processes and patterns of adaptation better expressed than under urgent threats to survival. Societies under extreme stress, both recursive and progressive, are "laboratories" for partially controlling variables crucial to societal adaptation. They represent an especially valuable arena for testing models of social dynamics and adaptation and thereby for increasing our comprehension of the structure and function of adaptive infrastructures under normal conditions.

The study of systems under stress is not a new idea, of course. It has been recognized and used to great advantage in a number of other fields. For example, much of what is known about the functions of the central nervous system in human beings, especially the neocortex, has been obtained from lesion studies, that is, studies of the systemic effects of temporary or permanent damage to portions of neural tissue. By studying functional deficits and compensatory operations in the brain, neurophysiologists have been able to construct a viable profile of the functions of healthy, undamaged brains (see Worden et al. 1975). Similarly, cognitive psychologists have shown that assigning special attention to psychopathologies as systemic "errors" in functioning can shed considerable light on the normal functions of human conceptual systems (see Giora 1975; McManus 1975).

In the same spirit, we would argue that there is much to be learned about human adaptation by carefully researching the responses of adaptive infrastructures to natural catastrophes and disasters on a cross-cultural, comparative basis (cf. Baker and Chapman 1962). These studies would complement longitudinal field research on sociocultural systems confronting deprivation—such as many of those described in the present work. Moreover, the model presented in article 1 of this volume provides an analytic framework for integrating studies of both types, that is, of deprivation as well as disaster. What remains to be determined is just how far our present efforts will take us in increasing our understanding of the larger issues at stake in studies of human adaptation and evolution generally.

Bibliography

Ackerman, Charles. 1975. "A Tsimshian Oedipus." MS.

Adams, John. 1973. *The Gitksan Potlatch*. Toronto: Holt, Rinehart and Winston.

Adams, Richard. N.d. "Harnessing Technology." MS.

Alejo, Javier. 1973. "Crecimiento demográfico y empleo en la economía mexicana." Paper presented at the 73rd Annual Meeting of the American Anthropological Association, Mexico City.

Alkire, William H. 1965. *Lamotrek Atoll and Inter-Island Socioeconomic Ties*. Illinois Studies in Anthropology No. 5. Urbana: University of Illinois Press.

Allan, W. 1967. *The African Husbandman*. New York: Barnes and Noble.

Alland, Alexander, Jr., and Bonnie McCay. 1973. "The Concept of Adaptation in Biological and Cultural Evolution." In J. Honigmann, ed., *Handbook of Social and Cultural Anthropology*. Chicago: Rand McNally.

Anonymous. 1732. *A Detection of the State and Situation of the Present Sugar Planters of Barbados and the Leeward Islands*. London: J. Wilford.

—— 1823. *Description of the Different Modes of Cultivation and Manufacturing Sugar in the East and West Indies*. London.

—— 1824. *Report of the Trial of 14 Negroes at . . . . Montego-Bay, January, 1824, . . . on a Charge of Rebellious Conspiracy, with the Arguments of the Advocates and the Speeches of the Judges*. Montego-Bay.

—— 1828. *Sketches and Recollections of the West Indies by a Resident*. London: Smith, Elder.

Atwood, Thomas. 1791. *The History of the Island of Dominica*. London.

Audy, J. R., and F. L. Dunn. 1973. "Health, Disease, and Community

Health." In Frederick Sargent, ed., *Human Ecology*. The Netherlands: North Holland Publishing.

Baker, George, and Dwight Chapman, eds. 1962. *Man and Society in Disaster*. New York: Basic Books.

Barber, J. 1968. *Imperial Frontier*. Nairobi: East African Publishing House.

Barnes, J. A. 1954. "Class Committee in a Norwegian Island Parish." *Human Relations* 7:39–58.

Barnett, Homer G. 1953. *Innovation: The Basis of Cultural Change*. New York: McGraw-Hill.

—— 1965. "Laws of Sociocultural Change." *International Journal of Comparative Sociology* 6:207–30.

—— 1971. "Compatibility and Compartmentalization in Cultural Change." In A. R. Desai, ed., *Essays on Modernization of Underdeveloped Societies*. Bombay: Thacker.

Barth, Fredrik. 1966. *Models of Social Organization*. Royal Anthropological Institute Occasional Paper No. 23. London: Royal Anthropological Institute.

Barth, Fredrik, ed. 1969. *Ethnic Groups and Boundaries*. Boston: Little, Brown.

Bateson, Gregory. 1936. *Naven*. Stanford, Calif.: Stanford University Press.

Baumgartner, T., W. Buckley, and T. R. Burns. 1975a. "Meta-Power and Relational Control in Social Life." *Social Science Information* 14:49–78.

Baumgartner, T., T. R. Burns, P. Deville, and D. Meeker. 1975b. "A Systems Model of Conflict and Change in Planning Systems." *General Systems* 20:167–83.

Beckford, William. 1788. *Remarks upon the Situation of the Negroes in Jamaica, Impartially Made from a Local Experience of Nearly 13 Years in that Island*. London: T. and J. Egerton.

—— 1790. *A Descriptive Account of the Island of Jamaica*. 2 vols. London.

Bee, Robert L. 1974. *Patterns and Processes: An Introduction to Anthropological Strategies for the Study of Sociocultural Change*. New York: Macmillan.

Beidelman, Thomas. 1961a. "Hyena and Rabbit: A Kaguru Representation of Matrilineal Relations." *Africa* 31:61–74.

—— 1961b. "Right and Left Hand among the Kaguru." *Africa* 31:250–57.

—— 1963. "Witchcraft in Ukaguru." In J. Middleton and E. Winters, eds., *Witchcraft and Sorcery in East Africa*. London: Routledge and Kegan Paul.

—— 1967. *The Matrilineal Peoples of Eastern Tanzania*. London: International African Institute.

Belgrove, William. 1755. *A Treatise upon Husbandry or Planting*.

Belisario, I. M. 1838. *Sketches of Character, in Illustration of the Habits, Occupation, and Costume of the Negro Population in the Island of Jamaica*. Kingston.

Bennett, J. Harry. 1958. *Bondsmen and Bishops, Slavery and Apprenticeship on the Codrington Plantations of Barbados, 1710–1838*. Berkeley: University of California Press.

Bennett, John W. 1969. *Northern Plainsmen*. Chicago: Aldine.

Bernal, Ignacio. 1973. "Teotihuacan y los destinos mexicanos." *Plural* 22:7–12.

Berndt, Ronald and Catherine. 1954. *Arnhem Land: Its History and Its People*. Melbourne: Cheshire.

Binford, Lewis R. 1968. "Post-Pleistocene Adaptations." In Sally R. and Lewis R. Binford, eds., *New Perspectives in Archeology*. Chicago: Aldine.

Birch, L. C. 1957. "The Meanings of Competition." *American Naturalist*. 91:5–18.

Birdsell, Joseph B. 1970. "Local Group Composition among Aborigines: A Reply." *Current Anthropology* 11:138–39.

Bishop, Charles A. 1970. "The Emergence of Hunting Territories among the Northern Ojibwa." *Ethnology* 9:1–15.

—— 1972. "Demography, Ecology and Trade among the Northern Ojibwa and Swampy Cree." *Western Canadian Journal of Anthropology* 3:58–71.

—— 1974. *The Northern Ojibwa and the Fur Trade: An Historical and Ecological Study*. Toronto: Holt, Rinehart and Winston.

—— 1975. "Ojibwa, Cree and the Hudson's Bay Company in Northern Ontario: Culture and Conflict in the Eighteenth Century." In A. W. Rasporich, ed., *Western Canada Past and Present*. Calgary: McClelland and Stewart West.

—— 1976. "The Emergence of the Northern Ojibwa: Social and Economic Consequences." *American Ethnologist* 3:39–54.

Bishop, Charles A., and M. Estellie Smith. 1975. "Early Historic Populations in Northwestern Ontario: Archaeological and Ethnohistorical Interpretations." *American Antiquity* 40:54–63.

Blau, Peter. 1964. *Exchange and Social Power*. New York: Wiley.
Bleby, Henry. 1854. *Scenes in the Caribbean Sea: Being Sketches from a Missionary's Notebook*. London: Hamilton, Adams.
Blome, R. 1678. *A Description of the Island of Jamaica*.
Boas, Franz. 1902. *Tsimshian Texts*. Washington, D.C.: Bureau of American Ethnology.
—— 1912. *Tsimshian Texts*. (N.S.) Seattle: Publications of the American Ethnological Society III.
—— 1916. *Tsimshian Mythology*. Washington, D.C.: Bureau of American Ethnology.
—— 1935. "Kwakiutl Culture as Reflected in Mythology." *Memoirs of the American Folklore Society* 28:1–190.
Boissevain, Jeremy. 1968. "The Place of Non-Groups in the Social Sciences." *Man* (N.S.) 3:542–56.
Brady, Ivan A. 1970. "Land Tenure, Kinship and Community Structure: Strategies for Living in the Ellice Islands of Western Polynesia." Ph.D. diss., University of Oregon.
—— 1972a. "Kinship Reciprocity in the Ellice Islands: An Evaluation of Sahlins' Model of the Sociology of Primitive Exchange." *Journal of the Polynesian Society* 81:290–316.
—— 1972b. "Population Structure and Distribution in the Ellice Islands." Paper presented at the Atoll Populations Conference, East-West Population Institute, Honolulu.
—— 1974. "Land Tenure in the Ellice Islands: A Changing Profile." In H. Lundsgaarde, ed., *Land Tenure in Oceania*. ASAO Monograph No. 2. Honolulu: University Press of Hawaii.
—— 1975a. "The Structural Nexus of Kinship: Mud and Blood Reexamined." Paper presented at the 74th annual Meeting of the American Anthropological Association, San Francisco.
—— 1975b. "Christians, Pagans and Government Men: Culture Change in the Ellice Islands." In Ivan A. Brady and Barry L. Isaac, eds., *A Reader in Culture Change, Vol. II: Case Studies*. Cambridge: Schenkman.
—— 1976a. "Problems of Description and Explanation in the Study of Adoption." In Ivan A. Brady, ed., *Transactions in Kinship*. . . . ASAO Monograph No. 4. Honolulu: University Press of Hawaii.
—— 1976b. "Socioeconomic Mobility: Adoption and Land Tenure in the Ellice Islands." In Ivan A. Brady, ed., *Transactions in Kinship*. . . . ASAO Monograph No. 4. Honolulu: University Press of Hawaii.

——— 1976c. "Adaptive Engineering: An Overview of Adoption in Oceania." In Ivan A. Brady, ed., *Transactions in Kinship*. . . . ASAO Monograph No. 4. Honolulu: University Press of Hawaii.

——— 1976d. "The Sociobiology of Hoarding: Some Preliminary Theory." MS.

———, ed. 1976e. *Transactions in Kinship: Adoption and Fosterage in Oceania*. ASAO Monograph No. 4. Honolulu: University Press of Hawaii.

Brady, Ivan A., and Barry L. Isaac, eds. 1975. *A Reader in Culture Change*. Vols. I and II. Cambridge: Schenkman.

Bridges, George W. 1828. *The Annals of Jamaica*. 2 vols. London: John Murray.

Britan, Gerald, and Bette S. Denich. 1976. "Environment and Choice in Rapid Social Change." *American Ethnologist* 3:55–72.

Brown, Joseph Epes. 1953. *The Sacred Pipe*. Baltimore: Penguin.

Bryant, Josua. 1824. *Account of an Insurrection of the Negro Slaves in the Colony of Demerara which Broke Out on the 18th August, 1823*.

Buckley, Walter. 1967. *Sociology and Modern Systems Theory*. Englewood Cliffs, N.J.: Prentice-Hall.

Burling, Robbins. 1962. "Maximization Theories and the Study of Economic Anthropology." *American Anthropologist* 64:802–21.

Burns, Sir Alan. 1965. *History of the British West Indies*. London: Allen and Unwin.

Burns, T. R. 1973. "A Structural Theory of Social Exchange." *Acta Sociologica* 16:188–208.

Burns, T. R., and Charles D. Laughlin. 1978. "Ritual and Social Power." In E. G. d'Aquili et al., eds., *The Spectrum of Ritual*. New York: Columbia University Press.

Burns, T. R., and D. Meeker. 1975. "A Multi-Level, Structural Model of Social Behavior." *Quality and Quantity* 9:51–89.

Butterworth, D. 1971. "Migración rural-urbana en América Latina: el estado de nuestro conocimiento." *América Indígena* 31:85–106.

Caines, Clement. 1801. *Letters on the Cultivation of Otabeite Cane, the Manufacture of Sugar and Rum, the Saving of Molasses, the Care and Preservation of Stock, with the Attention and Anxiety which is Due to Negroes*. London: Robinson.

Calhoun, J. B. 1972. "Plight of the Ik and Kaiadilt Is Seen as a Chilling Possible End for Man." *Smithsonian Magazine*, November.

The Canadian Council on Nutrition. 1963. *Dietary Standard for Canada*. Bulletin on Nutrition 6 (1).

Cancian, Frank. 1976. "Social Stratification." In B. J. Siegel, A. R. Beals, and S. A. Tyler, eds., *Annual Review of Anthropology* 5:227–48. Palo Alto, Calif.: Annual Reviews.

Carmichael, A. C. 1833. *Domestic Manners and Social Conditions of the White, Coloured and Negro Populations of the West Indies*. 2 vols. London: Whittaker.

Carneiro, Robert L. 1968. "Slash-and-Burn Cultivation among the Kuikuru and Its Implications for Cultural Development in the Amazon Basin." In Yehudi A. Cohen, ed., *Man in Adaptation: The Cultural Present*. Chicago: Aldine.

—— 1970. "A Theory of the Origin of the State." *Science* 169:733–38.

Cawte, John. 1972. *Cruel, Poor and Brutal Nations: The Assessment of Mental Health in an Australian Aboriginal Community by Short-Stay Psychiatric Field Team Methods*. Honolulu: University Press of Hawaii.

—— 1974. *Medicine Is the Law*. Honolulu: University Press of Hawaii.

Chakravarti, M. R., and T. V. Haurav. 1966. "Relation between Incidence of Small Pox and the OAB System of Blood Groups." In M. S. Malhotra, ed., *Human Adaptability to Environments and Physical Fitness*. New Delhi: Ministry of Defense, Government of India.

Chapman, Dwight, ed. 1954. "Effects of Social and Cultural Systems in Reactions to Stress." Social Science Research Council Pamphlet 14. New York: Social Science Research Council.

Chapple, E. D. 1970. *Culture and Biological Man*. New York: Holt, Rinehart and Winston.

Chisholm, C. 1801. *An Essay on the Malignant Pestilential Fever Introduced into the West India Islands from Boullam, on the Coast of Guinea in 1793, 1974, 1796*. 2 vols. London.

Clark, Lincoln D. 1965. "Aggressive Behavior and Factors Affecting It." In *Symposium on Medical Aspects of Stress in the Military Climate*. Sponsored by Walter Reed Army Institute of Research. Washington, D.C.: Government Printing Office.

Cochrane, Glynn. 1971. *Development Anthropology*. New York: Oxford University Press.

Codere, Helene. 1950. *Fighting with Property*. American Ethnological Society, Monograph 18. Seattle: University of Washington Press.

Cohen, Yehundi A. 1968. *Man in Adaptation: The Cultural Present.* Chicago: Aldine.

—— 1971. *Man in Adaptation: The Institutional Framework.* Chicago: Aldine.

Coke, Thomas. 1808. *A History of the West Indies.* 3 vols. Liverpool.

Colonial Office (British). 1701. "Communications Relating to the Murder of Samuel Martin." C.O. 152/4, Nos. 73, 73i–iii, C.O. 153/7, pp. 418–24.

—— 1718. "Mr. Nivine to Council of Trade and Plantations." C.O. 152/12, No. 100.

—— 1726. "Governor John Hart to Board of Trade." C.O. 152/15, R166.

—— 1737a. "Governor Mathew to Council of Trade and Plantations." C.O. 152/22, fos. 302–03d, 306–07d, 311–23d.

—— 1737b. "Governor Mathew to Alured Popple." C.O. 152/23, fos. 5–19d.

—— 1737c. "Petition of John Yeamans, Agent for Antigua and of Planters and Merchants, to King." C.O. 152/40, fox. 288b, 288c.

—— 1768. "Letters from Governor Woodley, Nos. 1 and 3." C.O. 152/48.

—— 1778. "Deposition of Mrs. Alice Carroll." C.O. 152/58, p. 34.

—— 1788a. "List of Accounts Demanded by the Agent for the Island of Antigua by his Letter to the President and Speaker of that Island." C.O. 157/67.

—— 1788b. "Answers by the Council and Assembly of the Island of Montserrat to Several Heads of Enquiry sent to the West India Islands." C.O. 152/67.

—— 1789. "Answers to Queries to Lord Sydney." C.O. 152/67.

—— 1806. "Letter from Lavington, No. 6." C.O. 152/88.

Cook, Scott. 1968. "The Obsolete 'Anti-Market' Mentality: A Critique of the Substantive Approach to Economic Anthropology." In E. E. LeClair and H. Schneider, eds., *Economic Anthropology.* New York: Holt, Rinehart and Winston.

—— 1971. "Production Strategy in Economic Anthropology." Paper presented at the 70th Annual Meeting of the American Anthropological Association, New York.

Cooper, Thomas. 1824. *Facts Illustrative of the Condition of the Negro Slave in Jamaica.* London: Hatchard.

Copeman, W. S. C. 1960. *Doctors and Disease in Tudor Times.* London: Dawson's of Pall Mall.

Count, Earl W. 1973. *Being and Becoming Human.* New York: Van Nostrand Reinhold.

Cove, John. 1975a. "The Boasian Problem: Reconstruction of Culture through Myth." MS.

—— 1975b. "The Spider and the Widow's Daughter: Famine and Authority in Tsimshian Myth." MS.

Craton, Michael. 1971. "Jamaican Slave Mortality: Fresh Light from Worthy Park, Longville and the Tharp Estates." *Journal of Caribbean History* 3:1–27.

Craton, Michael, and James Walvin. 1970. *A Jamaican Plantation: The History of Worthy Park, 1670–1970.* London: W. H. Allen.

Dancer, Thomas. 1819. *The Medical Assistant, or Jamaica Practice of Physic.* Kingston: Smith and Kinnear.

Danielsson, Bengt. 1955. *Work and Life on Raroia: An Acculturation Study from the Tuamotu Group.* Stockholm: Saxon and Lindstrom.

Dasen, P. 1972. "Cross-Cultural Piagetian Research: A Summary." *Journal of Cross-Cultural Psychology* 3:23–40.

d'Aquili, E. G., Charles D. Laughlin, and J. R. McManus, eds. 1978. *The Spectrum of Ritual.* New York: Columbia University Press.

de Castro, Josué. 1952. *The Geography of Hunger.* Boston: Little, Brown.

De La Beche, H. T. 1825. *Notes on the Present Condition of the Negroes in Jamaica.* London: T. Cadell.

DeVore, I, ed. 1965. *Primate Behavior: Field Studies of Monkeys and Apes.* New York: Holt, Rinehart and Winston.

Demerath, Nicholas J. 1957. "Some General Propositions: An Interpretive Summary." In Nicholas J. Demerath and A. F. C. Wallace, eds., *Human Adaptation to Disaster.* Special Issue, *Human Organization* 16:2:28–29.

Demerath, Nicholas J., and A. F. C. Wallace, eds. 1957. *Human Adaptation to Disaster.* Special Issue, *Human Organization* 16:2.

Dickson, William. 1814. *Mitigation of Slavery.* London.

Dirks, Robert. 1972. "Networks, Groups, and Adaptation in an Afro-Caribbean Community." *Man* (N.S.) 7:565–85.

—— 1975a. "Ethnicity and Ethnic Group Relations in the British Virgin Islands." In John Bennett, ed., *The New Ethnicity.* Minneapolis: West.

—— 1975b. "Slaves Holiday." *Natural History* 84:82–91.

—— 1976. "Sociobehavioral Responses to Famine (Review and Synthesis)." Paper presented at the 75th Annual Meeting of the American Anthropological Association, Washington, D.C.

Dirks, Robert, and Virginia Kerns. 1976. "Patterns of Mating and Adaptation in Rum Bay, 1823–1970." *Social and Economic Studies* 25:34–54.

Dobzhansky, Theodosius. 1965. "Biological Evolution in Island Populations." In F. R. Fosberg, ed., *Man's Place in the Island Ecosystem*. Honolulu: Bishop Museum Press.

Domar, Evsey D. 1970. "The Causes of Slavery or Serfdom: A Hypothesis." *Journal of Economic History* 30:18–32.

Dumond, Don E. 1972a. "Population Growth and Political Centralization." In Brian Spooner, ed., *Population Growth: Anthropological Implications*. Cambridge: M.I.T. Press.

—— 1972b. "Prehistoric Population Growth and Subsistence Change in Eskimo Alaska." In Brian Spooner, ed., *Population Growth: Anthropological Implications*. Cambridge: M.I.T. Press.

Dunn, Frederick L. 1970. "Cultural Evolution in the Late Pleistocene and Holocene of Southeast Asia." *American Anthropologist* 72:1041–54.

Dunn, Richard S. 1972. *Sugar and Slaves: The Rise of the Planter Class in the English West Indies, 1624–1713*. Chapel Hill: University of North Carolina Press.

Durkheim, Emile. 1938. *The Rules of Sociological Method*. S. Solvay and J. Mueller, trans.; G. E. G. Catlin, ed. Chicago: University of Chicago Press.

—— 1963. *The Division of Labor in Society*. Chicago: Aldine.

Dyson, W. S., and V. E. Fuchs. 1937. "The Elmolo." *Journal of the Royal Anthropological Institute* 67:327–38.

Dyson-Hudson, N. 1966. *Karimojong Politics*. London: Oxford University Press.

Eclectic Review. 1832. Art. IV. The Anti-Slavery Reporter. *Eclectic Review* (N.S.) 7:244–60.

Edwards, Bryan. 1819. *The History, Civil and Commercial of the British Colonies in the West Indies*. 5 vols. 5th ed: London.

Eitinger, L., and A. Strom. 1973. *Mortality and Morbidity after Excessive Stress: A Follow-Up Investigation of Norwegian Concentration Camp Survivors*. New York: Humanities Press.

Elton, Charles. 1927. *Animal Ecology*. London: Sidgwick and Jackson.

Ember, Melvin. 1966. "Samoan Kinship and Political Structure: An Archaeological Test to Decide between Two Alternative Reconstructions." *American Anthropologist* 68:163–68.

Erlich, Cora. 1937. "Tribal Culture in Crow Mythology." *Journal of American Folklore* 50:307–408.

Evans-Pritchard, E. D. 1940. *The Nuer*. Oxford: Clarendon.

Fiedler, F. E. 1962. "Group Climate and Group Creativity." *Journal of Abnormal and Social Psychology* 65:308–18.

Finney, Ben. 1966. "Resource Distribution and Social Structure in Tahiti." *Ethnology* 5:80–86.

Firth, Raymond. 1959. *Social Change in Tikopia*. London: Allen and Unwin.

—— ed. 1970. *Themes in Economic Anthropology*. ASA Monograph No. 6. London: Tavistock.

Flannigan, Mrs. 1844. *Antigua and the Antiguans*. 2 vols. London: Saunders and Otley.

Foley, J. T. 1966. *Droughts in Australia*. Bureau of Meterology Bulletin No. 43. Canberra: Commonwealth Bureau of Meterology.

Food and Agricultural Organization (FAO). 1957. *Protein Requirements*. FAO Nutritional Studies, no. 16. Rome: Food and Agricultural Organization of the United Nations.

—— 1962. *Nutrition and Working Efficiency*. Freedom from Hunger Campaign Basic Studies Series, 5. Rome: Food and Agriculture Organization of the United Nations.

Ford, Clellan. 1941. *Smoke from Their Fires*. New Haven: Yale University Press.

Fortes, Meyer. 1969. *Kinship and the Social Order: The Legacy of Lewis Henry Morgan*. Chicago: Aldine.

Fosberg, F. R., ed. 1965. *Man's Place in the Island Ecosystem*. Honolulu: Bishop Museum Press.

Foster, George M. 1973. *Traditional Societies and Technological Change*. New York: Harper and Row.

Foulkes, Theodore. 1833. *Eighteen Months in Jamaica with Recollections of the Late Rebellion*. London: Whittaker, Treacher, and Arnott.

Franklin, Joseph E., Burtrum C. Schiele, Josef Brozek, and Ancel Keys. 1948. "Observations on Human Behavior in Experimental Semistarvation and Rehabilitation." *Journal of Clinical Psychology* 4:28–44.

Freeman, Derek. 1961. Review of Marshall D. Sahlins, *Social Stratification in Polynesia*. *Man* 180:146–48.

—— 1962. "Environment and Culture in Polynesia." *Man* 20:24–25.

—— 1964. "Some Observations on Kinship and Political Authority in Samoa." *American Anthropologist* 66:553–68.

Fried, Morton H. 1957. "The Classification of Corporate Unilineal

Descent Groups." *Journal of the Royal Anthropological Institute* 87:1–29.

Geertz, Clifford. 1957. "Ritual and Social Change: A Javanese Example." *American Anthropologist* 59:32–54.

—— 1963. *Agricultural Involution: The Process of Ecological Change in Indonesia*. Berkeley: University of California Press.

—— 1966. "Religion as a Cultural System." In M. Banton, ed., *Anthropological Approaches to the Study of Religion*. ASA Monograph No. 3. New York: Praeger.

—— 1973. *The Interpretation of Cultures*. New York: Basic Books.

Genovese, Eugene D. 1967. "Rebelliousness and Docility in the Negro Slave: A Critique of the Elkin's Thesis." *Civil War History* 13:293–314.

Gibson, Captain H. W. S. 1892. "A Report on the Visit of H. M. S. Curaçao to the Ellice Islands in 1892." MS in Turnbull Library, Wellington.

Giesel, James T. 1974. *The Biology and Adaptability of Natural Populations*. St. Louis: Mosby.

Gill, W. W. 1885. *Jottings from the Pacific*. London.

Giora, Zvi. 1975. *Psychopathology: A Cognitive View*. New York: Gardner Press.

Gluckman, Max. 1954. *Rituals of Rebellion in South-East Africa*. Manchester: Manchester University Press.

Goffman, Irving. 1966. *Behavior in Public Places*. New York: Free Press.

Goldman, Irving. 1970. *Ancient Polynesian Society*. Chicago: University of Chicago Press.

Goodenough, Ward H. 1955. "A Problem in Malayo-Polynesian Social Organization." *American Anthropologist* 57:71–83.

—— 1959. Review of Marshall D. Sahlins, *Social Stratification in Polynesia*. *Journal of the Polynesian Society* 68:255–58.

—— 1971. *Culture, Language and Society*. Reading, Mass.: Addison-Wesley.

Gould, R. 1970. "Journey to Pulykara." *Natural History* 79:57–66.

Goveia, Elsa V. 1965. *Slave Society in the British Leeward Islands at the End of the Eighteenth Century*. New Haven: Yale University Press.

—— 1970. *The West Indian Slave Laws of the 18th Century*. Barbados: Caribbean Universities Press.

Government of Barbados. 1972. *The National Food and Nutrition Survey of Barbados*. Pan American Health Organization Scientific Publication No. 237. Washington, D.C.: Pan American Health Organization.

Gray, R. F. 1960. "Sonjo Bride-Price and the Question of African 'Wife Purchase.' " *American Anthropologist* 62:34–57.

Gross, Daniel, and Barbara Underwood. 1975. "Technological Change and Caloric Costs: Sisal Agriculture in Northeastern Brazil." In Ivan A. Brady and Barry L. Isaac, eds., *A Reader in Culture Change, Vol. II: Case Studies*. Cambridge: Schenkman.

Guetzkow, M. H., and P. H. Bowman. 1946. *Men and Hunger*. Elgin, Ill.: Brethren Publishing House.

Gurney, John Joseph. 1840. *A Winter in the West Indies, Described in Familiar Letters to Henry Clay, of Kentucky*. London: John Murray.

Hainline, Jane. 1965. "Culture and Biological Adaptation." *American Anthropologist* 67:1174–97.

Hall, Tim. 1972. "Hurricane Bebe—Special Report." *Atoll Pioneer*, Nov. 2.

Hamblin, R. L. 1958. "Leadership and Crisis." *Sociometry* 21:322–35.

Hamburg, D. A. 1971. "Crowding, Stranger Contact, and Aggressive Behavior." In Lennart Levi, ed., *Society, Stress, and Disease*. London: Oxford University Press.

Harris, Marvin. 1959. "The Economy Has No Surplus?" *American Anthropologist* 61:185–200.

Harvey, O. J., D. E. Hunt, and H. M. Schroder. 1961. *Conceptual Systems and Personality Organization*. New York: John Wiley.

HBC Arch. N.d. The Hudson's Bay Company Archives in Winnipeg (formerly in London, England) and on microfilm in the Public Archives, Ottawa.

Herskovits, Melville. 1926. "The Cattle Complex in East Africa." *American Anthropologist* 28:230–72, 361–88, 424–528, 630–64.

Hibbert, Robert, Jr. 1825. *Hints to the Young Jamaica Sugar Planter*. London: Underwood.

Hickerson, Harold. 1960. "The Feast of the Dead among the Seventeenth Century Algonkians of the Upper Great Lakes." *American Anthropologist* 62:81–107.

—— 1962. "The Southwestern Chippewa: An Ethno-Historical Study." *American Anthropological Memoir* 92.

—— 1967. "Some Implications of the Theory of Particularity, or "Atomism' of Northern Algonkians." *Current Anthropology* 8:313–43.

Hiernaux, Jean. 1968. *La Diversité humaine en Afrique Subsaharienne.* Editions de l'Institut de Sociologie. Bruxelles: Université Libre de Bruxelles.

Hobbes, Thomas. 1651. *The Leviathan: Part 1, of Men.* Chicago: Encyclopedia Britannica, Great Books of the Western World.

Holmberg, Allan R. 1950. *Nomads of the Long Bow.* Washington, D.C.: Smithsonian Institution, Institute of Social Anthropology.

Homans, G. C. 1958. "Social Behavior as Exchange." *American Journal of Sociology* 62:597–606.

House of Commons (British). 1789. *House of Commons Accounts and Papers.* Vol. 26.

—— 1790a. *House of Commons Accounts and Papers.* Vol. 29.

—— 1790b. *House of Commons Accounts and Papers.* Vol. 30.

—— 1791. *House of Commons Accounts and Papers.* Vol. 34.

Howard, Alan. 1963. "Land, Activity Systems, and Decision-Making Models in Rotuma." *Ethnology* 2:407–40.

—— 1970. "Adoption on Rotuma." In Vern Carroll, ed., *Adoption in Eastern Oceania.* ASAO Monograph No. 1. Honolulu: University Press of Hawaii.

Hutchinson, G. Evelyn. 1957. "Concluding Remarks." In *Population Studies: Animal Ecology and Demography, Cold Spring Harbor Symposia on Quantitative Biology.* Vol. xxii. Cold Spring Harbor, N.Y.: Biological Laboratory.

Jamaican Archival Collection. 1823. C.S. 102/5, No. 73.

Joseph, Edward L. 1836. *History of Trinidad.* London.

Kates, R. W., et al. 1973. "Human Impact of the Managua Earthquake." *Science* 182:981–90.

Keesing, Roger, M. 1967. "Statistical Models and Decision Models of Social Structure." *Ethnology* 6:1–16.

—— 1970. "Kwaio Fosterage." *American Anthropologist* 72:991–1019.

—— 1972. "Simple Models of Complexity: The Lure of Kinship." In P. Reining, ed., *Kinship Studies in the Morgan Centennial Year.* Washington, D.C.: The Anthropological Society of Washington.

—— 1975. *Kin Groups and Social Structure.* New York: Holt, Rinehart and Winston.

Kelly, James. 1838. *Voyage to Jamaica, and Seventeen Years' Resi-*

304   BIBLIOGRAPHY

dence in that Island: Chiefly Written with a View to Exhibit Negro Life and Habits. 2nd ed. Belfast: Wilson.

Kemper, Robert V. 1970. "El estudio antropológico de la migración a las ciudades en América Latina." *América Indígena* 30:609–34.

Kennedy, Donald G. 1931. *Field Notes on the Culture of Vaitupu.* Wellington: Polynesian Society Memoir 9.

Kerns, Virginia. N.d. "Feast and Famine: Slave Hunger and Theft in the British West Indies." MS.

Keys, Ancel, et al. 1950. *The Biology of Human Starvation.* 2 vols. Minneapolis: University of Minnesota Press.

King, J. T., Y. Chuing Puk Lee, and M. R. Visscher. 1955. "Single versus Multiple Cage Occupancy and Convulsive Frequency in C_3H Mice." *Proceedings of the Society for Experimental Biological Medicine* 88:661–63.

Kluckhohn, Clyde. 1962. "Universal Categories of Culture." In Sol Tax, ed., *Anthropology Today.* Chicago: University of Chicago Press.

Kohlberg, L. 1969. "The Cognitive Developmental Approach to Socialization." In D. A. Goslin, ed., *The Handbook of Socialization Theory and Research.* Chicago: Rand McNally.

Köngäs Maranda, Elli. 1973. "Five Interpretations of a Melanesian Myth." *Journal of American Folklore* 86:3–13.

Kroeber, A. L. 1944. *Configurations of Culture Growth.* Berkeley: University of California Press.

Landtmann, Gunnar. 1938. *The Origin of the Inequality of the Social Classes.* New York: Greenwood.

Lang, Kurt, and Gladys Engel Lang. 1964. "Collective Responses to the Threat of Disaster." In George H. Grosser et al., eds., *The Threat of Impending Disaster.* Cambridge: M.I.T. Press.

Laughlin, Charles D. 1972. "Economics and Social Organization among the So of Northeastern Uganda." Ph.D. diss., University of Oregon.

—— 1974a. "Maximization, Marriage and Residence among the So." *American Ethnologist* 1:129–41.

—— 1974b. "Deprivation and Reciprocity." *Man* 9:380–96.

—— 1975. "Lexicostatistics and the Mystery of So Ethnolinguistic Relations." *Anthropological Linguistics,* Oct.:325–41.

—— 1975. "Myth, Language and the Brain: The Evolutionary Importance of Vicarious Experience." MS.

—— 1978. "Ritual and Stress." In E. G. d'Aquili et al., eds., *The Spectrum of Ritual*. New York: Columbia University Press.

Laughlin, Charles D., and E. G. d'Aquili. 1974. *Biogenetic Structuralism*. New York: Columbia University Press.

Laughlin, Charles D. and J. J. Cove. 1977. "Myth, Cognition, and Adaptation." Paper presented at the Annual Meeting of the Canadian Ethnological Society, Halifax, Nova Scotia.

Laughlin, Charles D. and E. R. 1972. *"Kenisan:* Economic and Social Ramifications of the Ghost Cult among the So of Northeastern Uganda." *Africa* 42:9–20.

—— 1973. "Attitudes, Beliefs and Practices Relevant to Family Planning among the So." In A. Molnos, ed., *Cultural Source Materials for Population Planning in East Africa*. Nairobi: East African Publishing House.

—— 1974. "Age Generations and Political Process in So." *Africa* 44:266–79.

Lazarus, Richard S. 1964. "A Laboratory Approach to the Dynamics of Psychological Stress." In George H. Grosser et al., eds., *The Threat of Impending Disaster*. Cambridge: M.I.T. Press.

Leach, Edmund. 1960. "The Sinhalese of the Dry Zone of Northern Ceylon." In G. P. Murdock, ed., *Social Structure in Southeast Asia*. Chicago: Quadrangle.

Lee, Richard B. 1966. "Subsistence Ecology of Kung Bushmen." Ph.D. diss., University of California, Berkeley.

—— 1972. "Population Growth and the Beginnings of Sedentary Life among the Kung Bushmen." In Brian Spooner, ed., *Population Growth: Anthropological Implications*. Cambridge: M.I.T. Press.

Lee, R., and I. Devore, eds. 1968. *Man the Hunter*. Chicago: Aldine.

Leeds, A., and A. P. Vayda, eds. 1965. *Men, Culture, and Animals: The Role of Animals in Human Ecological Adjustment*. American Association for the Advancement of Science, Publication No. 78. Washington, D.C.: American Association for the Advancement of Science.

Leighton, Alexander. 1959. *My Name Is Legion: Foundation for a Theory of Man in Relation to Culture*. New York: Basic Books.

—— 1972. "The Other Side of the Coin." *American Journal of Psychiatry* 127:123–25.

Leslie, Sir Charles. 1740. *A New and Exact Account of Jamaica*. Edinburgh.

Lessa, William. 1966. "Discoverer-of-the-Sun: Mythology as Reflection of Culture." *Journal of American Folklore* 79:3–51.
—— 1968. "The Social Effects of Typhoon Ophelia (1960) on Ulithi." In Andrew Vayda, ed., *Peoples and Cultures of the Pacific*. New York: Natural History Press.
Lévi-Strauss, Claude. 1963. *Structural Anthropology*. New York: Doubleday.
—— 1967. "The Story of Asdiwal." In Edmund Leach, ed., *The Structural Study of Myth and Totemism*. London: Tavistock.
—— 1969. *The Elementary Structures of Kinship*. (1st pub. 1949.) Rpt. Boston: Beacon Press.
Lewis, Matthew Gregory. 1834. *Journal of a West India Propietor Kept during a Residence in the Island of Jamaica*. London: John Murray.
—— 1845. *Journal of a Residence among the Negroes in the West Indies in 1815–16 and 1817*. London: John Murray.
Lewis, Oscar. 1966. "The Culture of Poverty." *Scientific American* 215:19–25.
—— 1969. *La anthropología de la pobreza*. Mexico City: Fondo de Cultura Económica.
Leyton, G. B. 1946. "The Effects of Slow Starvation." *Lancet* 251:73–79.
Lieber, Michael. 1970. "Adoption on Kapingamarangi." In V. Carroll, ed., *Adoption in Eastern Oceania*. ASAO Monograph No. 1. Honolulu: University Press of Hawaii.
—— 1974. "Land Tenure on Kapingamarangi." In H. Lundsgaarda, ed., *Land Tenure in Oceania*. ASAO Monograph No. 2. Honolulu: University Press of Hawaii.
Ligon, Richard. 1657. *A True and Exact History of the Island of Barbados*. London: Humphrey Moseley.
Littleton, Edward. 1689. *The Groans of the Plantations*. London.
Lomnitz, Larissa. 1971. "Reciprocity of Favors among the Urban Middle Class of Chile." In George Dalton, ed., *Studies in Economic Anthropology*. Washington, D.C.: American Anthropological Association.
—— 1973. "Supervivencia en una barriada de la ciudad de Mexico." *Demografía y Economía* 7(1).
—— 1974. "The Social and Economic Organization of a Mexican Shantytown." In *Latin American Urban Research*, Vol IV. New York: Sage.

Long, Edward. 1774. *The History of Jamaica.* 3 vols. London: T. Lowndes.

Luffman, John. 1789. *A Brief Account of the Island of Antigua, together with the Customs and Manners of Its Inhabitants, as well Whites as Blacks.* London: T. Cadell.

MacArthur, Robert H. 1972. *Geographical Ecology.* New York: Harper and Row.

MacArthur, Robert H., and Edward O. Wilson. 1967. *The Theory of Island Biogeography.* Princeton: Princeton University Press.

Macdonald, Barrie. 1971a. "Policy and Practice in an Atoll Territory: British Rule in the Gilbert and Ellice Islands, 1892–1970." Ph.D. diss., Australian National University.

—— 1971b. "Local Government in the Gilbert and Ellice Islands, 1892–1969." Part I. *Journal of Administration Overseas* 10:280–93.

—— 1972. "Local Government in the Gilbert and Ellice Islands, 1892–1969." Part II. *Journal of Administration Overseas* 11:11–27.

Madden, Richard. 1835. *A Twelve-Month's Residence in the West Indies during the Transition from Slavery to Apprenticeship.* 2 vols. Philadelphia.

Malinowski, Bronislaw. 1922. *Argonauts of the Western Pacific.* London: Routledge.

—— 1962. *Sex, Culture, and Myth.* New York: Harcourt, Brace and World.

Manocha, S. 1972. *Malnutrition and Retarded Human Development.* Springfield: Thomas.

Maragos, James, G. B. K. Baines, and P. J. Beveridge. 1973. "Tropical Cyclone Bebe Creates a New Land Formation on Funafuti Atoll." *Science* 181:1161–63.

Martin, M. Kay. 1974. "The Foraging Adaptation—Uniformity or Diversity?" Addison-Wesley Module in Anthropology, No. 56. Reading, Mass.: Addison-Wesley.

Mason, Leonard. 1968. "The Ethnology of Micronesia." In Andrew Vayda, *Peoples and Cultures of the Pacific.* New York: Natural History Press.

Maude, Harry E. 1950. "The Cooperative Movement in the Gilbert and Ellice Islands Colony." In *Proceedings of the Seventh Pacific Science Congress* 7:63–76.

—— 1959. "Spanish Discoveries in the Central Pacific." *Journal of the Polynesian Society* 68:285:326.

Mauss, Marcel. 1954. *The Gift*. New York: Free Press.

McFee, Malcolm. 1968. "The 150% Man: A Product of Blackfeet Acculturation." *American Anthropologist* 70:1096–1107.

McManus, John. 1975. "Psychopathology: Errors in Cognitive Adaptation." Paper presented at the 74th Annual Meeting of the American Anthropological Association, San Francisco.

—— 1978. "Ritual and Social Cognition." In E. G. d'Aquili et al., eds., *The Spectrum of Ritual*. New York: Columbia University Press.

McNeill, Hector. 1788. *Observations on the Treatment of Negroes in the Island of Jamaica*. London.

McPherron, Alan. 1967. "The Juntunen Site and the Late Woodland Prehistory of the Upper Great Lakes Area." *Anthropological Paper No. 30*. Museum of Anthropology. Ann Arbor: University of Michigan.

Mead, Margaret. 1930. *Social Organization of Manua*. Honolulu: Bishop Museum Bulletin 76.

—— 1966. *Cooperation and Competition among Primitive Peoples*. Boston: Beacon Press.

Miller, James C. 1964. "A Theoretical Review of Individual and Group Psychological Reactions to Stress." In George H. Grosser et al., eds., *The Threat of Impending Disaster*. Cambridge: M.I.T. Press.

Miller, Richard S. 1967. "Pattern and Process in Competition." In J. B. Cragg, ed., *Advances in Ecological Research*. Vol. IV. London: Academic Press.

Mintz, Sidney W. 1959. "The Plantation as a Socio-Cultural Type." In *Plantation Systems of the New World*. Social Science Monograph 7. Washington, D.C.: Pan American Union.

Moreton, J. B. 1793. *West India Customs and Manners*. London: W. Richardson, Royal Exchange.

Morrell, W. P. 1960. *Britain in the Pacific Islands*. London: Oxford University Press.

Moseley, Benjamin. 1787. *A Treatise on Tropical Diseases*. London: T. Cadell.

—— 1799. *A Treatise on Sugar*. London: Robinson.

Murdock, George P. 1949. *Social Structure*. New York: Macmillan.

Murray, Rev. A. W. 1876. *Forty Years Mission Work in Polynesia and New Guinea*. London: Nisbet.

Murray, Henry A., et al. 1938. *Explorations in Personality*. London: Oxford University Press.

Naroll, Raoul, and William T. Divale. 1976. "Natural Selection in Cultural Evolution: Warfare versus Peaceful Diffusion." *American Ethnologist* 3:97–130.

Nash, Manning. 1966. *Primitive and Peasant Economic Systems.* San Francisco: Chamber Publishing.

Newton, W. F. 1967. "The Early Population of the Ellice Islands." *Journal of the Polynesian Society* 76:197–204.

Nicholson, A. J. 1957. "Self-Adjustment of Populations to Change." In *Population Studies: Animal Ecology and Demography, Cold Spring Harbor Symposia on Quantitative Biology.* Vol. xxii. Cold Spring Harbor, N.Y.: Biological Laboratory.

Nieboer, H. J. 1900. *Slavery as an Industrial System.* The Hague: Martinus Nijhoff.

Orans, Martin. 1966. "Surplus." *Human Organization* 25:24–32.

Orderson, J. W. 1800. *Directions to Young Planters for the Care and Management of a Sugar Plantation in Barbados.* London: T. Bensley.

Pares, Richard. 1960. *Merchants and Planters.* Economic History Review Supplement, No. 4. London: Cambridge University Press.

Park, Thomas. 1954. "Experimental Studies in Interspecies Competition ii: Temperature, Humidity, and Competition in Two Species of Tribolium." *Physiological Zoology* 27:177–238.

Parra, Rodrigo. 1972. "Marginalidad y subdesarrollo." In Ramiro Cardona, ed., *Migraciónes Internas.* Bogota: Editorial Andes.

Patterson, Orlando. 1969. *The Sociology of Slavery.* Rutherford, N.J.: Fairleigh Dickinson Press.

Phillippo, James Mursell. 1843. *Jamaica: Its Past and Present State.* London: John Snow.

Phillips, Ulrich B. 1926. "An Antigua Plantation, 1769–1818." *North Carolina Historical Review* 3:439–45.

Piaget, Jean. 1952. *The Origins of Intelligence in Children.* New York: International Universities Press.

—— 1971. *Biology and Knowledge.* Chicago: University of Chicago Press.

Piaget, Jean, and Barbel Inhelder. 1969. *The Psychology of the Child.* New York: Basic Books.

Piddocke, Stuart. 1965. "The Potlatch System of the Southern Kwakiutl." *Southwestern Journal of Anthropology* 21:244–64.

Pinkard, George. 1816. *Notes on the West Indies, Including Observa-*

tions Relative to the Creoles and Slaves. 2nd ed. 2 vols. London: Baldwin, Cradock and Jay.

Pitman, Frank Wesley. 1926. "Slavery on the British West India Plantations in the Eighteenth Century." *Journal of Negro History* 11:584–668.

Polanyi, Karl. 1968. *The Great Transformation.* Boston: Beacon Press.

Powers, William T. 1973. *Behavior: The Control of Perception.* Chicago: Aldine.

Poyer, John. 1801. *The History of Barbados, from the First Discovery of the Island in the Year 1605, till the Accession of Lord Seaforth.* Rpt. 1971. London. Frank Cass.

A Professional Planter. 1811. *Practical Rules for the Management and Medical Treatment of Negro Slaves, in the Sugar Colonies.* London: Vernor, Hood, & Sharp.

Quijano, Anibal. 1970. "Refefinición de la dependencia y proceso de marginalización en América Latina." MS.

Ragatz, Lowell J. 1928. *The Fall of the Planter Class in the British Caribbean, 1763–1833.* Rpt. 1963. New York: Octagon Books.

—— 1931. "Absentee Landlordism in the British Caribbean, 1750–1833." *Agricultural History* 5:7–24.

Rappaport, Roy A. 1965. "Aspects of Man's Influence upon Island Ecosystems: Alteration and Control." In F. R. Fosberg, ed., *Man's Place in the Island Ecosystem.* Honolulu: Bishop Museum Press.

—— 1967. "Ritual Regulation of Environmental Relations Among a New Guinea People." *Ethnology* 6:17–30.

—— 1968. *Pigs for the Ancestors: Ritual in the Ecology of a New Guinea People.* New Haven: Yale University Press.

—— 1971. "Nature, Culture, and Ecological Anthropology." Warner Modular Publication No. 799. Andover, Mass.

Renny, Robert. 1807. *A History of Jamaica.* London: J. Cawthorn.

Reynolds, L. 1966. "Open Groups in Hominid Evolution." *Man* 1:441–52.

Riland, John. 1827. *The Memoirs of a West Indian Planter.* 3 vols. London: Hamilton Adams.

Roberts, George W. 1952. "A Life Table for a West Indian Slave Population." *Population Studies* 5:238–43.

—— 1957. *The Population of K Jamaica.* Cambridge: Cambridge University Press.

Roberts, R. G. 1958. "Te Atu Tuvalu: A Short History of the Ellice Islands." *Journal of the Polynesian Society* 67:394–423.

Rogers, Edward S. 1966. "Subsistence Areas of the Cree-Ojibwa of the Eastern Subarctic: A Preliminary Study." *National Museum of Canada Bulletin 204.* Contributions to Anthropology 1963–64, Part II. Ottawa.

Rogers, Edward S., and Mary B. Black. 1976. "Subsistence Strategy in the Fish and Hare Period, Northern Ontario: The Weagamow Ojibwa, 1880–1920." *Journal of Anthropological Research* 32:1–43.

Roughley, Thomas. 1823. *The Jamaica Planters' Guide; or, A System for Planting and Managing a Sugar Estate or Other Plantations in that Island and throughout the British West Indies in General.* London: Longman, Hurst, Rees, Orme, and Brown.

Rubinstein, Robert A., and Charles D. Laughlin, Jr. 1977. "Bridging Levels of Systemic Organization." *Current Anthropology* 18:459–81.

Ruddell, Rosemary. 1973. "Chiefs and Commoners: Nature's Balance and the Good Life among the Nootka." In B. Cox, ed., *Cultural Ecology.* Toronto: McClelland Stewart.

Russell, Bertrand. 1956. "The Philosophy of Logical Atomism." In R. C. March, ed., *Logic and Knowledge.* New York: Macmillan.

Sade, Donald Stone. 1974. "The Vertebrate Ego." Paper presented at the 73rd Annual Meeting of the American Anthropological Association, Mexico City.

Sahlins, Marshall D. 1957. "Differentiation by Adaptation in Polynesian Societies." *Journal of the Polynesian Society* 66:291–300.

—— *Social Stratification in Polynesia.* Seattle: University of Washington Press.

—— 1961. "The Segmentary Lineage: An Organization of Predatory Expansion." *American Anthropologist* 63:322–45.

—— 1963. "Poor Man, Rich Man, Big-Man, Chief: Political Types in Melanesia and Polynesia." *Comparative Studies in Society and History* 5:285–303.

—— 1965a. "On the Sociology of Primitive Exchange." In M. Banton, ed., *The Relevance of Models for Social Anthropology.* London: Tavistock.

—— 1965b. "Exchange Value and the Diplomacy of Primitive Trade." In J. Helm, ed., *Essays in Economic Anthropology.* Seattle: University of Washington Press.

—— 1968. *Tribesmen.* Englewood Cliffs, N.J.: Prentice-Hall.

—— 1971a. "Tribal Economics." In G. Dalton, ed., *Economic Development and Social Change.* New York: Natural History Press.

Sahlins, Marshall D. 1971b. "The Intensity of Domestic Production in Primitive Societies: Social Inflections of the Chayanov Slope." In G. Dalton, ed., *Studies in Economic Anthropology*. American Anthropological Association Monograph 7.

—— 1972. *Stone Age Economics*. Chicago: Aldine-Atherton.

—— 1976. *The Use and Abuse of Biology*. Ann Arbor: University of Michigan Press.

Sahlins, Marshall D., and Elman Service, eds. 1960. *Evolution and Culture*. Ann Arbor: University of Michigan Press.

Saint Clair, Thomas S. 1834. *A Residence in the West Indies and America*. 2 vols. London: Bentley.

Schaw, Janet. 1923. *Journal of a Lady of Quality; Being a Narrative of a Journey . . . to the West Indies, North Carolina, and Portugal, in the Years 1774 to 1776*. Ed. E. W. Andrews and C. M. Andrews. New Haven: Yale University Press.

Schombrugk, Robert H. 1848. *The History of Barbados*. London: Longman, Brown, Green and Longman.

Schneider, David M. 1957. "Typhoons on Yap." In Nicholas J. Demerath and A. F. C. Wallace, eds., *Human Adaptation to Disaster*. Special Issue, *Human Organization* 16:2:10–15.

—— 1968. *American Kinship: A Cultural Account*. Englewood Cliffs, N.J.: Prentice-Hall.

Schroder, H. M., M. J. Driver, and S. Streufert. 1967. *Human Information Processing*. New York: Holt, Rinehart and Winston.

Scot's Magazine. 1775. "West Indies." *Scot's Magazine* 37:105.

—— 1777. "British West Indies." *Scot's Magazine* 39:449.

—— 1784. "Affairs in the West Indies." *Scot's Magazine* 46:545–46.

Scott, H. Harold. 1939. *A History of Tropical Medicine*. 2nd ed. 2 vols. London: Edward Arnold.

Seaton, Richard W. 1962. *Hunger in Groups: An Arctic Experiment*. Chicago: Quartermaster Food and Container Institute, U.S. Army.

Sells, William. 1823. *Remarks on the Condition of Slaves in the Island of Jamaica*. London: Richardson, Cornhill and Ridgways.

Selye, Hans. 1973. "The Evolution of the Stress Concept." *American Scientist* 61:692–99.

Senior, Bernard M. 1835. *Jamaica as It Was, as It Is, as It May Be*. Rpt. 1969. New York: Negro Universities Press.

Service, Elman. 1966. *The Hunters*. Englewood Cliffs, N.J.: Prentice-Hall.

—— 1971. *Cultural Evolutionism: Theory in Practice.* New York: Holt, Rinehart and Winston.

—— 1975. *Origins of the State and Civilization.* New York: Norton.

Sharp, Lauriston. 1934. "The Social Organization of the Yir Yoront Tribe, Cape York Peninsula." *Oceania* 4:404–31.

Shaughnessey, J. D. 1973. *The Roots of Ritual.* Grand Rapids, Mich.: William B. Eerdmann.

Sheridan, Richard B. 1957. "Letters from a Sugar Plantation in Antigua, 1739–1758." *Agricultural History* 31:3–23.

—— 1970. *The Development of the Plantations to 1750.* Barbados: Caribbean Universities Press.

—— 1973. *Sugar and Slavery.* Baltimore: Johns Hopkins University Press.

Sherif, Muzafer. 1967. *Social Interaction.* Chicago: Aldine.

Sherif, Muzafer and C. W. 1953. *Groups in Harmony and Tension.* New York: Harper and Row.

—— 1969. *Social Psychology.* New York: Harper and Row.

Silverman, Martin G. 1970. "Banaban Adoption." In V. Carroll, ed., *Adoption in Eastern Oceania.* ASAO Monograph No. 1. Honolulu: University Press of Hawaii.

—— 1971. *Disconcerting Issue: Meaning and Struggle in a Resettled Pacific Community.* Chicago: University of Chicago Press.

Simmons, Donald. 1961. "Analysis of Cultural Reflection in Efik Folktales." *Journal of American Folklore* 74:126–41.

Simmons, R. T., J. J. Graydon, and N. B. Tindale. 1964. "Further Blood Group Genetical Studies on Australian Aborigines of Bentinck, Mornington, and Forsyth Island and the Mainland, Gulf of Carpenteria." *Oceania* 35:1–66.

Singer, Milton. 1975. "The Indian Joint Family in Modern Industry." In Ivan A. Brady and Barry L. Isaac, eds., *A Reader in Culture Change, Vol. II: Case Studies.* Cambridge: Schendmann.

Singh, S. 1968. "Dermatoglychics of Australian Aborigines, Mornington Island, Australia." *Archaeology and Physical Anthropology in Oceania* 3:41–48.

Sloane, Sir Hans. 1707. *A Voyage to the Islands Maglera, Barbados, Nieves, S. Christophers, and Jamaica, with the Natural History . . . of the Last of These Islands.* 2 vols. London.

Smith, S. Percy. 1897. "The First Inhabitants of the Ellice Group." *Journal of the Polynesian Society* 6:209–10.

Smith, William. 1745. *A Natural History of Nevis and the Rest of the*

English Leeward Charibbee Islands in America. Cambridge: W. Thurlborn.

Southey, Thomas. 1827. *Chronological History of the West Indies.* 3 vols. Rpt. 1968. London: Frank Cass.

Spicer, Edward H., ed. 1961. *Perspectives in American Indian Culture Change.* Chicago: University of Chicago Press.

Spillius, James. 1957. "Natural Disaster and Political Crisis in a Polynesian Society: An Exploration of Operational Research." *Human Relations* 10:3–27, 113–25.

Stair, J. B. 1897. *Old Samoa.* London: Religious Tract Society.

Stephen, James. 1824. *The Slavery of the British West India Colonies Delineated, As It Exists Both in Law and Practice, As Compared to the Slavery of Other Countries, Ancient and Modern.* 2 vols. London: Joseph Butterworth.

Stewart, John. 1808. *An Account of Jamaica and Its Inhabitants.* London: Longman, Hurst, Rees, and Orme.

Suggs, Robert, 1961. *The Archaeology of Nukuhiva, Marquesas Islands, French Polynesia.* Anthropological Papers of the American Museum of Natural History 9.

Sunkel, Osvaldo. 1971. *El Subdesarrollo Latinoamericano y la Teoría del Desarrollo.* Mexico City: Siglo XXI.

Suttles, Wayne. 1960. "Affinal Ties, Subsistence, and Prestige among the Coast Salish." *American Anthropologist* 62:296–305.

—— 1968a. "Variation in Habitat and Culture on the Northwest Coast." In Yehudi A. Cohen, ed., *Man in Adaptation: The Cultural Present.* Chicago: Aldine.

—— 1968b. "Coping with Abundance: Subsistence on the Northwest Coast." In R. Lee and I. Devore, eds., *Man the Hunter.* Chicago: Aldine.

Teleki, G. 1973. *The Predatory Behavior of Wild Chimpanzees.* Lewisburg, Pa.: Bucknell University Press.

Thom, René. 1975. *Structural Stability and Morphogenesis.* Reading, Mass.: W. A. Benjamin.

Thome, James A., and J. Horace Kimball. 1838. *Emancipation in the West Indies.* New York: American Anti-Slavery Society.

Tindale, N. B. 1962a. "Geographical Knowledge of the Kaiadilt People of Bentinck Island, Queensland." *Records of the South Australia Museum* 14:259.

—— 1962b. "Some Population Changes among the Kaiadilt People of Bentinck Island, Queensland." *Records of the South Australia Museum* 14:297.

Trivers, R. L. 1971. "The Evolution of Reciprocal Altruism." *Quarterly Review of Biology* 46:35–57.

Tuckman, B. W. 1964. "Personality Structure, Group Composition, and Group Functioning." *Sociometry* 27:469–81.

Turnbull, Colin. 1967. "The Ik: Alias the Teuso." *Uganda Journal* 31:63–71.

—— 1972. *The Mountain People*. New York: Simon and Schuster.

Valentine, Charles. 1972. *Culture and Poverty*. Chicago: University of Chicago Press.

Van Lawick-Goodall, Jane. 1968. "A Preliminary Report on Expressive Movements and Communication in the Gombe Stream Chimpanzees." In P. Jay, ed., *Primates*. New York: Holt, Rinehart and Winston.

Vandermeer, John H. 1972. "Niche Theory." *Annual Review of Ecology and Systematics*. Vol. 3. Palo Alto, Calif.: Annual Review.

Vayda, Andrew. 1961. "A Re-Examination of Northwest Coast Economic Systems." *Transactions of the New York Academy of Sciences*. Series ii. 23:618–24.

Waddell, Eric. 1975. "How the Enga Cope with Frost: Responses to Perturbations in the Central Highlands of New Guinea." *Human Ecology* 3:249–72.

Waddington, C. H. 1957. *Strategy of the Genes*. London: Allan and Unwin.

Wagner, Roy. 1975. *The Invention of Culture*. New Jersey: Prentice-Hall.

Wallace, Anthony F. C. 1956. "Revitalization Movements." *American Anthropologist* 58:264–81.

—— 1966. *Religion: An Anthropological View*. New York: Random House.

Ward, Captain E. V. 1967. *Sailing Directions: Navigation in and between the Atolls of the Gilbert and Ellice Islands Colony*. Tarawa, Gilbert Islands: Government Printer.

Washburn, Sherwood. 1961. *Social Life of Early Man*. Chicago: Aldine.

Webb, P., and V. Blockley. 1962. *N.A.S.A. Life Sciences Data Book*. N.A.S.A. Washington, D.C.: Government Printing Office.

Welch, Bruce L. 1965. "Psychophysiological Response to the Mean Level of Environmental Stimulation: A Theory of Environmental Integration." In *Symposium on Medical Aspects of Stress in the Military Climate*. Sponsored by Walter Reed Army Institute of Research. Washington, D.C.: Government Printing Office.

Wentworth, Trelawny. 1834. *The West India Sketch Book*. 2 vols. London: Whittaker.

Whitehead, Alfred North. 1960. *Process and Reality*. New York: Harper Torchbooks.

Whitmee, Rev. S. J. 1871. *A Missionary Cruise in the South Pacific*. London.

Whitten, Norman E., Jr., and John F. Szwed. 1970. "Introduction." In Norman E. Whitten, Jr., and John F. Szwed, eds., *Afro-American Anthropology*. New York: Free Press.

Wiens, Harold J. 1962. *Atoll Environment and Ecology*. New Haven: Yale University Press.

Williams, Cynric R. 1826. *A Tour Through the Island of Jamaica . . . in the Year 1823*. London: Hunt and Clarke.

Williamson, John. 1817. *Medical and Miscellaneous Observations, Relative to the West India Islands*. 2 vols. Edinburgh.

Wilson, Edward O. 1971. *The Insect Societies*. Cambridge: Harvard University Press.

—— 1975. *Sociobiology*. Cambridge: Harvard University Press.

Wittgenstein, L. 1961. *Tractatus Logico-Philosopicus*. New York: Humanities Press.

Wittkower, E. D. 1962. "Perspectives of Transcultural Psychiatry." *International Journal of Psychiatry* 8:811–24.

Wolf, Eric R. 1966. *Peasants*. Englewood Cliffs, N.J.: Prentice-Hall.

Wolf, Eric R., and Sidney W. Mintz. 1957. "Haciendas and Plantations in Middle America and the Antilles." *Social and Economic Studies* 6:380–412.

Wolff, K. H., ed. 1964. *The Sociology of George Simmel*. New York: Free Press.

Woodburn, J. 1968. "An Introduction to Hadza Ecology." In R. Lee and I. Devore, eds., *Man the Hunter*. Chicago: Aldine.

Worden, Frederic G., Judith P. Swazey, and George Adelman. 1975. *The Neurosciences: Paths of Discovery*. Cambridge: M.I.T. Press.

Worsley, Peter. 1957. "Millenarian Movements in Melanesia." *Rhodes-Livingstone Institute Journal* 21:18–31.

Young, Sir William. 1807. *The West India Common-Place Book*. London: Phillips.

Zeeman, E. C. 1976. "Catastrophe Theory." *Scientific American* 234:65–83.

Zwart, F. H. and Ko Groenewegen. 1970. *A Report on the Results of the Census of the Population, Gilbert and Ellice Colony, 1968*. New South Wales: Government Printer.

Index